HISTORY

OF

MONTGOMERY COUNTY

WITHIN

THE SCHUYLKILL VALLEY:

CONTAINING

Sketches of all the Townships, Boroughs and Villages, in said limits, from the earliest period to the present time; with an account of the Indians, the Swedes, and other early settlers, and the local events of the Revolution; besides notices of the Progress in Population, Improvements, and Manufactures;

PREPARED CHIEFLY FROM ORIGINAL MATERIALS:

BY WILLIAM J. BUCK,

Author of the "History of Bucks County," "History of Mooreland," &c., &c., Member of the Historical Society of Pennsylvania, and Auditor of Montgomery County.

NORRISTOWN:
PRINTED BY E. L. ACKER.
1859.

PREFACE.

For the last fifteen years, the author has been diligently engaged in collecting materials for the histories of Bucks and Montgomery counties. The various articles that he has already written, relating more or less to those counties, and published either in books, magazines, or newspapers, if collected, would amount to several volumes; but these have been but a portion of what he has still on hand, besides what further research may secure. Thus however long he has been engaged as a collector, he still owes an apology to his readers for the imperfections of this work. These arise, chiefly, from the hasty manner in which he was necessitated to prepare it for the press. The life of the writer has not been one of leisure; and the work as it now appears, was written under great disadvantages — it can be said, amidst many interruptions which necessarily arise from one's business, independent of those of an official character. It had been the intention of the author to delay the publication of this work for several years, but owing to the encouragement offered by Dr. E. L. Acker, the editor and proprietor of the *Norristown Register*, he was induced to prepare it for that paper, to be afterwards issued in a volume. It was this unexpected offer and its acceptance that has occasioned its early appearance. Immediately after this arrangement, in the last two weeks of August, 1858, the writer set out on a pedestrian tour of the entire Schuylkill Valley, as embraced within the limits of Montgomery county, and visited, personally, every township, borough, village, and other objects of interest herein described. The distance traveled for this purpose was about two hundred and eighty miles, and to be more accurate, all the notes taken were made on the spot. Just previous to setting out, all the requisite preparations were made to add to the success of this undertaking, in regard to procuring the information that was still wanting and unsupplied in our materials: for this purpose maps of all the townships and boroughs were taken along to assist in our visits, besides numerous queries made up from our collections on which additional information was desirable. In procuring the matter embodied in this work we were quite successful, even beyond our most sanguine expectations. There was no necessity with us to be diffuse, that too common fault of authors; on the contrary, we have tried to condense our matter as much as was practicable with the general plan of the work. For its size, we are pursuaded few works on American history contain more information derived from unpublished sources. It was this motive that prompted us in the undertaking—namely, of contributing something additional to our country's annals—even if it should be a mite of local history. The reader must bear in mind, however imperfect this work may be in its present edition, that the result has not been achieved without great personal labor and expense; and had no higher motives than those to be derived from mere pecuniary profit actuated the author, the work would never have been undertaken; though if this had been the reality, no doubt, the field would have been occupied long ago by the reapers for the harvest it would bring. But, in our opinion, money cannot wholly make up the many hours spent in the solitude of the closet in concentrated study, away from society and the beautiful face of nature, but not absent from the midnight lamp, in digesting a mass of often crude and conflicting materials.

Partly in illustration of the foregoing assertions, we will give our readers a few extracts from the writings of distinguished literary persons. Mr. Griswold, in his Prose Writers of America, remarks that "There are few if any kinds of composition requiring a higher order of genius or more profound acquirements than History; and it might be supposed, therefore, that it would be amongst the last of the fields in which the authors of a new nation would be successful." Mrs. Sarah J. Hale, in her biography of Agnes Strickland, quite philosophically remarks: "We know nothing among the aims of literature more difficult than to write history well: learning conscientiousness, the patient spirit of research, time and opportunities for such research, unflagging industry, penetration into character, a philosophic power of observation and reflection, are some of the requisites for an historian." Of late years there has been an increasing taste for local literature, aided, as it has been, by a more general diffusion of knowledge amongst the people by our common school system. This we can say is known to us from experience. On this matter, S. G. Goodrich, in his "Recollections," published in 1857, remarks: "The last ten years have been noted for the production of local, state, town, and city histories. Many of these are of great interest, going back to the lights and shadows of colonial periods. Here are the future resources of historic poetry and romance, of painting and sculpture." From this it will be seen that this kind of composition will have a tendency to Americanize, not only our literature, but our arts. This is what is wanting in us—more nationality in our thoughts and feelings—the future basis of originality.

Of course, the principal object of this work has been to collect together and preserve much valuable and interesting matter relating to our history which otherwise might have been lost. In its compilation, care has been taken to give whatever information could be derived from authentic documents the preference; the authorities are given for that which has been obtained through traditionary sources. In all instances attention has been given to dates, which possess a particular importance and may well be called the mile-stones of time: without them, it would be difficult to show what progress is made. It will be extremely difficult, where information has been derived from a thousand sources, to be entirely correct, but we have followed that which we believed to be the most reliable. Independent of our own collections and researches made in the records of Philadelphia, Bucks, and Montgomery counties, and in the Philadelphia, Pennsylvania Historical Society and Hatborough libraries, we are indebted for some information, and which merit an acknowledgement, to Lossing's Field Book of the Revolution, Ferris's Original Settlements on the Delaware, the Journal of the Rev. Henry M. Muhlenberg, the Rev. J. W. Richard's Centennial Sermon at the Trappe, Rev. J. C. Clay's Annals of the Swedes, Hazard's Annals of Pennsylvania, Gordon's Gazateer, and Day's Historical Collections. We are also indebted for favors to Dr. G. W. Holstein, of Bridgeport, Abel Rambo, A. M., of Trappe, Rev. Edmund Leaf, of Douglasville, and Dr. E. L. Acker, of Norristown. To Henry Woodman, formerly of Upper Merion, we are quite grateful for a loan of his manuscript History of Valley Forge.

It may be necessary to state why this work was not made a complete history of Montgomery County, instead of that part of it lying in the Schuylkill valley. There are several reasons for this present design. To have prepared a work on the same scale on the entire county, would have made it entirely too large and expensive to have met with any degree of success as a local work. In the present undertaking are contained ten townships and four boroughs, which, in 1810, contained 12,252 inhabitants, and which now must be near 50,000; which alone is three times greater than the entire population of the county at the time of its formation in 1784. The aforesaid fourteen townships and boroughs in 1856 contained 8,838 taxables. There are in the entire county, thirty townships and four boroughs, leaving therefore undescribed in this work twenty townships, which, were they to receive the same space, would make a volume of nearly twice the present size. However, it may be well enough to state that the author contemplates, at a future time, to write a history of the county, when he expects to be better prepared than he now otherwise could he, both as regards time and materials.

Within the limits of Montgomery County, the Schuylkill valley is rich in historical associations. Here have lived, at various times, the Indians, Swedes, Dutch, Welsh, English and Germans. In the lapse of two centuries the Indians have passed away, and the numerous descendants of the others remain. The struggles of the navigators and shoremen, the Revolutionary events of Whitemarsh and Valley Forge, the philosophical observations of David Rittenhouse, and the great and magnificent undertaking of John James Audubon, on American birds, are not without interest. In these limits, too, was born a Major-General of the American Revolution, a Speaker of the first Congress of 1789, and two Governors of Pennsylvania. We cannot pass up or down the valley of the Schuylkill, without feeling emotions for the great events that have transpired there in the past, and the present astonishes us for the enterprise it exhibits on every hand, and the future puzzles us to judge what will happen in the next two centuries.

It will be observed in this work that, though every article is complete in itself, there is a connection in the manner they are placed, from the beginning to the end, each being introductory to the other. As the plan is our own, it perplexed us at first what to do with the various biographies now placed in the appendix. At first we had concluded to place them in the townships or boroughs where they originally belonged, but on consideration, from their length and want of connection with the other local matter, this arrangement was thought best. At the present termination of our labors, it was not without feelings of pride that we reflect that this was the result of an unoccupied field, which we were the first to enter, explore, and take possession. In all our rambles along this beautiful and interesting valley, to all our numerous inquiries, which brought us so often in contact with strangers, we were always treated kindly, and on stating our object, it often appeared to create some interest in the undertaking. At different times an amount of intelligence was received from mechanics and laborers that quite surprised us, from the scant opportunities the nature of those occupations afford. This, with us, is a source of pride, and shows the elevating tendencies of our institutions and the interest the masses are taking in subjects connected with literature and science. No doubt many important facts will be found wanting which will be supplied. The houses and shops of the villages we entered were counted. This, now, may seem of little moment, but in our estimation will be hereafter one of the important features of the book. Thirty, sixty, or a hundred years from this, may show thus better the progress they may make.

Could a book now be found giving, for a certain year, the number of houses and shops in every village of Pennsylvania, say a hundred years ago, it would prove quite a desideratum and would furnish information which could not otherwise be obtained. That a work of this kind is wanted, whatever encouragement this may meet with, can be proven by repeated paragraphs which have at different times appeared in our local newspapers, inviting to such an undertaking. In closing our labors, we are led sincerely to believe that we were engaged in a laudable work, and that many a one, as he arises from its perusal, will feel himself (so we hope) a better and a wiser man.

W. J. B.

WILLOW GROVE, *July*, 1859.

HISTORY OF MONTGOMERY COUNTY

WITHIN THE SCHUYLKILL VALLEY.

I.

THE SCHUYLKILL.

The river Schuylkill has its origin from two small streams which rise in the Broad Mountain, in Rush township, Schuylkill county. Following its meanderings to where it empties into the Delaware, which is five miles below Philadelphia, its total length is about one hundred and twenty-five miles, and its general course is south-easterly. Its principal tributaries, in Schuylkill county, are the Little Schuylkill, Bear, and Tumbling creeks; in Berks county, Maiden and Tulpehocken creeks; in Montgomery county, Manatawny and Perkiomming creeks; in Chester county, Pigeon and French creeks; and in Philadelphia, the Wissahickon creek. Following its courses, the Schuylkill laves the shores of Montgomery county for about forty miles.

On it in this distance are located ten townships and four boroughs, of whose history it is our intention to treat, viz: Pottsgrove, Limerick, Upper Providence, Lower Providence, Norriton, Plymouth, Whitemarsh, Springfield, Upper Merion and Lower Merion townships; and Pottstown, Norristown, Bridgeport and Conshohocken boroughs. Within these limits it is spanned by no less than eleven noble bridges; railroads pass on its eastern and western margins, while itself is made navigable for boats of one hundred and eighty tons. These grand improvements, wonderful to relate, have been effected in less than half a century. They show the energy, the thrift and enterprise of our countrymen in these latter days, for two hundred and forty-two years have passed away since its first discovery by the European. What a subject is here offered for reflection!

Within these limits there are no mountains, though the country is most agreeably diversified by undulating hills and valleys, interspersed with towns, villages, and various manufacturing establishments, all beautifully situated by its banks, or nestled near by in some lateral valley. Though not on a grand scale, yet few valleys in any country, for the same distance, can boast of more lovely and varied picturesque scenery. Sometimes meandering through broad cultivated fields and fertile plains, on which are studded, like gems in a casket, substantial stone houses and barns. Next, on some eminence, may be seen an elegant country seat; then it sweeps past bits of woodland, tufting the hill-slopes, or contracted by a bolder bluff of rocks; then, again, follow in succession, the park-like islands, so gently reposing in its bosom, and the long stretches of green meadow. Here is to be found the *utile et dulce* of the ancients to a greater degree than, perhaps, in any other section of equal extent in our wide-spread republic. To one that has never before traversed this part of the valley, and however much the hand of improvement may alter it, it will still present those ever varying succession of scenes which charm the landscape and are the admiration of every traveler.

In the year 1609, Captain Henry Hudson, an Englishman in the service of the Dutch East India Company, it is believed, touched at the mouth of what is now known as Delaware Bay; but finding shoal water, and fearful of grounding, he retired, and in a few days after entered the harbor of New York, and sailed up the river to which his name has been given. In the summer of 1610, it is said, Lord Delaware, while on his voyage to Virginia, as governor, entered the bay which now bears his name, as well as the large river that empties into it. In 1612 the Dutch commenced settlements at Fort

Orange, now Albany, and at Manhattan Island, the present site of the city of New York. Captain Hendrickson, a Dutchman, having built a yacht at Manhattan, called the "Onrust," which in English means *Restless*, of only sixteen tons burthen, set out on a voyage of discovery in 1616. From a map which he made of this expedition, it would appear as if he had sailed along the coast from Nova Scotia to the Capes of Virginia. While on this trip, he entered Delaware Bay, and ascended its river as far as the Schuylkill, which he entered a short distance, and in consequence, is, therefore, entitled to the honor of being its discoverer. In 1633 orders were given to Arent Corsson, the commissary of Fort Nassau, by authority of Governor Van Twiller, of Manhattan, to purchase a tract of land on the Schuylkill, on which to erect a fort. In 1648, Corsson concluded a purchase from several Indian chiefs to the satisfaction of the West India Company, which was placed on record in their office. Soon after a fort was erected, which was called "Beversrede," and was said to be a place remarkably well situated, and was named thus on account of the beaver trade, which was carried on there extensively with the Indians. This fort, it is believed, stood at or near the present Gray's Ferry, at the lower extremity of the city of Philadelphia. This trade or traffic in beaver skins, it appears, increased so by 1656 that the documents of the company speak of it as the "great beaver trade of the Schuylkill."

The origin of any name that has, for a long time, been applied to any object, which in itself is permanent and likely to remain so, is ever interesting, especially when of a local nature, to the inhabitants of its vicinity. In consequence, before we proceed further in this undertaking, we shall venture on an explanation, if not rather an investigation, of the name of Schuylkill, as well as of several others which have been applied to it. The Indians, it appears, had several names for this stream. One was "Nittabockunk," which we know was applied in 1655, if not earlier. In the deeds of purchase from the Indians to William Penn, in 1683 and 1685, it is called "Manaiunk." John Heckewelder, the missionary, says it was called by the natives "Ganschowehanne," which signified, in their language, a stream whose falls and ripples make a noise. Mr. Heckewelder's statement is doubted, for the reason that no authority has yet been found to corroborate that the Indians had ever called it by this name. The Swedes, as may be seen on Peter Lindstrom's map of "New Sweden," made in 1655, also called it the "Linde Kilen," or Linden stream, from the large trees of this kind that grew on its banks. Its present name of Schuylkill was given it by the Dutch, very probably by Captain Hendrickson, in 1616; if not, it bore this name at least seventeen years later. By means of a rare work, entitled "Woordenbock Der Nederduitsche in Fransche Taalen, by Francois Halma," published at Amsterdam, in 1729, we are enabled to give some light as to the origin of the Dutch name of this stream. Schuil, or Schuilen, in the Dutch, signifies *concealed*, or *hidden*, that is, by land or otherwise. Kil, signifies a *channel*, *stream*, or *river*. Therefore, the meaning of Schuil-Kil, or Schuilen-Kil, (the way it is spelled in the Dutch, and as it should be now written,) is, Hidden river, or Concealed stream. This name was given it by its discoverers, from the fact of its mouth being so concealed by several low islands that the river can not be found till actually entered; to the truth of which I can vouch from personal observation, while ascending both the Delaware and entering the Schuylkill.

The Schuylkill, though unknown to the generality of our citizens, was, a century and a quarter ago, the scene of a violent struggle between those who resided on its shores in this county and those who navigated its waters in canoes from the upper country, now better known as Berks, while on their voyages with produce to the Philadelphia markets. This was a contest that lasted many years, and in which both parties warmly contended for their respective interests, which here came in conflict. With what novelty, at the present day, must we view such a struggle, when we reflect on the many and mighty changes that man and time have wrought on this river. When we behold its canals with their deeply laden boats, its railroads with their long, dark trains, the many thriving towns and villages that adorn its banks, and the many busy manufactories, and quiet, pleasant villa residences—what a tale is told of progress! To the period to which we refer, hamlets and villages were unknown; even the spot where is now our populous county seat, was then unmarked by a single house. The hills and the valleys were covered with their majestic ancient forests to the very shores, with the exception of here and there, where occasionally the hardy settlers had effected clearings and erected rude log dwellings. The contrast is enough to make one smile, especially now, when we reflect that the dispute which we intend to speak of, simply originated from the obstructions placed in the channels of the Schuylkill, by the shoremen, for the purpose of assisting them to catch fish, and which considerably impeded, if it did not really render the navigation thereof dangerous.

It appears, that as early as 1683, when William Penn and his colonists had not been a year in this country, that an act had been passed against the erecting of racks, wears, or dams, in any navigable waters, which might otherwise hinder the free intercourse thereon, and also tend greatly to diminish the brood of fish. Through the influence of Governor Penn, another act was passed, in the year 1700, with the intent of more effectually securing this object. After this, from what we have been enabled to ascertain, the matter remained quiet for a number of years, or with but little agitation, till in May, 1724, when the Governor's Council introduced "A bill, entitled an act for demolishing and removing fishing dams, wears, and kedles, set across the river Schuylkill, was read and ordered to be returned with amendments." It next appears, that the Council, on the 15th of August, 1730, passed a law, entitled "An act to prevent the erecting of wears, dams, &c., within the river Schuylkill." Yet, even this was found to be not altogether sufficient. It was, by an act passed in 1734, further strengthened and rendered more effectual. The shoremen made a strong effort, in the years 1735 and 1736, to get an amendment, or rather a repeal, so as to get permission to erect wears in the months of April and May of every year, which was warmly opposed by the navigators, or those living on the upper parts of the Schuylkill. The Governor, Patrick Gordon, being also opposed to any permission of the kind being given, the shoremen at length yielded, so far as to look for any redress for their grievances from the legislature. It became a matter of complaint against the shoremen, that for several miles above the racks and wears, they were in the practice to commence with their horses in the river and strike the water as they came downwards with stakes and long brushes as they proceeded, so as to drive and frighten the fish into them, to their great diminution—that they carried stones into the river to hold the stakes and wears, which not only obstructed but rendered navigation difficult and dangerous. They were also charged on these occasions, while chasing fish, of bringing the young people together, who would become riotous and quarrelsome, "which was a reproach to good order, peace and tranquility." A number of depositions were taken in March, 1732, by George Boone, a justice of the peace, residing in the township of Oley, in the present Berks county, which then belonged to Philadelphia, as did likewise the intervening territory now comprised in Montgomery. These, Mr. Boone, who was equally interested with his neighbors, transmitted to the Governor and Legislature, and the result was, the stringent enactment of 1734, to which reference has been made. To these depositions we are indebted for the following adventures encountered by the navigators of Amity and Oley townships, while on their canoe voyages to Philadelphia, in 1731 and 1732.

Marcus Hulings states, that as he was going down the Schuylkill with a canoe, loaded with wheat, which, by striking against a fish-dam took in a great deal of water, which damaged the wheat considerably, and came near being totally lost. He also further says, that on another occasion, his canoe got in a similar predicament, and would have lost his whole load of wheat, if he had not leaped into the river, and with much labor, succeeded in preventing his canoe from swinging around, which otherwise would have been capsized by the current. In so doing, he "suffered very much in his body by reason of ye water and cold." Again, on another occasion, he got fast on one of the rack-dams, and only by great hazard escaped with his life and freight. In the month of February, while it was extremely cold, Jonas Jones relates that he got "fast on a fish-dam, and to save his load of wheat was obliged to leap into ye river to ye middle of his body, and with all his labour and skill could not get off in less than half an hour; afterwards proceeding on his journey with ye said clothes, they were frozen stiff on his back, by means whereof he underwent a great deal of misery." The next sufferer we shall mention was Jacob Warren, who relates that his canoe, loaded with wheat, got fast on a dam, when he and his partner were forced into the river, and while one, with all his power, was obliged to hold the canoe, the other had to open a passage, with great difficulty, to get through. Isaac Smally affirms, that in going down the river, with one hundred and forty bushels of wheat, he got fast on a rack-dam, "and, in order to save ye load from being all lost, he was, much against his mind, obliged to leap into ye river, the water being to his chin, frequently dashed into his mouth, where between whiles he breathed, and he and his partner held ye canoe with great labour, while a young man there present, ran above a mile to call help to get off." Jonas Yocum and Richard Dunklin say that they got fast on a fish-dam with their canoe, on board of which was Dunklin's wife and child, besides sixty bushels of wheat, and that for more than an hour were in imminent danger of being overset and drowned. Barnaby Rhoades relates, that he got fast with his canoe on a fish-dam for several hours in the winter season, when, being without any assistance, he had to suffer considerably from the severity of the cold, besides being in great danger of losing both his life and load. The sufferings of the complainants might be much extended, but shall let it suffice to say, without going into details, that among them can also be mentioned Walter Campbell, George Boone, John Boone, and several others, who had been at divers times fast with their canoes on the fish and rack-dams in the Schuylkill, and to preserve their loads had been forced at different times to leap into the river at the peril of their lives to save their property.

The freight carried in some of their canoes, shows to what a prodigious size the timber had attained at the arrival of the early settlers;—for it should be recollected that they were always hewn from out a single trunk. William Penn, in a letter from Philadelphia, dated the 30th of 5th month, 1683, to Henry Savell, in England, mentions of his having seen a canoe, made from a poplar tree, that carried four tons of bricks. Isaac Smally's canoe, as has been stated, carried one hundred and forty bushels of wheat, which is a still heavier load, and consequently must have been larger. Our information, so far, has been to favor the cause of the navigators, but the shoremen no doubt believed that they had just reasons to complain, from the stringent enactments passed against them. Their dams and wears were formed at a considerable expense and labor, for the sole purpose of supplying fish to their families. They were always placed convenient to their residences, and by their own lands. Generally the most advantageous places for them were, where they were the most detrimental to the interests of navigation, such as below the mouths of creeks, and where islands and shallows rendered them of easy construction. The navigators, too, on many occasions, did much injury by breaking through their dams, and maliciously destroying them, with the racks, wears, and baskets. Nay, the shoremen charged them with stealing, at divers times, the proceeds of their honest labor—the fish. Thus, between 1731 and 1740, there was an intense excitement produced by these conflicting interests, along the peaceful valley of the Schuylkill. Many deeds of heroism were achieved on both sides, and prodigies of valor performed, which no chronicler has thought proper to transmit to posterity. The result, however, was, that at length it terminated in open war between the parties. Fleets of canoes would put off on the voyage together, for the purpose of mutual protection to themselves and the mutual destruction of all fish-dams, wears, and baskets. On the other hand, the shoremen would congregate in their respective neighborhoods, for the protection of their property thus assailed, and should any unlucky wights get fast with their canoes, or venture too near the shore, they would bring their artillery to bear on them in a shower of—stones. The navigators being generally the greatest sufferers, at length concluded to call on the magistrates for assistance, when William Richards, the constable of Amity township, received a warrant from George Boone, Esq., "one of His Majesty's Justices of the Peace" for Philadelphia county, to remove the said obstructions as the true authors of the mischief. What Mr. Richards accomplished in the undertaking, we shall leave him state in his own words, given on oath before Ralph Asheton, Esq., and corroborated by Benjamin Milliard, who was one of his assistants on this memorable affair, which happened the 20th of April, 1738.

Having "received a warrant, requiring him, this deponent, to take to his assistance such persons as this deponent should think proper, and go down the river Schuylkill, and remove all such obstructions as should be found in the said river.—In obedience to which warrant this deponent took several persons, inhabitants of the said county, as his assistants, and together with one Robert Smith, constable of the township of Ouly, (Oley,) who had received a warrant to the same purpose, went down the said river, in three canoes, to Mingo creek, where they found a large number of racks and obstructions in the said river, and saw four men upon an island near the said racks—that this deponent and company removed the said racks without receiving any opposition. From thence they proceeded down the river to the mouth of Pickering's creek, near which they found several racks which reacht across the said river to an island, which racks this deponent and company also removed—that immediately after the said racks were removed, about the number of two hundred men came down on both sides of the said river, and were very rude and abusive, and threatened this deponent and his company—that the said deponent, expecting, from the ill-language and threats given, that some mischief, or a quarrel would ensue, he took his staff in his hand and his warrant, and commanded the said men, in the King's Name, to keep the peace, and told them that he came there in a peaceable manner, and according to law, to move the racks and obstructions in the river, upon which some of the said men damned the laws and the law-makers, and cursed this deponent and his assistants—that one James Starr knockt this deponent down in the river with a large club or stake; after which several of the said men attackt this deponent and said company with large clubs, and knockt down the said Robert Smith, the constable, as also several of this deponent's assistants—that one John Wainwright, in company with this deponent, was struck down with a pole or staff, and lay as dead, with his body on the shore and his feet in the river. That this deponent and company, finding that they were not able to make resistance, were obliged to make the best of their way in order to save their lives; after which, this deponent, together with the constable of Ouly, and some of their company, proceeded down the river, in order to go to Philadelphia, to make complaint of the ill usage they had received—that as they came near Parkyooman (Perkiomen) Creek, they found another set of racks, which were guarded by a great number of men. That this deponent and company requested the said men to let them go down the river, and if they would suffer them to pass that they would not meddle with their racks. Upon which the said men abused and cursed this deponent in a very gross manner, telling the said deponent and his company, that they should not pass them—that one of the said men called out aloud, and offered five pounds for Timothy Miller's head, the said Timothy being one of the deponent's assistants; and afterwards the said men pursued this deponent and company, who, for fear of being murthered, made the best of their way, with their canoes, to the mouth of Parkyooman Creek, and then went ashore, and left their canoes there with several cloathes, which canoes are since split (as reported) in pieces, and several of the cloathes turned adrift."

This affair having reached the heads of the government, whereupon the Hon. James Logan, President of the Council, issued a proclamation and a warrant, the 25th of April, 1738, for the arrest of the "rioters," who are "to be proceeded against according to law, and that they, the said Justices, exert the powers wherewith they are invested, for the preservation of His Majesty's Peace and the good order of government in those parts where the late tumult arose, or others may be likely to arise. And the sheriffs of the said counties of Philadelphia and Chester, respectively, are hereby enjoined and required, with a sufficient assistance, if need be, to cause the warrants to be duly executed." This is the last official act we have been enabled to find on the subject, from whence we conclude that the shoremen, after contending for half a century, at length gave way before the majesty of the law, and the navigators, the fish, and the waters of the Schuylkill, were permitted to pass on uninterrupted, till a recent time. Mingo, Pickering, and Perkiomen Creeks still retain their time-honored names—the same islands and channels are there, but the people are changed. The inhabitants of Limerick, and Upper and Lower Providence townships, are reckoned now among our most peaceable citizens. The contest between the navigators and shoremen is long, long past—I might have said, long, long forgotten; but the wand of the antiquary is mighty—out of old musty tomes it may re-create a world to live again in imagination as it once did in reality.

That considerable importance was attached to the navigation of the Schuylkill, at an early period, has been already shown in the contest between the navigators and the shoremen. Even William Penn, in his proposals for a second settlement in the province of Pennsylvania, published in 1690, alludes to the practicability of effecting a communication by water between a branch of the Schuylkill and the Susquehanna. This, my readers should remember, was at a period when canals were unknown even in Great Britain. However, nothing was done, we believe, towards improving its navigation for a considerable length of time, though the matter was occasionally agitated. To promote the same, an act was passed by the Assembly the 14th of March, 1761, and from which we give the following extract: "Whereas, the river Schuylkill is navigable for rafts, boats, and other small craft, in times of high freshes only, occasioned by the obstruction of rocks and bars of sand and gravel, in divers parts of the same: And whereas, the improving the navigation of the said river, so as to make it passable at all times, will be very advantageous to the poor, greatly conducive to the promotion of industry, and beneficial to the inhabitants residing on or near said river, by enabling them to bring the produce of the country to the market of the city of Philadelphia, and thereby increase the trade and commerce of the province: And whereas, divers of the inhabitants of this province, desirous to promote the welfare of the public, have subscribed large sums of money for the purpose aforesaid, and, by petition to the Assembly, have requested that commissioners may be appointed by law to take, receive and collect the said subscriptions, and such others as shall hereafter be given or subscribed, and to apply and appropriate the same for and towards the clearing, scouring and rendering the said river navigable, as aforesaid." To carry out the measure, Joseph Fox, John Hughs, Samuel Rhoades, John Potts, William Palmer, David Davis, Mordecai Moore, Henry Pawling, James Coultas, Jonathan Coates, Joseph Millard, William Bird, Francis Parvin, Benjamin Lightfoot, and Isaac Levan, were appointed commissioners. This act had also for its object the preservation of fish, especially the shad, herring and rockfish, which ascended this stream annually, in great shoals, from the sea. For this purpose, the commissioners were empowered not only to destroy but to prevent the erection of all wears, racks, fish-dams and baskets within the same. At this time, it also appears that at the several ferries established along the Schuylkill for the transportation of passengers and freight, there were ropes stretched across the same for the purpose of drawing the boats. These were frequently cut by some evil-minded persons who were either going up or down the stream, in consequence of which the ferrymen petitioned to the Assembly for protection from these outrages, when an act was passed the 8th of February, 1766, making such offences finable ten pounds each.

Several of the commissioners mentioned having died, a new board was appointed by the Assembly, in 1773, to carry out the measures contained in the act of 1761. For this purpose, David Rittenhouse, Anthony Levering, John Roberts, William Dewees, Jr., David Thomas, James Hockley, Thomas Potts, Mark Bird, James Star, Jacob Kern, and John Pawling, Jr., were selected. In 1781, a change was made, when the board consisted of David Rittenhouse, Owen Biddle, Mark Bird, Baltzer Gehr, Thomas Potts, David Thomas, Patrick Anderson, John Mear, Isaac Hughs, Nathan Levering, George Douglass, John Heister and Christian Steer. An act was passed the 29th of September, 1791, to incorporate a company to connect the Schuylkill with the Susquehanna by a canal and slackwater navigation, and also to improve the navigable waters of the Schuylkill from the lower falls, a few miles above Philadelphia, to Reading, for which purpose the Assembly appropriated £2500, as an encouragement to the enterprise. By an act of the 10th of April, 1792, a company was incorporated to make a canal from Norristown to the river Delaware, at Philadelphia, a distance of seventeen miles. From the former place the Schuylkill was to be temporarily improved, and thus form, with the works of the Schuylkill and Susquehanna company, an uninterrupted water communication with the interior of the State, and which, it was expected, would be eventually extended to connect with the waters of the Ohio and Lake Erie.

One of the objects, also, in constructing the canal from Norristown was, by this means to furnish Philadelphia with water. The undertaking was commenced by the two companies, and at the close of 1794 they had expended $440,000, and had nearly completed fifteen miles of the most difficult part of the two works. Some of the principal stockholders having become involved at the time in commercial difficulties, the consequence was, the two companies were compelled to suspend operations. As an additional inducement to revive the companies, the State passed an act the 17th of April, 1795, to empower them to raise, by way of lottery, the additional sum of $400,000 for the purpose of completing their works, as mentioned in the acts of incorporation. But naught availed, though this offer induced several abortive attempts, which only tended to continue in these companies a languishing existence. Below Norristown, beginning at the Swedes' Ford bridge by the banks of the Schuylkill, may be seen the excavation made for this canal for some distance down the river. It remains there a monument of an undertaking commenced in 1792, but never finished.

In the year 1811, the two companies were united as the Union Canal Company, and in 1819 and 1821 the State granted further aid by a guarantee of interest and a monopoly of the lottery privilege. In consequence of this legislative encouragement, there were additional subscriptions obtained to the stock of the company to resume operations in 1821. The line was re-located, the dimensions of the canal changed, and the whole work finished in about six years from this period—after thirty-seven years had elapsed from the commencement of the work, and sixty-five from the date of the first survey by David Rittenhouse and Rev. William Smith.

This canal is eighty miles in length, extending from the Schuylkill four miles below Reading, where it connects with the works of the Schuylkill Navigation Company; thence up the Tulpehocken creek to the Swatara, and thence down the same to Middletown, on the Susquehanna—thus connecting the two rivers—which idea William Penn conceived in 1690, but which required an interval of one hundred and thirty-seven years to be put into practical operation. The whole cost of this work was about $2,000,000.

The Schuylkill Navigation Company was incorporated under the act of the 8th of March, 1815, by which they were required to commence operations at each end of the route simultaneously; their labors, in consequence, were rendered nearly useless until the whole line would be completed. This certainly was an ingenious plan in the Assembly to ensure the completion of the undertaking. This work is about one hundred and ten miles in length, beginning at Fairmount, Philadelphia, and extending to Mill creek, at Port Carbon, in Schuylkill county. It consists of a series of canals, sixty-three miles in length, and slackwater-pools for forty-seven miles, produced by thirty-four dams, which feed the canals. This work in its whole length was made three and a-half feet deep, with a width of no less than thirty-six feet at the top. There are one hundred and nine locks of six hundred and twenty feet ascent, each eighty feet long and seventeen broad, and one tunnel three hundred and eighty-five feet in length—the first, it is said, attempted in the United States. The whole cost of the line was $2,966,180. It was commenced immediately after its incorporation, and finished in 1826. In 1818, it was sufficiently completed to allow the descent of a few boats, on which tolls were collected to the amount of $230, which comprised the total of its first year's receipts. Chiefly in consequence of the great increase of the coal trade, it was determined to enlarge the capacity of the canal for a greater amount of business, which was accordingly done in 1846. Hitherto it had only admitted the passage of boats of sixty-six tons, but, by the enlargement, boats of one hundred and eighty-six tons are enabled to pass through its whole length of one hundred and ten miles, being one of the grandest works of the kind in the Union. A great improvement was made. The locks were reduced in number from one hundred and nine to seventy-one, and enlarged to one hundred and ten by eighteen feet; the width of its canals to not less than sixty feet, with a depth of at least five and a-half feet. To guard against the danger of a deficiency of water, to which the navigation is exposed in dry seasons, the company has erected several large dams upon tributary streams at the head of navigation, from which to draw supplies in cases of deficiency. The dam at Silver creek covers nearly sixty acres, and is estimated to hold sufficient water of itself to float about 120,000 tons of coal, annually, to market. As may be expected, the business of this great work has increased wonderfully. In 1825, this line brought about 5000 tons of coal to market; in 1827, 31,360 tons; and in 1857, it was 1,275,988 tons—showing that forty tons had now gone over the works when, thirty years previously, but one had gone. It is stated, on reliable authority, that the coal consumed by the various furnaces, forges and manufactories, in the Valley of the

Schuylkill, amounts now to 450,000 tons annually. Thus we see how greatly important this trade has become, and in which we are all more or less interested. We have said that the Schuylkill flows by Montgomery county about forty miles, in which distance the navigation company has erected six dams across it, which, at Norristown and Conshehocken, afford valuable water-power. We wish to be prophetic when we say that we really believe the day is not far distant when this line will be further enlarged and that vessels of two hundred and fifty tons will ascend, by steam or otherwise, as far as Port Kennedy, where they will load and then return to the ocean to discharge their freight at the cities of our sea-board. Young reader, you may live to see it!

II.

THE INDIANS.

The aborigines found by the early European adventurers inhabiting this part of Pennsylvania, called themselves the *Lenni Lenape*, or the *original people*. They also assumed unto themselves the name of *Woapanachki*, or the *people from the east*. These names, it would appear, they adopted from a belief of being superior in all respects to any of the adjacent tribes. The territory they lived on lay between the Hudson and the Susquehanna rivers, and consequently inhabited both sides of the Delaware and Schuylkill. It was from this circumstance that they early received from the whites the name of Delawares. Under this general name they comprehended a number of distinct tribes, but speaking dialects of a common language, and uniting around the same great council fire. Mr. Jefferson, in his Notes on Virginia, says, that the Lenni Lenape were a taller people generally than the Europeans. Oldmixon, who visited Pennsylvania, in 1708, speaks of the Indians as being generally tall, straight, and exceedingly well proportioned, and that they were in the common practice of anointing themselves with clarified bear's fat. He says he saw some as handsome faces among them, of both sexes, as any in England, and that many had fine Roman features. He also mentions that they were very civil and friendly to the English, and that he had not heard of an instance where they had done an injury to any of the whites. Mons Rambo, who was born near the Schuylkill, in 1693, and settled in Upper Merion in 1712, often related in his latter days, the great kindness shown by the Indians to the whites of his neighborhood. In a letter sent to Gottenburg, in 1692, by some of the Swedes here, they make mention that the Indians had not molested them for many years. William Penn, shortly after his first arrival in Pennsylvania, sent a letter to England, in which, among other matters, he gives the following interesting character of the Indians: "In liberality they excel: nothing is too good for their friend; give them a fine gun, coat, or other thing, it may pass twenty hands before it sticks; light of heart, strong affections, but soon spent. The most merry creatures that live, feast and dance perpetually; they never have much, nor want much. Some kings have sold, others presented me with several parcels of land. The pay, or presents I made them, were not hoarded by the particular owners; but the neighboring kings and their clans being present when the goods were brought out, the parties chiefly concerned consulted what and to whom they should give them. To every king then, by the hands of a person for that work appointed, is a proportion sent, so sorted and folded, and with that gravity that is admirable. They care for little, because they want but little; and the reason is, a little contents them. In this they are sufficiently revenged on us; if they are ignorant of our pleasures, they are also free from our pains. We sweat and toil to live; their pleasure feeds them; I mean their hunting, fishing, and fowling; and this table is spread everywhere."

The Rev. John Campanius, Swedish chaplain of Governor Printz, and who resided on Tinicum Island, near the mouth of the Schuylkill, from 1642 to 1648, gives us, in his "Nya Swerige," an excellent account of the Indians, and which contains information we have been unable to find in any other work. What adds to the interest of his description is, that he wrote it from his own actual observations, and that, too, at a period dating back nearly to the first landing of the Europeans in this part of the country. His arrival here was forty years previous to the first landing of Penn; yes, even two years before he was born. On account of the rarity of Mr. Campanius' work, and its appropriateness at this place, is our apology for the following extract:—

"Their way of living was very simple. With arrows, pointed with sharp stones, they killed the deer and other creatures. They made axes from stones, which they fastened to a stick, to kill the trees where they intended to plant. They cultivated the ground with a sort of hoe, made from the shoulder-blade of a deer, or a tortoise shell, sharpened with stones, and fastened to a stick. They made pots of clay, mixed with powdered muscle shells burnt in fire, to prepare their food in. By friction, they made fire from two pieces of hard wood. The trees they burnt down and cut into pieces for firewood. On journeys they carried fire a great ways in spunk, or sponges found growing on the trees. They burnt down great trees, and shaped them into canoes by fire, and the help of sharp stones. Men and women were dressed in skins; the women made themselves under garments of wild hemp, of which also they made twine to knit the feathers of turkeys, eagles, &c., into blankets. The earth, the woods, and the rivers were the provision stores of the Indians; for they eat all kinds of wild animals and productions of the earth, fowls, birds, fishes, and fruits, which they find within their reach. They shoot deer, fowls, and birds with the bow and arrow; they take the fishes in the same manner; when the waters are high, the fish run up the creeks and return at ebb tide; so that the Indians can easily shoot them at low water, and drag them ashore."

"They eat, generally, but twice a day, morning and afternoon; the earth serves them for tables and chairs. They sometimes broil their meat and their fish; other times, dry them in the sun, or in the smoke, and thus eat them. They make bread out of the maize or Indian corn, which they prepare in a manner peculiar to themselves: they crush the grain between two great stones, or on a large piece of wood; they moisten it with water, and make it into small cakes, which they wrap up in corn-leaves, and thus bake them in the ashes. In this manner they make their bread. The Swedes made use of it when they first came. They can fast, when necessity compels them, for many days. When traveling, or lying in wait for their enemies, they take with them a kind of bread made of Indian corn and tobacco juice, to allay their hunger and quench their thirst, in case they have nothing else at hand. The drink, before the Christians came into this country, was nothing but water; but now they are very fond of strong liquors. Both men and women smoke tobacco, which grows in their country in great abundance. They have, besides corn, beans, and pumpkins, a sort of *original dogs* with short pointed ears."

"The American Indians had no towns or fixed places of habitation. They mostly wandered about from one place to another; and generally went to those places where they could find the most likely means of support. In spring and summer they preferred the banks of rivers, where they found plenty of fish; but in winter, they went up into the country, where they found abundance of venison. When they travel, they carry their game with them wherever they go, and fix it on poles, under which they dwell. When they want fire they strike it out of a piece of dry wood, of which they find plenty; and, in that manner, they are never at a loss for fire to warm themselves, or to cook their meat. Their principal articles of furniture are a kettle, in which they boil their meat, and some dishes or plates of bark and cedar wood, out of which they eat; for drinking they use commonly the shell of the calabash."

"When a Christian goes to visit them in their dwellings, they immediately spread on the ground pieces of cloth, and fine mats or skins; then they produce the best they have, as bread, deer, elk, or bear's meat, fresh fish and bear's fat, to serve in lieu of butter, which they generally broil upon the coals. These attentions must not be despised, but must be received with thankfulness, otherwise their friendship will turn to hatred. When an Indian visits his friend, a Christian, he must always uncover his table at the lower end, for the Indian will have his liberty; and he will immediately jump upon the table, and sit on it with his legs crossed, for they are not accustomed to sit upon chairs; he then asks for whatever he would like to eat of. When the Swedes first arrived, the Indians were in the habit of eating the flesh of their enemies. Once on an occasion they invited a Swede to go with them to their habitation in the woods, where they treated him with the best the house afforded. Their entertainment was sumptuous; there was broiled, boiled, and even hashed meat, all of which the Swede partook with them, but it seems it did not well agree with him. The Indians, however, did not let him know what he had been eating; but it was told him some time after by some other Indians, who let him know that he had fed on the flesh of an Indian of a neighboring tribe, with whom they were at war."

If we compare the American Indians with the natives of Europe, or Asia, we shall find that the superiority displayed by the latter in conducting the operations of agriculture, depended chiefly on two circumstances, the use of tame animals and the possession of iron and other hard metals. But the aborigines of America had not reduced animals to subjugation; and they were completely ignorant of the harder and more useful metals. Gold, with the exception of a little silver and copper, was the only metal known in America before the discovery; and the use of this was chiefly confined to ornament. The principal tool in the possession of the natives were hatchets of stone; and with these the labor of a year was requisite to cut down a tree and hollow it into a canoe. In agriculture their progress was equally slow. The trees with which the forests were crowded, were of the hardest wood, and the shrubs so thickly interwoven, that the efforts of a whole tribe were scarcely sufficient to clear a small piece of ground, and adapt it to the purposes of cultivation. The fertility of the soil, rather than the industry of the people, secured to them an increase equal to their wants. Necessity, chiefly, compelled them, for subsistence, to depend on hunting and fishing.

The language of the Indians has been to us an interesting subject of study, we mean by this more particularly their numerous speeches which have been handed down to us in the Colonial Records and Archives of Pennsylvania. We know it is customary to laud the languages of ancient Greece and Rome; but it is doubtful with us but what there are finer passages to be found in some of the speeches made by the unlettered savages that roamed our forests, not two centuries ago, than can be found in many of the more celebrated worthies of the nations referred to. There are in those Indian speeches some of the most splendid poetical images that the mind of man has ever conceived; such expressions, we might say, of natural beauty that we could almost doubt any language could furnish, much less that of our American Indians. It is confidently believed, though now so little known, that the time is not far distant when these speeches will become a part of the study of every lover of elegant literature. William Penn, in his "Present State of America," printed in London, in 1687, at page 69, says: "Their language is lofty, yet narrow, but like the Hebrew; in signification full; like short hand in writing, one word serveth in the place of three, and the rest are supplied by the understanding of the hearer; imperfect in their tenses, wanting in their moods, participles, adverbs and conjunctions: I have made it my business to understand it, that I might not want an interpreter on any occasion; and I must say, I know not a language spoken in Europe that has words of more sweetness or greatness in accent and emphasis than theirs; for instance, Octorocken, Rancocas, Oricton, Schakamaxon, Poquesin, all which are names of places, and have grandeur in them of words of sweetness. *Anna* is mother; *Isamus*, brother; *Netap*, friend; *Usque oret*, very good; *Poru*, bread; *Metse*, eat; *Matto*, no; *Natta*, have; *Payo*, to come. If one ask them of any thing they have not, they will answer, *matta ne hotta*, which, translated, is, *not I have*, instead of *I have not.*" The name they applied to the Swedes was, *Akoores*, and to the Dutch and English, *Senaares*. The Rev. John Campanius, of whom we have alluded, represents the Indians as having been frequent visitors at his house, and that, in his conversation with them, generally succeeded in making them understand the leading truths and doctrines of the gospel. He was so much encouraged, that he learned their language, and translated the Lutheran catechism into it, and which was published at Stockholm in 1696. In our next article on the Swedes, extracts from it will be given, both in the Indian and Swedish. In this work he calls the Indian language the "American Virginiske spraket." It is much to be regretted that so few of those beautiful, sonorous-sounding Indian names have been retained, for no language has given any more agreeable to the ear. They even won the admiration of Charles Dickens, who could find so little in America to praise. As far as our investigations have been made, the following constitute all the Indian names we were enabled to ascertain, as now existing in this county: Manatawny, Perkiomen, Wissahickon, Pennypack, Skippack, Saratoga, Tacony, Towamencin, Mingo, Mashilmac, Goshehoppen, Sciota and Macovy creeks, and Methacton and Conshehocken hills. These names, it is hoped, may prove as lasting as the streams and hills to which they were originally applied, for it should be remembered that they are now almost the only mementos of a departed race. What a strange fatality! While the once lords of creation here have forever disappeared, they have left those names behind to linger by our valleys and our hill-tops. An allusion has been made to Indian speeches. We have concluded, partly in corroboration of our remarks, to give a short extract of one delivered at the court house at Lancaster, in this State, June 30th, 1744, by Gachradodow, a chief, in reply to the commissioners of Virginia, concerning some lands. It is taken from Colden's History of the Five Indian Nations, published at London, in 1755, pages 86–7 of vol. ii. What renders this effort the more extraordinary is that the name of the speaker is only found in connection with this speech, otherwise, like nearly all the others, it would have passed into oblivion. It was translated at the time into English by Conrad Weiser, who was the interpretor. Where an uncultivated mind can give expression to such striking, original and concise ideas, what might it have been made if properly educated by the best schools of this day?

"The world at first was made on the other side of the Great Water, different from what it is on this side, as may be known from the different colors of our skin, and of our flesh, and that which you call justice may not be so amongst us; you have your laws and customs, and so have we. The Great King might send you over to conquer the Indians, but it looks to us that God did not approve of it; if he had, he would not have placed the sea where it is, as the limits between us. You know very well, when the white people came first here they were poor; but now they have got our lands, and are by them become rich, and we are now poor; what little we have had for the land goes soon away, *but the land lasts forever.*"

There are numbers of persons tolerably familiar with Indian history, yet if they were asked to explain fully what was meant by wampum and the calumet, would be unable to give a satisfactory answer. These are so often mentioned in our colonial records and archives as to merit some description. Wampum passed as current money between the early whites and Indians. There were two kinds of it, the white and purple. They were both worked into the form of beads, generally each about half an inch long, and one-eighth broad, with a hole drilled through them so as to be strung on leather or hempen strings. The white was made out of the great conch or sea-shell, and the purple out of the inside of the muscle shell. These beads, as we shall call them, after being strung, were next woven by the Indian women into belts, sometimes broader than a person's hand, and about two feet long. It was these that were given and received at their various treaties as seals of friendship; in matters of less importance, only a single string was given. Two pieces of white wampum were considered to equal in value one of the purple. The calumet was a large smoking pipe, made out of some soft stone, commonly of a dark red color, well polished, and shaped somewhat in the form of a hatchet, and ornamented with large feathers of several colors. It was used in all their treaties with the whites, and it was considered by them as a flag of truce between contending parties, which it would be a high crime to violate. In fact, the calumet by them was considered as sacred and as serious an obligation as an oath among the Christians. The late Matthias Holstein found on his farm, near Norristown, while ploughing, a number of years ago, an Indian head, ingeniously carved in stone. Axes and arrow-heads are still occasionally found along the entire valley of the Schuylkill, which, in a reflecting mind, will awaken an interest in the people to whom they once belonged.

The early history of Pennsylvania is not one of bloodshed, like that of New England. One great reason of this is the fair and honorable purchases made here for the lands of the Indians. From the earliest period, both the Swedes and the English recognized in the natives a right to the soil. We have looked in vain to find an instance of even a single murder or outrage having been committed between the Indians and the whites within the present limits of Montgomery county. At the time of the first settlement of the Swedes along the Delaware in 1638, they purchased the lands from the natives. We learn from Campanius, that during the administration of John Claudius Risingh, the successor of Governor Printz, that on the 17th of June, 1654, there was held on Tinicum Island, near the mouth of the Schuylkill, a great treaty, at which were present ten neighboring chiefs, besides many Indians. The right of the Queen of Sweden was admitted to all the lands which they had sold, and the old league of friendship was duly confirmed. Naoman, a firm friend of the Swedes, was the principal speaker on this occasion. The covenants then entered into, it is perhaps needless to add, were never violated. After the business of the treaty had been concluded, two great kettles of *sappan*, as the Swedes called mush made of Indian corn, were produced. At one the chiefs sat, and around the other, the common Indians, all seated on the floor. Campanius says they "fed heartily and were satisfied."

Immediately after the arrival of William Penn, he at once entered upon treaties with the Indian chiefs for the purchase of lands. By the royal charter granted him no other had the right, and he therefore stipulated with the purchasers under him to extinguish the right of the Indians to the same. His religious principles would not permit him to wrest the soil from those to whom Nature had given it, and therefore under the shade of the lofty trees of the forest did he make his treaties, and which were duly sanctified by smoking incense from the calumet of peace. In these early purchases the boundaries are often vague and undefined, and the stations cannot always be precisely ascertained at the present day. The earliest purchase by Penn, of any part of what now constitutes Montgomery county, was made the 25th of June, 1683, of Wingebone, for all his right to lands lying on the west side of the Schuylkill, beginning at the lower falls of the same, and so on up, and backwards of said stream as far as his right goes. The next purchase was made the 14th of July, of the same year, from Secane and Idquoquehan and others, for all the land lying between the Manayunk or Schuylkill River and Macopanackhan or Chester River, and up as far as the Conshehocken Hill, which is opposite the present borough of that name. On the same day, another purchase was made of Neneshickan, Malebore, Neshanocke and Oscreneon, for the lands lying between the Schuylkill and Pennepack streams, and extending as far north-west as Conshehocken, but now better known as Edge Hill. On the 3d of June, 1684, all the right of Maughhongsink to the land along the Perkiomen Creek, was duly sold and conveyed. On the 7th of the same month and year, Mettamicont relinquished all his right to lands on both sides of the Pennepack. July 30th, 1685, Shakhoppa, Secane, Malebore and Tangoras conveyed all their right to lands situated between Chester and Pennepack Creeks, and extending up into the country, in a north-west direction from the sources of those streams, two full days' journey. This almost takes in the whole of the county, excepting only that portion lying east of the Pennypack Creek. July 5th, 1697, another purchase was made from Tamany, Weheeland, Wehequeekhon, Yaqueekhon and Quenamockquid, for all their right to lands lying between the Pennepack and Neshaminy creeks, and extending in a north-west direction from the Delaware as far as a horse could travel in two days. Thus was finally extinguished by purchase all the right and title of the Indians to any portion of the soil now embraced within the limits of Montgomery County.

An Indian council was held by previous appointment, at the house of Edward Farmer, where is now the village of Whitemarsh, on the 19th of May, 1712. The Governor, Charles Gookin, was present, with the Sheriff, John Budd, Coroner Richard Walker, and others. A delegation of eleven Delaware Indians was present, Sassunan being the principal chief, accompanied by Ealochelan and Scholichy, the latter being speaker. Edward Farmer, who was quite familiar with the Indian language, performed the duties of interpretor. Scolitchy, in his address to the Governor, mentioned, that as the Delawares had been made tributary to the Mingoes, or Five nations, many years ago, they had thought proper to call on him previous to their seeing those tribes, and that they had brought their tribute along, which was duly presented to the Governor, and consisted of thirty-two belts of wampum, of various figures, and a long Indian pipe called the calumet, made of stone, the shaft of which was adorned with feathers resembling wings, besides other ornaments. Their business was amicably adjusted to the entire satisfaction of all parties. On this occasion the Governor and his friends, thirteen in number, came from Philadelphia on horseback.

III.

THE SWEDES.

The credit is due to the Swedes of having made the first permanent settlements in Pennsylvania. The Dutch founded Fort Orange and New Amsterdam, on the Hudson River, in 1612. These settlements proved so successful that it was not long before they arrested the attention of Gustavus Adolphus, the illustrious monarch of Sweden. William Usselinx, a Hollander by birth, but now a distinguished merchant of Stockholm, conceived the idea, in 1624, of starting a company somewhat similar to the Dutch, for trading and colonizing purposes, on the west side of the Delaware River. All the necessary stock was subscribed, and every thing arranged for the successful prosecution of the matter, when a German war broke out, which checked the enterprise, and resulted in the death of the monarch, at the battle of Lutzen, in November, 1632. However, the project was not allowed to slumber, and during the minority of Queen Christina, her excellent prime minister, Oxenstiern, revived it on a somewhat smaller scale. Two vessels, the "Key of Calmar" and the "Bird Grip," were despatched from Gottenburg to the Delaware, in the fall of 1637, with colonists, provisions, ammunition and merchandise for traffic. Peter Minuet, who had formerly been Governor of New Amsterdam, but had become dissatisfied with the company, offered his services to the Swedes, and was appointed to the command of the expedition. They arrived safely at Cape Henlopen, near which place they first landed. A clergyman, the Rev. Reorius Torkillus, accompanied them as chaplain. They made a purchase from the natives, in 1638, of the lands on the west side of the bay, from Cape Henlopen to Santhicon, or the falls of the Delaware, which they called "New Sweden." They next proceeded up the river and built a town and fort, on the north side of Minquaas, or Mingo Creek, three miles from its mouth, which they called Christina, in honor of their sovereign, which name was also given to the stream. Tradition has it that the ancestors of the Rambos, the Holsteins, the Yocums, and the Matsons and others, now so numerous in Montgomery county, arrived in these vessels. The Swedes zealously endeavored to cultivate peace with the Indians and Dutch, who had settled and taken possession of the country on the opposite side of the river. Minuet, after three years' administration, died, and Peter Hollendare, his successor, after ruling a year and a half, returned home. Immediately on this event John Printz was appointed Governor, and the Rev. John Campanius chaplain of the colony. They sailed from Stockholm August 16th, 1642, in the ship Fame, accompanied by two other vessels of war, the Swan and the Charitas, and proceeded up the Delaware to the low alluvial island called by the natives Tinicum or Tinnekonk, situated below, but near the mouth of the Schuylkill. This spot Governor Printz selected both for a colony and his future residence, and in consequence landed here in February, 1643. A strong fort was immediately erected of large green hemlock logs, and a handsome palace for the Governor, called Printz Hall, which was surrounded with a fine orchard and pleasure grounds. Near by, on the same island, were also erected a number of houses and plantations for the most respectable colonists. The whole was called New Gottenburg, and enjoyed the dignity for twelve years of being the metropolis and capital of New Sweden. Queen Christina, this same year, on hearing of Governor Printz's valuable services and success in founding the colony, granted him the island and town thereon as a possession to be enjoyed by him and his heirs forever. In her instructions to the Governor, among other matters she strictly enjoined him to administer justice according to Swedish laws; to preserve, as far as practicable, the manners and customs of Sweden; to promote diligently all profitable branches of industry, such as the culture of grain, of tobacco, of the vine, and the mulberry for silk, the raising of cattle, to search for precious metals, diligently to cultivate a traffic with the Indians, and especially to be careful to undersell the English and the Dutch. With the Indians he was to confirm the former purchases of lands and treaties of peace; and as far as practicable to win them over to embrace Christianity, and adopt the manners and customs of civilized life. Under these wholesome instructions the Swedish colony abundantly prospered.

The early Swedes undoubtedly were a moral and religious people, and under the most adverse circumstances never lost sight of their faith. As soon as opportunities permitted a commodious church of wood was built, which was consecrated by the Rev. Mr. Campanius, on the 4th of September, 1646, and was the first house of worship erected in Pennsylvania. A burying ground was laid out adjacent, and the first corpse interred was that of Catharine, the daughter of Andrew Hansen, on the following 28th of October. This church has long since been destroyed, and in consequence of the scarcity of stone on the island and its vicinity, bricks were used in its foundation, one of which may now be seen in the collections of the Pennsylvania Historical Society. It is made of clay, slightly burnt, and of a light amber color, its dimensions are six and a half by three inches, being smaller than bricks made at the present day. In consequence, it appears, of a too rigid exercise of authority, Governor Printz became quite unpopular among the colonists, and after a residence of ten years returned in 1652, leaving his son-in-law, Pappegoia, in temporary charge of the colony. The Swedes about this time also formed a settlement a few miles below New Gottenburg, on the Delaware, which they called Upland, which continued to bear this name till the arrival of Penn, in 1682, when it was called Chester. They also had two settlements and forts on the Schuylkill, a short distance above its mouth, which they called Gripsholm and New Wasa. In 1654, Peter Lindstrom, the royal Swedish engineer, made a map of New Sweden, which included the bay and river Delaware, with the adjacent country on the west side, up as far as the falls at Trenton. It has also the Schuylkill marked as far up as to contain a part of the territory now comprised in Montgomery county. Though this map is not a correct one, yet there is enough delineated to show that the Swedes at this time were tolerably familiar with the country. A few English families from Maryland settled upon the Schuylkill as early as 1642. They were, however, soon after driven away by the Hollanders. The Dutch West India Company having for some time had possession of the opposite shores of the Delaware, now New Jersey, began to covet the western side also, at length in 1644, laid claim to this territory under a grant from the government of Holland, and the year after was subdued by Stuyvesant, the Dutch Governor of New Amsterdam, now New York, and the government transferred there. On the 5th of December of this year, (1655), a great fire broke out in New Gottenburg, which consumed the fort and the town. Whether this disaster was brought about by the Dutch, while taking or holding possession of the place, we are unable to tell, but the circumstance was sufficient to bring on a decline from which it never recovered, and its existence is only now a matter of history. It cannot be denied that the principal object of the Dutch and Swedes in their settlements along the Delaware from 1623 to 1665, was the prosecution of the fur trade, with the Minqua Indians. The documents of the Holland Company in 1656, speak of the great beaver trade of the Schuylkill, and along which for the more successful operations of this traffic they erected several forts. But the Dutch were more actuated by selfish considerations—a mere love of gain—while the Swedes, by cultivating the soil to some extent, gave permanency and success to the colony. However much the kind-hearted Swedes had been wronged by their masters, retaliatory justice was approaching to teach them that the way of the transgressor is hard. The English, in 1664, conquered the whole country of New Netherlands, and Sir Robert Carr became deputy governor here, under Richard Nichols, of New York. At the lower end of the present city of Philadelphia the Swedes had a small settlement, which was called Wicaco, where a block house, in 1669, was built for the purposes of defence, armed with "loop-holes," which in 1677 was converted into a house of worship. The spot is still used for this purpose to the present day, being the site of the Swedes Church, the Rev. Jacob Fabricius being the first pastor. Three Swedes of the name of Swanson owned the land on which the city stands, which they relinquished to Penn, shortly after his arrival, for a small consideration. Upland, the English, in 1673, made the chief place of a judicial district. From the "Court Records" of this place we learn that in 1677, Laer Colman, Pell Laerson, and Peter Erickson took up three hundred acres near the "Falls of Schuylkill." Having proceeded so far in chronological order, we will fall back to say that a ship, called the Mercurius, arrived from Sweden, in 1656, filled with emigrants. As the Dutch had the year previous taken possession of the country, they tried to prevent her from ascending the river, but the Indians, ever the true friends of the Swedes, interposed their authority, when the ship was permitted to pass on and discharge her passengers and freight.

The Rev. John Campanius, of whom we have several times spoken, deserves at our hands a further notice. He was born in the village of Frost Hult, Sweden, in the year 1600. His works show that while young he must have received a good education, and that at no period of his long life had been an idle student. Doubtless owing to his abilities he received the appointment of preceptor of the Orphans' House at Stockholm. This post he held till he received the appointment of Chaplain, under Governor Printz, of the colony about to be established in New Sweden. He sailed with the expedition in August 1642, and arrived at Tinicum Island, below the mouth of the Schuylkill, in February of the next year. A church was erected here in 1646, having no doubt previously held worship in Governor Printz's mansion. A desire to be spiritually useful to the Indians, induced him to study their language, which he acquired at length with tolerable proficiency. During his residence here he laid the foundation of his two principal works: Luther's Catechism in the Swedish and Indian languages, with a vocabulary, and the Description of New Sweden. It is much regretted that he never finished these works himself. He returned, with his family, from Elfsborg, in the ship Swan, on the 13th of May, 1648, and landed at Stockholm, July 3d, making the voyage in sixty-three days, which was considered a remarkably short passage. Soon after his arrival he was made first preacher of the Admiralty, and afterwards pastor of Upland, where we believe he continued to preside till his death. He died the 17th of September, 1683, at the advanced age of eighty-three years, and was interred in the Church of Frost Hult, where a monument is erected to his memory. There is commonly attached to his name the word *Holm*, which has led several to presume it to be his surname, but in fact was intended to imply that he was from Stockholm, such affixes being customary in those days. His son, it appears, was in this country with him, and from the papers of the former and the relations of the latter, with perhaps some other traditionary matter, *his son*, Thomas Campanius, who was never in America, prepared and published the aforesaid works. These labors of Campanius possess a particular value, and go to supply what otherwise would have been a considerable gap in the early history of Pennsylvania. What adds to their interest at this day is their remarkable originality and vigor of mind which they display. There are a few defects in them which we must overlook on account of the manner under which they were prepared. These consist, chiefly, of a few inaccuracies as regards dates, and an occasional tinge of exaggeration. There is reason to believe that he was the first missionary among the Indians in Pennsylvania, if not within the limits of the thirteen original colonies. He began the translation of the Catechism in the Lenni Lenape language, in 1646, being fifteen years before the publication of the New Testament of John Elliot into the Indian language in New England.

The works of Campanius, as may well be expected, at this day, are extremely rare. There is a copy of each in the Philadelphia Library, and a copy of his New Sweden in the Library of the Historical Society; none other is known to us, at least in Pennsylvania. The Catechism, which was printed in 1696, is a small duodecimo of 160 pages, to which is appended a vocabulary of 28 pages of the Indian, or, as he calls it, Virginian language. The following is copied from its title page and is in the Swedish: "Lutheri Catechismus Ofwersatt pa American-Virginiske Spraket. Stockholm, Tryct vthi, thet af Konigl-Maytt, privileg. Burchardi Tryckeri af I.I. Genath, f. Anno. MDCXCVI." Following, from page 130, is the Lord's Prayer, in the Indian and also in the Swedish. These are given chiefly to show to our readers what comparison may exist between those two languages and the English or German.

"Nooshun Kesukquot, Quittiana tamunach Koowesuonk. Peyaumoontch Kukke tussoo tamoonk. Kutte nautamoonk neu nach ohkeit neane Kesukquut. Nummeet suongash ascke-sukokish assamaijnean yeuyeu kesukod Kah ahquontamaj innean numat cheseongash Neane matchenehu queagig nuta quonta mounnonog. Ah que sagkom pagunainnean en qutchhuaon-ganit. Webe pohquoh Wussinean wutch machitut. Amen."

"Fader war som ast i Himblom. Helgat warde tikk Namn. Tilkomme tikk Rijke. Skee tin Wilie, sason i Himmelon, sa ock pa

Jordenne. Wart dageligit Brod gif ofz i Dag. Och forlat osz wara skulder, sasam ock wij forlate them osz skyldige aro. Och inled osz icke i Trestelsen. Vtan frals osz ifran Ondo. Ty tikk ar Rijket, Machten och Harligheten i Eweghet, Amen."

The other work of Campanius was also printed at Stockholm, in the Swedish, in 1702, the title of which is "Kort Beskyrfunnig om Provincian Nya Swerige callas Pennsylvania," which literally translated reads "Brief Description of the Province of New Sweden, now Pennsylvania." It contains several maps of the country which were made before 1655, besides several curious copper-plate engravings. We shall now give a few additional extracts from this work which relate to this section of the country, and from their novelty cannot fail to interest the reader.

"About the Falls there grow walnut, chestnut, peach and mulberry trees, and several sorts of plum trees, and grape vines; hemp and hops grow in abundance. On this river there grows a plant, the fruit of which is round, and is called *Calabash.* It is a vine that runs along the ground. The fruit is shaped like a pear. Some are as large as a great pumpkin, and others are as small as a snuff-box. The skin is yellow, smooth, and thin as glass; it is hard and tough as horn. If they chance to fall on the ground they will not split to pieces. Within, they are full of seeds; when these are taken out the fruit serves as a vessel for several uses. If sawed in two they will make bottles, cups and dishes, and for variety's sake they may be rimmed with silver. Some of them are so large that they will hold a gallon or more. There is also a kind of fly, which the Indians call Cucuyo, which in the night gives so strange a light that it is sufficient, when a man is traveling, to show him the way: one may also write and read the smallest print by the light which they give. When the Indians go in the night a hunting, they fasten these in ects to their hands and feet, by which they can see their way as well as in the day time. One night those flies frightened all the soldiers that were on guard at Fort Christina: they thought they were enemies advancing toward them with lighted matches. There is here, also, a large and horrible serpent, which is called a rattlesnake. It has a head like a dog, and can bite off a man's leg as if cut with an axe. There are horny joints in their tails, which make a noise like children's rattles, and when they see a man they wind themselves in a circle, and shake their heads, which can be heard at the distance of a hundred yards, so that one may put himself on his guard. These snakes are three yards long, and thick as the thickest part of a man's leg; they are as many years old as they have rattles in their tails; their color is brown, black and yellow."

It appears that the calabash is a native of this country, and that its name is of Indian origin, a circumstance we have not seen mentioned in any other work. It seems as if Mr. Campanius had no knowledge of the poisonous qualities of the rattlesnake. The Rev. Andrew Sandel, who was the Swedish minister at Wicaco, from 1702 to 1719, and if not a native of Sweden was at least educated there, and belonged to what was called the "mission." The following is his account of the appearance of the locusts, as published in Clay's Swedish Annals:—

"In May, 1715, a multitude of locusts came out of the ground, everywhere, even on the solid roads. They were wholly covered with a shell, and it seemed very wonderful that they could penetrate the hard earth. Having come out of the earth, they crept out of the shells, flew away, sat down on the trees, and made a peculiar noise till evenings. Being spread over the country in such numbers, the noise they made was so loud that the cow-bells could scarcely be heard in the woods. They pierced the bark on the branches of the trees, and deposited their eggs in the opening. Many apprehended that the trees would wither in consequence of this, but no symptom of it was observed the next year. Hogs and poultry fed on them. Even the Indians did eat them, especially when they first came, boiling them a little. They did not continue long, but died in the month of June. The same year was very fruitful."

Accustomed as we now are to those things, they seem of little moment, but to the early Europeans they justly excited astonishment, being so unlike anything found in their own country.

The charter of Pennsylvania was granted by Charles II., March 4th, 1681. William Penn, the founder of Pennsylvania, landed at Upland, now called Chester, on the 8th of November, (new style) 1682, from the ship Welcome, commanded by Robert Greenaway. Richard Townsend, a passenger in this vessel, states in his "Testimony," that "At our arrival we found it a wilderness; the chief inhabitants were Indians, and some Swedes, who received us in a friendly manner, and though there was a great number of us the good hand of Providence was seen in a particular manner, in that provisions were found for us, by the Swedes and Indians, at very reasonable rates." Penn proceeded at this place to establish his government over the infant province, and convened an assembly which met on the 4th of December following. This session only lasted three days and enacted three laws. One was to naturalize the Swedes, Dutch and other foreigners in the province. Late in the year 1682, assisted by Thomas Holme, the Surveyor General, Penn laid out Philadelphia on land purchased from three Swedes. The Proprietary, it appears, was delighted with the kind reception he received from the gentle-hearted Swedes. After his departure from this country he sent a letter from London, dated the 16th of 1st mo., 1684-5, to Thomas Lloyd, President of Council, in which he says, "Salute me to the Swedes, Captain Cock, old Peter Cock, and Rambo, and their sons, the Swansons, Andrew Binkson, P. Yoakum, and the rest of them. Their ambassador here dined with me the other day." Penn, again, in his "Present State of America," printed in London, in 1687, at page 106 says, "I must needs commend the Swedes' respect to authority, and kind behavior to the English; they do not degenerate from the old friendship between both kingdoms. As they are people proper and strong of body, so they have fine children, and almost every house full, rare to find one of them without three or four boys, and as many girls; some six, seven, eight sons: And I must do them that right, I see few young men more sober and industrious."

We can well imagine the condition of any people living for so many years as isolated as the Swedes did from their mother country, that any occurrence which would throw light on their kindred and friends abroad, would stir up within their breasts, as it would in most human beings similarly situated, the strong and warm sparks of affection which still binds the race to the land of its fathers. About the year 1690, Andrew Printz, a nephew of Governor Printz, unexpectedly visited his countrymen along the Delaware, and was hailed with delight, affection and warm hospitality. He was from the "fatherland," and could tell them much about their own dear Sweden. Two men, at least, were still living who had crossed the ocean with their first Governor: old Peter Bonde and Peter Rambo. Young Printz returned to Sweden, and at Gottenburg met with John Thelin, the postmaster of the place, and to whom he related the circumstances of his journey, and particularly of the discovery he had made of a settlement of "old Swedes," on the Delaware, who lived comfortably, had good land, dwelt together in harmony, and used the old Swedish way in every thing. Communication between Sweden and Pennsylvania at this time, it should be remembered, was very rare. John Thelin was acquainted with a sister of old Peter Rambo, who lived in Gottenburg, and through her aid sent a letter of inquiry to the Swedes along the Delaware, dated November 16th, 1692, and which was received the 23d of May, of the following year. A reply was sent eight days after, by Charles Springer, of Christina, in which it was stated that they were in want of two ministers of the "true Lutheran faith," 3 books of sermons, 12 bibles, 42 psalm books, 100 tracts, with 200 catechisms, and as many primers, and for which punctual payment was offered. With this letter was sent an interesting account of the mode of life among the Swedes, of which the following is an extract: "As to what concerns our situation in this country, we are for the most part husbandmen. We plough and sow and till the ground; and as to our meat and drink, we live according to the old Swedish custom. This country is very rich and fruitful, and here grow all sorts of grain in great plenty, so that we are richly supplied with meat and drink, and we send out yearly to our neighbors on this continent and the neighboring islands, bread, grain, flour and oil. We have here all sorts of beasts, fowls and fishes. Our wives and daughters employ themselves in spinning wool and flax, and many of them in weaving; so that we have great reason to thank the Almighty for his manifold mercies and benefits. We also live in peace and friendship with one another, and the Indians have not molested us for many years. Further, since this country has ceased to be under the government of Sweden, we are bound to say, for the sake of truth, that we have been well and kindly treated, as well by the Dutch as by his Majesty, the King of England. We have always had over us good and gracious magistrates, and we live with one another in peace and quietness." The Swedish inhabitants were much gratified in receiving, shortly after, the ministers and books which they so earnestly desired, by order of the Swedish government, free of charge.

The present population of Swedish extraction in Pennsylvania must now be considerable. By order of Governor Stuyvesant, it was ascertained, in 1659, that there were one hundred and thirty Swedish families in New Sweden. In 1693 these had increased to one hundred and eighty-nine families, numbering upwards of nine hundred and thirty-nine inhabitants. Bancroft, in his History of the United States, estimates them now as being one part in two hundred of the present population. He supposes that at the time of their surrender to the Dutch, in 1655, that they may have exceeded seven hundred souls. So far we have rather generalized the subject, which was deemed necessary for a better understanding of the subsequent history of the Swedes, as they progressed up the Schuylkill, founded settlements, built churches, and gave names to places, around which have since clustered revolutionary associations.

Among our ancient Swedish families, none are, perhaps, as numerous, at this day, as that of Rambo. Whether there was more than one bearing this name that came from Sweden with Governor Minuet, in 1737, we are unable positively to tell, but we have reason to believe that Peter Rambo and his family included the whole. It appears that he was a conspicuous man in the early settlement, from what little has been handed down to us. In 1657, he was appointed by the Director-General one of the magistrates of the colony; he was also a commissary, which office he resigned in 1661. On the 1st of May, 1668, Colonel Francis Lovelace, of New York, made him one of the counsellors of Robert Carr, the deputy governor. He was appointed a justice of the peace, October 3rd, 1676, with five others, in the Jurisdiction of Delaware River and dependencies, any three or more to be a Court of Judicature for one year. As he had a sister living in Gottenburg, in 1692, and with whom he had a correspondence, the inference is that he may have been a native of that place. He was still living in 1693, and, with Andrew Boude, was perhaps the only survivor of those who came over in the first expedition. He had then four surviving sons; these were Peter, Gunner, Andrew and John.

Peter Rambo, Jr., we find first mentioned in Walter Wharton's Book of Surveys, at Harrisburg, from which we learn that there was a tract of land surveyed to him, called "Ramsdorp," extending from the Pennepack creek, northeasterly, fifty perches along the Delaware, and which contained three hundred acres. In December, 1681, he is mentioned in the Upland Court Records. He was present at the landing of Penn at Upland, now Chester, November 8, 1682. With Swan Swanson he was a witness to the Indians signing the deed of July 14th, 1683, for lands to William Penn. In the list of Swedish inhabitants, in 1693, he is mentioned as having six persons in his family. Charmed with the beauty and fertility of the Schuylkill valley, he removed with his family from the vicinity of Upland and settled in Upper Merion township, in 1712, where he had purchased a large tract of land adjoining the river, and on which he spent the remainder of his days.

Gunner Rambo, brother of the aforesaid, we find, was a member of the grand jury, at Philadelphia, the 27th of 12th month, 1683, and represented Philadelphia county in the Assembly, in 1685. In the list of 1693, he is represented as having six in his family. He moved into Upper Merion about the time his brother did, and took up a large tract above but adjacent to his, and fronting on the river. It was on a portion of his land that the Swedes' Church was built.

Andrew Rambo, we find, was appointed by the Court at Upland, March 14th, 1681, one of nine overseers of highways, whose jurisdiction extended from Marcus Hook to the Falls of Delaware. The portion assigned to him was from the Falls of Schuylkill to Tacony creek. We find he was continued in the same the year following. The law, at this time, required the roads to be repaired before the last day of May. In the list of 1693, he is represented as having nine persons in his family, and John Rambo, six.

Mons or Mounce Rambo was the son of Gunner Rambo, and was born in 1693, and accompanied his father to Upper Merion, where he spent the remainder of his days. He was a famous hunter, and his exploits still live in the traditions of the neighborhood. When he first came here, he used to say that there were numbers of friendly Indians about and among them. He stated that he had shot numbers of deer in the vicinity as late as the year 1770. Once he shot a panther which he found attempting to attack his dog. Another time, he wounded a large deer, and in stepping across it to cut its throat with a knife, the deer made off with him at full speed; however, he clung to its back and in this position succeeded in killing the animal. The Swedes' Church, in 1760, was built on a portion of his farm. In the grave-yard of the same may be seen a large stone which has inscribed on it, "In memory of Mons Rambo, who departed this life October the 23rd, 1782, aged 89 years." In the list of settlers of Upper Merion, in 1734, we find the names of Mounce, Gabriel, John and Elias Rambo, and, for the same year, Peter Rambo, in Providence township. In the ancient tomb-stones of the Swedes' Church, we find the names of Diana Rambo, who died January 30th, 1744-5, aged 36 years; Peter Rambo, June 18th, 1667, aged 42 years; and Mathias Rambo, October 10th, 1782, aged 66 years. In the list of voters in Upper Merion for 1858, we find registered six of the name of Rambo, and the same number for Upper Providence.

The earliest we know of the name of Holstein is in the list of Swedish settlers in 1693, where Mats Holstein is mentioned as having a family of four persons. There is a family tradition that he came over with Governor Minuet, in 1637, and that he is the ancestor of all those bearing the name and of Swedish descent to be found in Pennsylvania. Mats, or rather Mathias, Holstein, son of the aforesaid, in the year 1712, with Brita, his wife, moved up along the Schuylkill and took up his abode in "Ammasland," now called Upper Merion. Besides the native Indians, he found a few Welshmen scattered through the country, and who had preceded him. He purchased a tract containing one thousand acres of land, which lay directly opposite where Norristown now stands. It had a river-front of about a mile, and from thence extending back into the country some two miles, embracing all the territory upon which the borough of Bridgeport is now laid out, the Shainline farms, Peter Supplee's, and all the land from Red Hill to the river. Swedes' Ford was also on this, and which name we know it bore before the year 1723. In the year 1714, he built a stone house on his place, about one and a-half miles from the river, where he lived with his family. His children, grand-children, great-grand-children and great-great-grand-children have been born in that house, and its walls still stand, though they have been built upon and added to several times since. The aforesaid had a son, Mathias, who was born in 1717, and married Magdalena, daughter of Marcus Hulings, of Morlatton, a Swedish settlement on the Schuylkill, four miles above the present borough of Pottstown. Mrs. Holstein, who survived her husband many years, related several incidents in her early life, which at this day seem quite curious.

She well remembered, when quite young, being carried some distance on a squaw's back. The traveling then was chiefly performed in canoes. When married and brought to Swedes' Ford, near where her husband resided, she and all her wedding friends came down the river in canoes. In February, 1747, we find in the Colonial Records that a company of volunteers or Associators, as they were then called, was raised in Upper Merion, on account of the French and Indian troubles then raging on the frontiers. John Hughs was appointed captain, Mathias Holstein, lieutenant, and Frederick Holstein, ensign. But their services, we believe, were never required. This Mathias Holstein died December 10th, 1768, aged 51 years, and is buried at the Swedes' Church. It is said he was one of the most active in the erection of this church, in 1760. In the list of settlers, in 1734, we find there was a Henry Holstein living in Providence township. Samuel Holstein, who was a son of the last mentioned Mathias Holstein, owned six hundred acres of land in Upper Merion in the beginning of the Revolution. It is said that he could on this tract, as late as 1760, kill deer whenever he desired.

Major Mathias Holstein, a well known and highly respected citizen of Norristown and a son of the above Samuel Holstein, was born October 10th, 1772. He long kept the old Swedes' Ford tavern, standing within the present limits of the borough of Bridgeport. It is said that he often related that about the year 1790 he was the means of killing, on his father's farm, a very large bear by shooting him on a tree, where he had sought refuge from pursuit. He was a man endowed with more than ordinary powers of observation and withal enjoyed a strong retentive memory, and before his death few could be found in any neighborhood that were better stored with the reminiscences of the past. It is much regretted that with his abilities he did not endeavor to preserve his recollections in writing. We have been informed, on the authority of others, that he often wished that some would write a history of his neighborhood or county, and that he had even strongly pursuaded men of literary habits to undertake it; but, kind reader, it was invariably put—put—put off! till the present writer has attempted it out of a mere love of the thing.

It was on a beautiful afternoon in the latter part of August, 1858, that we stood alone in the ancient church-yard below Swedes' Ford. By our side stood a tall white marble monument, at least twelve feet high; on it was inscribed that it was erected to the "Memory of Mathias Holstein, who died August 10th, 1849." As we stood there, a stranger, and reflected on some of the above matters, strange ideas came into our head, but, however, the leading impulse was a strong trust in the future. On an adjoining tombstone, we are informed that Col. George W. Holstein died March 10th, 1841, aged nearly 63 years. In the list of voters of Upper Merion for 1858, we find but two bearing the name of Holstein.

The earliest we find of the name of Yocum is in the Upland Court records, where mention is made of Peter Yocum being on a jury, held there in December, 1681. He was appointed, March 14th, 1682, overseer of the highways for one year, from Karker's Mill to the Falls of Schuylkill. In the list of 1693, he is represented as having a family of nine persons. About the year 1712, he settled in Upper Merion where he had purchased a large tract of land which fronted on the river and extended some distance back into the country. It lay between the present Swedes' Ford Church and the Lower Merion line. In the list of settlers of Upper Merion, in 1734, we still find the name of Peter Yocum. Whether it was the same person or a son we are at present unable to tell. In the Colonial Records for 1693, mention is made of a Mounce Yocum, who probably was a brother. There was a Swan Yocum living in 1780, in Towamencin township. We are informed by a stone in the Swedes' church-yard, that a Moses Yocum died March 1st, 1787, aged 67 years. A Peter Yocum is buried at Morlatton, who died July 13th, 1794, aged 76. By the list of voters in Upper Merion, in 1858, it appears as if the name was now extinct there, but in Upper Providence the name is found; also in several of the adjoining townships.

Nils Matson was a native of Sweden, and was very probably the ancestor of John Matson, mentioned in the list of 1693. The latter is represented as having at that time a family of eleven persons. One of the same name, very likely a son, moved into Upper Merion in 1712, where he took up a large tract of land, fronting on the Schuylkill and lying adjacent to the township of Lower Merion. In the course of time, as the country became settled, a ford was established on the Schuylkill, and, as it lay partly on this tract, it received the name of Matson's Ford. A bridge is now built over the spot, at Conshehocken, and is called the Matson's Ford Bridg. During the Revolution, the American army crossed several times at this ford; it was then owned by Peter Matson, and on his death the land was divided among his four sons, leaving each a farm. Isaac Matson was one of those sons. A hill in his vicinity, on the Lower Merion line, is still called Matson's Hill. In the list of voters in Upper Merion for 1858, but one is now found bearing the name of Matson.

In the list of Swedish settlers, in 1693, we find the name of Lars Halling, or Hulings, mentioned. Probably he was the father of Marcus Hulings, an early settler at Morlatton, on the Schuylkill, two miles above the present Montgomery county line. We know that the latter resided here, previous to 1720. He appears to have been a prominent citizen, and took an early part in procuring the services of a preacher, and in getting the church built, in 1735. In the difficulties between the navigators and the shoremen, in 1731–2, he figures with his neighbors, Jonas Yocum and Jonas Jones. They all then lived in Amity township, in the present Berks county, and were in the practice of taking their wheat and produce every year to Philadelphia in canoes. Marcus Hulings died April 2d, 1757, aged 70 years. There is a stone also erected in the Morlatton church-yard to the memory of Peter Hulings, who died the 17th of August, 1739, aged 18 years.

As Jones is generally a name of Welsh or English origin, it is difficult to trace those bearing it of Swedish descent. The name originally was Jonasson, and is found mentioned in the list of 1693. This family of

Jones were early settlers at Morlatton. On the tombstones we find the names of Peter Jones, who died in 1739, aged 40 years; Jonas Jones, who died January 27th, 1777, aged 77 years, and his wife, Mary, who died September 11th, 1772, aged 68 years. Near the church is still standing a substantial house with a stone in its front wall, containing "I. M. I. 1716," which was owned by the aforesaid couple. In a list of settlers residing in Perkiomen township, in 1734, are mentioned the names of Peter and Mathias Janson. It is our opinion that those names are all corruptions from the one name of Jonasson.

We have spoken of the Swedes as being a religious people, and find that for some time previous to the Revolution they had erected at least four houses of worship in the valley of the Schuylkill. As we wish to be brief, we shall not dwell on the churches they built at Wicaco and Kingsessing. St. Gabriel's Church, at Morlatton, being built first, shall now deserve our attention. This name is supposed to have been given to this place from a church and district in Sweden. This neighborhood was early settled by several Swedish families, at least before 1716; among them can be mentioned the names of Hulings, Yocum, Jones, Kerlin, Anderson, Kerst, and very probably others. It appears that as early as 1720, Marcus Hulings secured the services of the Rev. Samuel Hesselius as pastor, who had arrived the year previous from Sweden. How long he resided in this relation, here, is not certain, but in consequence of the recall of his brother, from Wilmington, in 1723, he took charge of the church there, till 1731, when he returned to Sweden. We know the grave-yard was used here as a place of interment, by the tombstones, at least as early as 1719. The church was first commenced in 1735 and finished in 1737. The Rev. Gabriel Folk was its first pastor, and resided here in that capacity from 1735 to 1745. The earliest marriages and baptisms recorded in the church books begin in the year 1735. It appears, for most of the time, no regular preacher was stationed here. The Rev. Henry M. Muhlenberg, of the Trappe, preached at stated times for a number of years, after 1747. The Rev. Alexander Murray, a missionary sent from Europe by the Society for the Propagation of the Gospel, presided here from 1672 to 1768. The Rev. Edmund Leaf, formerly of Pottstown, is the present pastor. The church is a plain two-story stone building, about thirty-two by thirty-six feet in dimensions, and was erected in 1801. The grave-yard attached to it comprises nearly two acres of ground and is enclosed by a wall. The most common names on the tombstones are Yocum, Hulings, Jones, Kerst, Harrison, Koons, Lott, Dehaven, Eisenberg, Brower, Lear, Leaf, Douglas, Rahn, Ingles, Schunk, Bunn, Koop, Bird, Kerlin, Tea, Henton, Krouse, Rutter, Bell, Lake, Stanley, Robeson and Turner. This church is situated on the Reading turnpike, in Douglassville, a place of about fifty houses. The Reading railroad has a station here, and is forty-four miles from Philadelphia.

Christ church is situated about a mile below the Borough of Bridgeport, in the village of Swedesburg, on the west bank of the Schuylkill River, in Upper Merion Township. It is better known as the Swedes' church, and was built in 1760, on a portion of land belonging to Mons Rambo. Owing to a petition from the members of this and the two other churches at Wicaco and Kingsessing, they were all three, unitedly, incorporated by Lieutenant Governor John Penn, the 25th of September, 1765, as "Swedish Lutheran Churches." This charter, by a private act of Assembly, passed September 10th, 1787, was confirmed with several amendments. The Rev. Charles Magnus Wrangel was the first clergyman that attended this church. He had in charge, at the same time, the church of St. James, in Kingsessing. He was a very popular preacher, and great crowds were in the practice of attending his sermons. In 1768 he returned to Sweden, where he was shortly afterwards made a bishop. The Rev. Slater Clay officiated once a month here, from 1792 till his death, in 1821, when his son, the Rev. J. C. Clay, became his successor. The present pastor is Rev. Wm. Henry Rees, who resides in the village. The church was enlarged in 1837 to its present size. It is a handsome stone edifice, built in the form of a cross, and which is adorned with a spire upwards of fifty feet high, in which a bell was placed in 1855. Few churches have a more beautiful situation, and to the traveler, from the east side of the river, forms a picturesque object. It is surrounded by a large graveyard, enclosed by a wall, in which are planted maple, poplar and cedar trees. A great many are buried here, and some of the tombstones go back sixteen years before the erection of the church, thus showing that it was used as a place of interment some time previously. The late Major Mathias Holstein, of Norristown, related that about 1790 nearly all who attended this church came on horseback. The Rev. H. M. Muhlenberg speaks of being visited, at the Trappe, in October 1763, by the "Swedish Missionary Heggeblatt." No doubt he preached to this congregation and that of St. Gabriel's, at Morlatton.

Before we close this article there are yet a few matters deserving consideration. The Swedish language, it appears, was still spoken by their descendants in the county as late as the time of the Revolution. Mathias Holstein, who died in 1768, spoke it in his family. Andrew Rambo, now aged about seventy years, and living in Swedesburg, informed us, that when a young man, he attended worship in the Gloria Dei church at Wicaco, and heard the Rev. Dr. Colin preach in Swedish, but was unable to understand it; he also says that his grandfather, Tobias Rambo, spoke the language. It is believed that no preaching was ever done in the Swedish at Christ Church, Swedesburg, but that Dr. Colin, in preaching there, would now and then, from habit, use a Swedish word in his sermon, which he would, however, explain. What languages have been spoken along the valley of the Schuylkill within the last two hundred years! The Indian, the Swedish and the Welsh, once so prevalent, have been displaced by the English and the German. The latter, perhaps, in another century will follow. Though the Indians, the Swedes, the Welsh, the English and the Germans have lived here, and however much they differed in nationality, religion, manners and customs, they agreed in one thing, *to live peaceably together*. Perhaps no other country can show, amidst such a diversity, a similar parallel in ancient or modern times. Judging by this result within the last two centuries, who can say that man does not progress?

Mention has been made that in 1712, Mats Holstein, Peter Rambo, Gunna Rambo, Peter Yocum and John Matson, with their families, settled in "Ammasland," now called Upper Merion. As this "Ammasland" has puzzled some of our antiquaries, we will venture an opinion. In records of 1678 Darby Creek has been called "Amesland" Creek, and also the country lying between the Schuylkill and Ridley Creek. One has supposed that this name is derived from Aany, the Indian name for a road or path. It is probable that this name is derived from Ameland, an island in the North Sea belonging to Holland. As the Coateses, Hughses, Supplees, Ramseys, Stewarts and Robertses have intermarried, at an early time, with Swedish families, it has been supposed that some of those names, at least, were of Swedish origin, but this is quite a mistake, for none of these are Swedish names. From the earliest period the Swedes and their descendants have shown a predilection to settle along the banks of the Delaware and Schuylkill, and along those streams they still hold great quantities of our most fertile lands. As a people they are honest and industrious, and have been remarkable for pursuing the even tenor of their way to wealth and prosperity. Seldom, indeed, can it be said that any one of them forgot himself so far as to enter the vortex of speculation. In consequence, the late disastrous convulsion, though it wrecked numbers, has left them unharmed.

LOWER MERION.

The township of Lower Merion is bounded on the north by Upper Merion and the Schuylkill, south by Philadelphia, east by the Schuylkill, and west by Delaware county. Its greatest length is six and a-half miles, and width four miles, containing an area of fourteen thousand six hundred and eleven acres. In its situation it is the most southern in the county, and is also the greatest in extent and population. Its surface is rolling, and the soil is a rich loam. Extending through its breadth is a belt of serpentine, accompanied by steatite, or soapstone, which is quarried on the Schuylkill, about a mile above the mouth of Mill Creek. In connection with the aforesaid formation, talc, dolomite and some other minerals abound.

The surface of this township is agreeably diversified by a number of beautiful streams. Though none are large, yet they furnish valuable water-power. So well is Lower Merion watered that scarcely a large farm can be found which does not contain one or more excellent springs of living water. Mill Creek is the largest stream and lies wholly within the limits of this township. It has its source near the Green Tree Tavern, on the Gulf Road, and is a winding, rapid stream, about six miles in length. In this distance it receives eight or nine small streams, and a line of steep hills mark its course, but none are over one hundred feet in perpendicular height. It propels the machinery of one plaster, two grist and two saw mills, besides eleven manufactories of different kinds. Trout Run is a branch of Mill Creek, and following its course is about two miles long. It has received its name from the trout that abound in it. What is curious, though these fish have been known there from the earliest period, none have ever been found in Mill Creek. In the south part of the township the east and west branches of Indian Creek have their origin; also a branch of Cobb'sCreek, near Athensville. Rock Hill Creek and Frog Hollow Run are rapid streams, from one to two miles long, and empty into the Schuylkill opposite Manayunk.

As Lower Merion was first settled chiefly by the Welsh, so to this day their descendants constitute the majority of its population; next in order follow those of English and Irish origin. Those of Swedish or German descent are few. In 1741, this township contained one hundred and one taxables; in 1828, five hundred and twenty-two; in 1849, seven hundred and fourteen; and in 1856, one thousand and twenty-two. The census of 1810 gives the total population as one thousand eight hundred and thirty-five; in 1820, two thousand two hundred and fifty-six; in 1830, two thousand five hundred and twenty-four; in 1840, two thousand eight hundred and twenty-seven; and in 1850, three thousand five hundred and seventeen. The population at this time must be about five thousand five hundred, showing a rapid increase since 1840. The census of 1850 give the greatest number of colored persons here, being one hundred and forty-eight, out of seven hundred and nine in the remainder of the county.

The improvements of this township are very valuable: two railroads and one turnpike pass through it, and the census of 1850 gave five hundred and eighty-three houses and one hundred and ninety-five farms. According to the triennial assessment of 1856, the real estate was valued at one million one hundred and two thousand three hundred and fifty-one dollars, and the horses and neat cattle at thirty-seven thousand five hundred and eighty-four. In the spring of 1858 licenses were granted to eight public houses, ten stores, two lumber yards, four coal yards and three grist mills. Previous to 1830 there were no post offices in the township; now there are three, called General Wayne, Lower Merion and Cabinet. The turnpike road leading from Philadelphia to Lancaster, passes through the township a distance of about four and a-half miles. It was the first road of this kind made in Pennsylvania. It was commenced in 1792 and completed two years afterwards. It was effected, wholly, by individual subscription, and is sixty-two miles in length, and cost four hundred and sixty-five thousand dollars, or seven thousand five hundred dollars per mile. It was laid with broken stones twenty-four feet wide and eighteen inches deep. The Pennsylvania railroad was built by the State, and was originally made from Philadelphia to Columbia, on the Susquehanna River, a distance of eighty-two miles, where it connected with the canal to Pittsburg. It was nearly one of the first in the country, and was opened for use in April, 1834, and cost three million nine hundred and eighty-three thousand three hundred and two dollars. It was finished, a few years ago, all the way to Pittsburgh, a distance of three hundred and ninety-three miles, at a cost of six millions two hundred and sixty-six thousand nine hundred and eighty-one dollars. The State, in 1857, sold its right to the Pennsylvania Rail Road Company, under whose control it now is. This road, by its connections, recently formed, gives Philadelphia the advantages of a cheaper and more direct transportation to the West than any of the other Atlantic cities. This railroad passes through this township about four and a-half miles, and crosses not far east of Lancaster Pike, a branch of Indian Creek, on a large and substantial stone bridge, twenty-five feet above the water. The Reading railroad follows the Schuylkill the entire length of this township, a distance of about seven and a-half miles. It extends from Philadelphia to the coal region, in Schuylkill county, and was incorporated April 4th, 1833, and was put under contract the following year. Immediately below the Flat Rock Hotel, this railroad has a tunnel nine hundred and sixty feet long, nineteen feet wide and sixteen feet high, made through very hard solid rock, worked from the two ends, and at the deepest place is ninety-five feet below the surface. It is neatly arched and runs through in a straight line, with sufficient width for two tracks The entrance at the southern end of the tunnel is built of handsome cut stone, where the following inscription was copied, "Philadelphia and Reading Railroad, opened between Philadelphia and Reading the 9th day of Dec. 1839. President, Elihu Chauncey. Managers, Coleman Fisher, Wm. H. Keating, M. S. Richards, John A. Brown, Wm. F. Emlin, Chas. P. Fox; Engineers, M. and W. Robinson." It is commonly called the Manayunk tunnel, in consequence of being about half a mile above that place.

The manufactures of Lower Merion are considerable. It contains two saw mills, two rolling mills, one forge, two paper mills, one dye mill, one machine establishment and ten cotton and woolen factories. The census of 1840 gave but three cotton factories. The manufacture of paper has, however, decreased; about forty years ago there were some seven or eight engaged in this business, on Mill Creek alone, which have, in consequence, been converted into other manufacturing branches. To enter more fully into the details of the various manufacturing establishments of this township, we shall begin with the Pencoyd Iron Works, situated on the Schuylkill, near the Philadelphia line. These belong to A. and P. Roberts, and comprise a rolling mill and forge, which went into operation in 1852, and employ generally about thirty-six hands. Nearly opposite Manayunk, on Frog Hollow Run, and about half a mile from its mouth, is a cotton factory for yarn and bobbin, which formerly belonged to Isaac Wetherill. At the mouth of this stream is Grimrod's grist mill. Between the west end of Manayunk bridge and the Reading Railroad is the extensive logwood factory belonging to Samuel Grant, jr. & Co., called the "Ashland Dye Mills," who employ twenty-three hands. At West Conshehocken is the Merion Furnace, a large establishment belonging to Colwell & Co., and under the superintendence of J. B. Moorhead, where thirty hands are employed. Here was, also, the print and bleaching works of P. W. Bliss, which have been burned down. There is another block printing works which was not in operation when the author was here. Beginning at the mouth of Mill Creek and going up this stream, the first manufacturing establishment we come across is Joseph Stillwagon's paper mill, which usually employs about six hands. Next is Wm. Chadwick's lampwick factory and grist mill, which employs about the same number. Next is Daniel Nippes' manufactory, which was not in operation; then William Todd's factory of woolen and cotton filling, for carpets, which employs fifteen hands; then Hannah Hagy's factory, for woolen yarn, which was not in operation. Charles Greaves' Kentucky jean factory comes next, which employs six or eight hands; then Evan Jones' manufactory of carpet yarn, &c., which has about twelve hands; next Samuel L. Robeson's saw mill and manufactory of carpet filling, &c., which has twelve hands; then comes Samuel Croft's brass rolling mill and chandelier and lamp chain manufactory; next is Francis Sheetz's paper mill, which has usually employed about five or six hands; then Charles Humphrey's woolen factory and machine shop, for the manufacture of agricultural implements, where about twenty hands are employed. The last and the farthest up the stream is Levi Morris' grist, plaster and saw mill. Near the mouth of Mill Creek is a small stream which empties into it, on which James Dixon has a draper factory, which employs five or six hands. These constitute the principal, if not all the manufacturing establishments in the township, and the greater portion of them are propelled by water power.

There is considerable interest taken in education, and there are some very good two story school houses in the township. For the school year ending with June 1st, 1857, we learn there was six schools which were taught by five male and three female teachers. The pay of the former was forty-two, and the latter twenty-two dollars per month. These schools were open ten months, eight hundred and fifty-two scholars attended, and three thousand seven hundred dollars was levied as tax to pay the expenses of the same. Efforts are about being made to establish a library at Athensville.

Athensville is situated on the Lancaster turnpike, seven miles from Philadelphia, and is the largest village in the township. It contains twenty-eight houses, three stores and one hotel. Cabinet post office is at this place. The Odd Fellows hold their meetings in a two story hall, in which it is proposed to place a library now about starting. The old Red Lion tavern was at this place, which was torn down, and the present fine three story hotel erected in 1855, which is kept by H. Litzenberg. Public houses in this vicinity, it appears, are not numerous, the Eagle hotel being the first on the pike west of this, and is six and a half miles off, and the first below is at Hestonville, four and a half miles off. Several of the houses here have been built within the few past years. A short distance below the village, near the pike, is the handsome residence of the Hon. Owen Jones, late member of Congress, from the fifth district, comprising Montgomery County and the contiguous portion of Philadelphia. Humphreysville is near the Delaware county line, on the Lancaster pike, nine miles from Philadelphia, has twenty-one houses, a two story public schoolhouse and several handsome private residences. One mile below, on the pike, and eight from the city, is the Episcopal church, where there are fifteen houses, several of which are elegant structures. The church stands on the north side of the road, and is a low one story stone-pointed building with a steep roof and a tower forty feet high. The whole have been built within the last twelve years. A few yards to the south-west is a two story hall, in Delaware County. Immediately below this place the Pennsylvania railroad crosses the pike. The houses along the Lancaster turnpike, in this township, are pretty numerous, and among them are many elegant residences, with shady lawns and flower plats, often displaying considerable taste. These are often the country seats of retired Philadelphians or those who are still engaged in business in the city, and yet, with their families, prefer to live here to the noise and bustle of the town. In consequence many new houses have been built within the past five years, and if brought together would be enough to make an ordinary sized borough.

West Conshehocken is situated in the northern part of the township, on the line of Upper Merion, and immediately opposite the borough of Conshehocken. The Reading railroad has a station here, which is thirteen miles from Philadelphia. This village has grown up within the last twelve years, and contains in all about twenty-three houses, one store and a blacksmith shop. The "Merion Furnace," an extensive establishment, employing thirty hands, a block printing establishment, not now in operation, and a grist mill, formerly a bleaching works, are also here. This place possesses great advantages as a business location; two railroads and a canal pass by it, and a bridge connects it with the opposite side of the Schuylkill. This place, it is said, owes much of its prosperity to the enterprise of William Davis, who owned most of the land on which it is built. Formerly, here was Matson's Ford, which name it bore some time previous to the Revolution, being so called after the descendants of an early settler and landholder. The bridge here was incorporated in 1832, as the "Matson's Ford Bridge," and is still called by this name. By means of this bridge the Reading railroad has a connection with the Norristown railroad, on the opposite side. Nearly half a mile below this village a steep, conical hill rises from the Schuylkill, probably to an elevation of two hundred and fifty feet, and is believed to be the highest eminence in the township. It is a continuation of Edge Hill, which crosses the river below Spring Mill and then runs up the west side of the Schuylkill about a mile, and at West Conshohocken turns to the west and is then better known as the Gulf Hill. This is the same hill mentioned in the deeds of 1683 and 1685, which the Indians called Conshehocken.

Merion Square is situated nearly in the centre of the township, at the intersection of a cross roads, and contains twenty-six dwellings, two stores, a tavern, school-house, Methodist church, Odd Fellows' hall, and a wheelwright and blacksmith shop. Lower Merion post office is located here. Gabriel Thomas, in his account of Pennsylvania in 1696, speaks of the village of Merioneth, which, in all probability, was this place. We know, from its position, that it is this village which Lewis Evans, in his map of 1749, calls "Merion." It is therefore one of the oldest settlements in the county. Green Tree is the name of an inn kept by E. Ramsey, on the Gulf road, one and a-half miles south of the Gulf Mills, and twelve miles from Philadelphia. It is at the intersection of a cross roads, and there is a dwelling, wheelwright and blacksmith shop here. In this vicinity are several elegant country seats and farm houses, the land being rolling, fertile and well cultivated. Near this lived Charles Thompson, secretary of Congress from 1774 to 1789, and who died in 1824. His seat, called Harrington, is now owned by Levi Morris. A biographical sketch of Mr. Thompson is given in the appendix of this work.

General Wayne is the name of a small village and post office near the lower part of the township. It contains a Friends' meeting house, an inn, smith shop, and four or five dwellings. There is a plank road of two tracks from here to West Philadelphia, five miles in length, made in 1855, but which is now nearly worn out, and preparations, we understand, are about being made to get it piked. As the elections for the township are held here, a few words in their connection with the past may not be amiss. The voters, not only of Lower Merion, but of the whole county, before the revolution, gave their votes at the inn opposite the State House, in Chestnut street, Philadelphia. In 1778 the elections for this vicinity were ordered to be held at the public house of Jacob Coleman, in Germantown, where they were continued, till by an act of September 17th, 1785, they were transferred to the Court House, in Norristown, when by the act of March 31st, 1806, this township became a separate district, and the elections were ordered to be held at the house of Titus Yerkes. The land in the vicinity of this village is highly productive and well cultivated.

Opposite Manayunk there is a village which we believe stands in need of a name. Here are twelve dwellings, an inn, smith shop, logwood factory, grist mill and coal yard. Two bridges here span the Schuylkill. The lower one was built by the canal company for the crossing of boat horses from one side of the river to the other, as from here down the canal is on the Lower Merion side. This bridge is free to foot passengers, and it is thus far that steamboats ascend the Schuylkill. The upper Manayunk bridge was built in 1833, and it is at its west end where Rock Hill Creek empties into the river. The hills along the Schuylkill, in this vicinity, rise to the height of from fifty to one hundred feet, and are generally rocky, and covered with young timber. The stones consist chiefly of serpentine, interspersed with mica. The rocks, generally, are very hard and of a dark blue color, and approximate to the trap. From the advantages of this place in a business point of view, there is no doubt it will before long rise into importance and attain to the dignity of a name.

Croft's Mill, on Mill Creek, contains a store, six or seven dwellings and three factories. Chadwick's factory and grist mill has a store and seven houses. Here are several fine springs of water. The lampwick factory was built in 1836. The mouth of Mill Creek is an interesting place to visitors. This stream is here crossed by two bridges. The road passes over it on a frame-covered bridge, sixty-three feet long, and above and almost adjoining, the Reading railroad crosses it by a tressel bridge, twenty feet above the water. Near by is a beautiful small island in the Schuylkill, containing about a quarter of an acre, covered with buttonwood and willow trees, and is quite a feature in the scenery. From here up, and by the side of the creek for a quarter of a mile, to the paper mill, is a good, level road, which is beautifully shaded, and with the surrounding scenery makes a very attractive walk. About half a mile above this there is a batteau ferry across the Schuylkill, which lands passengers at the Soapstone station of the Norristown railroad.

Flat Rock is the name now generally given to a hotel situated on the west side of the Schuylkill, at the upper end of the Reading Railroad tunnel. It is a well conducted house, kept by William Williams, and has a beautiful and romantic location, and, from its retired position and surrounding attractions, could not help but prove a delightful place for city boarders. The name is derived from a huge bed of rocks extending here across the river. Righter's Ferry was established, at this place, by an Act of Assembly, in January, 1741. A bridge was built here in 1810, which was the first that spanned the Schuylkill, within the limits of Montgomery county. Some years afterwards, while several teams were crossing with marble, it broke down, but was rebuilt. In consequence of a great freshet on the night of September 2nd, 1850, the Conshehocken Bridge, four miles above, was washed away, and it came down with such force as to sweep this bridge entirely away, and which has not since been rebuilt. What at this time heightened the catastrophe was that the Conshehocken Bridge was firmly held together by the railroad crossing it. On this occasion, it took away one-half of the Manayunk bridge, which has since been repaired. From the masses of rock in the contracted bed of the river for half a mile below this, it is truly wonderful how persons with canoes could venture to pass through in safety, as we know they did, and which has been mentioned in our article on the Schuylkill. Just below this is a small island, covered with numerous willows, which is much the resort of game, and, in consequence, has received the name of Duck Island. From the western abutment of the bridge, which still remains by the roadside, a splendid view is obtained in a north-west direction of the falls of the Flat Rock dam and the Schuylkill, for the distance of three miles.

A mile and a-half above the Flat Rock hotel, on the Schuylkill, is the lumber yard of William Smith, where are four houses. This is nearly opposite to the Soapstone quarries of the late John Freedley. From here down to the Philadelphia line, in this township, there is a line of wooded hills along the Schuylkill, while from here up, a mile or more, the land is more level and cultivated. Below this, when we were here in August last, we observed a new branch of industry being vigorously prosecuted, namely: that of gathering elder and blackberries along the highway and railroad by wagon loads. There is a large three-story stone hotel by the roadside, opposite Spring Mill. It is in rather a retired place—no other house being near. A few yards below this hotel a beautiful crystal stream of water, which has no name and is very rapid, empties into the Schuylkill.

Among the ancient houses of worship still standing in Pennsylvania, the Friends' Meeting House of Lower Merion is the oldest. It is situated in the village of General Wayne, at the head of the West Philadelphia Plank-Road, five miles from the city. It was built in 1695, and in its ground plan is in the form of a T. It is a substantial stone edifice of one story, or about fourteen feet to the roof, with walls over two feet in thickness. Its greatest length is about thirty-six feet, and the end facing south-west is twenty by twenty-four feet. Originally it was stone-pointed, but in repairing it, in 1829, it was plastered over in imitation of large cut stone. It is surrounded by several large, venerable-looking buttonwood trees. The grave-yard, we regret to say, looks neglected, and, with all its antiquity, no old inscriptions abound to arrest the attention of the antiquary. There are now about a dozen low stones, of recent origin, that tell us the names of as many reposing beneath the sod, but beyond this, of those buried here we know not. Previous to the erection of this meeting-house, its members, with those residing in the adjacent townships of Haverford and Radnor, held private meetings as early as 1683. These were all Welsh Friends.

The second house of worship built in this township was by a number of German Lutherans, in 1769. This church is situated at the intersection of cross-roads, half a mile south-east of Athensville, near the Delaware county line. It was rebuilt in 1800, and further enlarged in 1833. It is a handsome one-story stone edifice, surrounded by shade trees. Adjoining is a very fine grave-yard, comprising about one and a-half acres, laid out in walks and planted with trees and shrubbery. There are many buried here. The most common names on the tombstones are West, Lainhoff, Knox, Kugler, Marten, Dalby, Colflesh, Sheaff, Pechen, Miller, Goodman, Litzenberg, Smith, Wagner, Fiss, Super, Bittle, Latch, Epright, Fimple, Poget, Hamell, Sibly, Zell, Nagle, Hoffman, Moyer, Krickbaum, Knoll, Horn, Trexler and Ott. The present pastor is the Rev. Timothy Tilghman Titus, who resides in the parsonage adjoining.

The Baptists have a church at the intersection of the Roberts and Gulf roads, eleven miles from Philadelphia. It is a large two-story stone edifice, situated on an elevated site, and is surrounded by several ancient forest trees. It was built in 1809. The grave-yard is laid out in gravelled walks, planted with shrubbery, and is neatly kept. The most common names on the tombstones are Taylor, Johnson, Curwen, Morris, Smith, Williamson, Gaskill, Righter, Matheys, Elliot, Owens, Lewis and Sheaff. The Gaskill family has a number of fine tombs here; they are related to the Penns. The present pastor is the Rev. Mr. Anderson. Before the erection of this church, the congregation worshipped in a small building near by, which had been originally a school-house, but it has some time since been demolished. The first clergyman of this congregation was the Rev. Horatio Jones, who officiated for nearly half a century, or till near his death, in 1853.

Having given, at length, a description of Lower Merion, with a few particulars of the past, we propose now to enter more fully on its early history. Its name is derived from Merioneth, or Merionethshire, a maritime county in North Wales. As the early settlers here were nearly all Welsh, and among them it is known that John Thomas, Robert Owen, Thomas Owen and Rowland Ellis came from Merioneth, will account why it was so called. What is now Lower and Upper Merion townships, Gabriel Thomas, in his account of Pennsylvania, in 1696, calls Merioneth, and in the Colonial Records of 1723, is still called Merion, which we know, however, was divided and known by their present names before 1734.

But a short time before the arrival of Penn, a number of Welsh, who proposed settling in Pennsylvania, purchased of Wm. Pennin, England, a tract of forty thousand acres of land, which subsequently was located in Merion, Haverford, Goshen, and several of the adjoining townships. How much of this tract lay in this township is unknown to us, but no doubt it covered more than half its present area. Thomas Holme, the surveyor-general, begun a map of original surveys, with the names of the first purchasers, in 1682, and as portions of it were sold kept filling it up to about the year 1695. From this map it is ascertained that the following persons purchased nearly all the lands in Lower Merion: John Holland, Christopher Pennock, William Wood, William Sharlow, Daniel Meredith, John Roberts, John Humphreys and others, Thomas Ellis and others, and Edward Jones with seventeen others in company. About 1683-4 several had already settled on their purchases and the number was yearly augmenting. J. Oldmixon, who was here in 1708, in speaking of this tract and the Welsh, says that it then was "very populous, and the people are very industrious; by which means this country is better cleared than any other part of the county. The inhabitants have many fine plantations of corn, and breed abundance of cattle, inasmuch that they are looked upon to be as thriving and wealthy as any in the province—and this must always be said of the Welsh, that wherever they come, 'tis not their fault if they do not live, and live well, too; for they seldom spare for labor, which seldom fails of success." We have made mention of the Friends having held meetings for worship, as early as 1683, and that the present meeting-house was built in 1695. Application was made to the Council, in 1706, for a road from this meeting-house to the Schuylkill, where a ferry was to be established.

Among the earliest settlers here was Benjamin Humphrey, who came over in 1683. He was a useful man in the colony, and through his hospitality enjoyed a wide-spread reputation. He died the 4th of November, 1737, aged 76 years. David Humphrey was commissioned a justice of the county courts, November 22d, 1738. There are persons of this name still residing in the township, and it is from members of this family that Humphreysville received its name. The Roberts family is another of early origin. Hugh Roberts came from Wales in 1684, and traveled here in the work of the ministry in Maryland, Long Island and New England, where it is said "his services were effectual to the people." He died in 1702, and was buried at the Merion meeting house. Robert Jones purchased of Penn, in England, in 1682, five hundred acres of land, which was afterwards located in this township. He was also an early settler, and was exceedingly popular among his neighbors. In June, 1715, he was appointed one of the justices of the county courts, which office he continued to hold for many years. Edward Jones was another early settler, "given to hospitality and generally beloved by his acquaintances." He died in February, 1737, aged 82 years. Jonathan Jones came here with his parents when only three years old, and continued a resident till June 30th, 1770, when he died, at the advanced age of 91 years. A company of Associators was formed in February, 1747, of which Edward Jones was chosen captain, and Griffith Griffith, first lieutenant. Edward Edwards purchased of Penn in England, two hundred and fifty acres, which was afterwards located here and which he settled upon. Robert Owen arrived from Wales in 1790. He was a minister among Friends, and traveled much on this account, both in his native country and America He died in July, 1797, and was interred at Merion meeting house. Benjamin Eastborn, an early settler, we learn from the Abington records, married Ann Thomas in 1722. Griffith Lewellen was commissioned a justice of the county courts in April, 1744, and was continued in said office for a number of years. The following is a list of landholders and tenants residing in Lower Merion in 1734, which is copied from the original manuscript, prepared for Thomas Penn. It contains fifty-two names and cannot fail to prove interesting at this day to their numerous descendants. It will also be observed that they are all Welsh, with the exception, probably, of two or three names: John, son of Mathias Roberts, Hugh Evans, Robert Jones, Robert Roberts, Robert Evan, Rice Price, Edward Jones, Abel Thomas, Benjamin Eastborn, Jonathan Jones, Wm. Havard, Richard Hughs, Morris Lewellen, Benjamin Humphrey, John Humphrey, Joseph

Williams, Rees Thomas, William Thomas, Peter Jones, Humphrey Jones, John Griffith, Catharine Pugh, Rees Phillip, Joseph Tucker, James John, Thomas John, John Lloyd, Griffith Lewellen, Robert Roberts, David Jones, William Walton, David Davis, Joseph Roberts, John Roberts, David Price, Isachar Price, David Price, Jr., Lewis Lloyd, John David, Robert, son of Peter Jones, Thomas David, John Evans, Eleanor Bevan, Owen Jones' plantation, Evan Harry, Nicholas Rapy, John Roberts, carpenter, Evan Ross, Samuel Jordan, James Dodmead, Edward Edwards and Garret Jones.

During the revolution, particularly while the British held possession of Philadelphia, from September, 1777, to June, 1778, the inhabitants of Lower Merion suffered severely from the depredations of the enemy, in consequence of living so near the city. Shortly after their departure an assessor was appointed to rate the damages, which amounted to three thousand two hundred and twelve pounds, or eight thousand five hundred and sixty-five dollars and eleven cents of our present currency. It appears that though no striking events of interest occurred here, yet this township bore its share of the trials. We have in our possession a list of all persons who stood attainted for treason during the revolution within the present limits of Montgomery county, being twenty-nine in number. Among these there is but one who was a resident of Lower Merion, thus showing that the people here were generally disposed to independence. The person alluded to was John Roberts, a descendant of one of its earliest and most respectable families. After the British had taken possession of Philadelphia, Mr. Roberts no doubt supposed that the subjugation of the country was a certainty, and therefore, as a man of property, it would redound to his interest to join their cause. The result was that he was induced to do acts through the power of those he considered his friends, which, on their departure, brought on him the vengeance of his countrymen. For his conduct he was arrested, tried, found guilty, and publicly executed in Philadelphia. His real estate, in this township, was confiscated, and consisted of three hundred and seventy-eight acres of land, besides two mills and several houses. A portion of said property now belongs to Samuel E. Robeson, on Mill Creek. A biographical sketch of Mr. Roberts is given in the appendix of this work.

UPPER MERION.

The township of Upper Merion is bounded on the north-west, north and north-east by the river Schuylkill, and also on the north-east by the borough of Bridgeport, on the south-east by Lower Merion township, on the south by the counties of Chester and Delaware, and on the south-west by Chester. Its greatest length is eight and a quarter miles, and its greatest width three and a-half. It will be observed that it lies wholly on the west side of the Schuylkill, and that its form must be very irregular. It formerly contained ten thousand seven hundred and seventy-five acres, but by the erection of the borough of Bridgeport, in 1851, four hundred and eighty acres were taken off, leaving its present area ten thousand two hundred and ninety-five acres. The surface is rolling and contains, generally, a lime-stone soil.

The principal elevations in this township are called Mount Joy, Red Hill, Flint Hill, North Valley Hill, and Conshehocken or Gulf Hill.

Mount Joy is of a conical form, and is wooded to its top, and forms a beautiful feature in the landscape, as seen from the old school house on the Valley Hill—half a mile west of Port Kennedy—from which place it is about one and a-half miles. This hill gave name to a manor which belonged to Letitia, daughter of William Penn. Tradition says that he gave this hill its name while on a visit to the neighborhood. It is the highest eminence in Upper Merion, in the vicinity of Valley Forge. In the time of the Revolution it was strongly fortified, and the remains of entrenchments are still visible on its top.

Red Hill is an eminence something over a mile south-west of Bridgeport. It is a well known tradition, handed down by several families, that two panthers were shot on it in the time of the early settlement.

The Conshehocken or Gulf Hill is a long narrow range that runs a great way into Chester county. It is a continuation of Edge Hill, which crosses the Schuylkill at Spring Mill, and extends east and west. It commences in New Jersey, and crosses the Delaware at Trenton. What is strange, in Montgomery county no iron, lime-stone, or marble, is found on the south side of it. Geologically speaking, it forms a narrow belt of the primary rocks with gneiss and talcon slate. The name of Gulf Hill has only been applied in this vicinity from the deep, narrow passage of Gulf Creek through it in its course to the Schuylkill. This natural curiosity will be more fully described when we speak of the villages of the township.

The North Valley Hill is a range following the Schuylkill, and commences a short distance above Bridgeport. It is only of moderate elevation, and is the highest between Port Kennedy and Valley Forge.

In walking along the Schuylkill canal from Bridgeport to Port Kennedy, we found the land chiefly cultivated to the river, with an occasional margin of trees, making it a shady and agreeable walk. Probably one of the most fertile tracts of land in Montgomery county is that portion of the township lying along the Schuylkill, between Bridgeport and Gulf Creek, and extending west for about a mile and a-half. Within this space lime-stone and iron ore is obtained in abundance; and the stranger views with regret the disfigurations occasioned in obtaining these materials from such beautiful and productive fields. Indeed, in few neighborhoods has Nature been so lavish of her choicest gifts. The soil is a loose loam, nearly level on its surface, and so free from stones that no country can produce probably any land of easier cultivation. The Swedes, in taking up and settling this tract, showed considerable foresight as to its future importance.

Generally speaking, for its size, this is not a well watered township. The streams do not rise from many springs, and are, therefore, too weak to furnish much valuable water-power. Elliott's Run, which rises from two branches near the Chester county line, and is three and a-half miles in length, propels only a saw mill, near its mouth. Frog Run, two and a half miles long, and Matsunk, a smaller stream, and both emptying into the Schuylkill below Swedesburg, propel no mills.

Mashilmac Creek rises in Chester county, and, after a course of about two miles, empties into the Schuylkill at the Catfish locks, below Port Kennedy. For its length, it is a pretty strong stream, and, on account of rising from several large springs, is not liable to be affected by draught or cold weather. Near its mouth, it turns a merchant and grist mill.

The largest and most important stream is Gulf Creek, in the south-east part, near the Lower Merion line. It is a rapid stream, which rises in Delaware county, and after a course of nearly four miles, empties into the Schuylkill about half a mile above the Conshehocken bridge. It propels one saw mill, two grist mills, and four or five cotton and woolen factories. Near its mouth, the highway and railroad cross it by substantial stone bridges. The East Valley Creek, for the distance of a mile, forms the western boundary of the township, and propels, within its limits, a cotton factory and a grist mill. These furnish all the water-power, and are much the largest streams. There is a fine spring at Port Kennedy and another in the borough of Bridgeport.

The wealth that the inhabitants of Upper Merion derive from its mines and quarries is probably not exceeded by that of any other township in the county. It contains three large furnaces for the manufacture of iron—one at Port Kennedy, and the other two on the Schuylkill, a mile below Swedesburg. The ore is dug now in considerable quantities in the vicinity of Valley Forge, especially on the farm of Richard Marten, on the Gulf Road. The most extensive bed of iron ore commences near what was formerly Henderson's marble quarry, and extends to the Swede furnaces on the Schuylkill, a distance of one and a-half miles, and is probably about half a mile in width. On this tract great quantities of ore have been extracted within the last ten years, and is now worked exclusively at three or four places. From the farm of George Henderson, particularly, considerable has been taken. The iron made from this ore is said to be of excellent quality.

In the manufacture and quality of its lime, Upper Merion is conspicuous. The lime-stone belt crosses the Schuylkill at and below Swedesburg, and has an average breadth of a mile, running in a western direction into Chester county. Its length, in this township, is nearly six miles. The marble prevails on its southern edge, and on its northern line the softer lime. It has been satisfactorily ascertained that the lime made from its northern edge is the best. The quarries of William B. Rambo, near Swedesburg, and those at Port Kennedy, have this position: while approaching the opposite edge, it increases in hardness till it terminates in white marble, which merges into the still harder blue marble. This lime-stone is placed in the primitive formation, and, as may be supposed from the aforesaid remarks, is by no means uniform in its quality, some of its beds yielding lime of much greater purity than others. But taken collectively, no lime in the United States surpasses it, especially for mechanical purposes. Mr. Trego, in his geography, thus speaks of the value and importance of this article: "It is scarcely possible to form an estimate of the incalculable advantages derived by Pennsylvania from the limestones so extensively diffused throughout the State. They impart fertility to the soil wherever found; they are used as a building stone for houses, barns, bridges, canal locks, &c., and they constitute an indispensable article of use in our furnaces for smelting iron ores. When burned into lime they yield a necessary ingredient in the mortar for stone-masons, bricklayers, plasterers, for whitewashing, and for several purposes in the manufactures and the arts. But it is from the benefits derived to our agriculture, from the use of lime as a manure for the soil, that our State is destined to be most enriched by this important article of her productions. At several points on our canals and railroads vast quantities of limestone are quarried and transported to places where it is required for use, and from the rapidly increasing demand it is becoming a considerable item in the tolls upon our public works." Oldmixon, in his British Empire in America, published in 1708, says that the first limestone dug in America was found in Letitia Penn's manor of Mount Joy. This probably was in the vicinity of the present Port Kennedy. The census of 1840 values the lime then manufactured in this township at seventy-four thousand seven hundred and seventy-two dollars, or about one third of that produced in the entire county. This business has since greatly increased through the additional facilities afforded for its transportation. It is said that Port Kennedy, for the year ending with June 1st, 1857, exported lime to the value of one hundred and forty thousand dollars. The whole county is represented in 1840 to have produced lime to the amount of two hundred and thirty-six thousand one hundred and sixty-two dollars. This sum, we have no doubt, is now exceeded in value by Upper Merion alone.

Marble is composed of chrystalized carbonate of lime, and the two are always found combined, more or less, together. The marble worked in this township runs in a long, narrow, perpendicular seam, extending down, no doubt, to a great depth. It is said the deeper it is obtained the better is its quality. What was formerly known as Henderson's quarry is now owned and worked by John Sandeman. It is situated about two miles south of Bridgeport. There is here an extensive steam mill for sawing marble. Thirty-five hands are generally employed in the mill and quarry. The greatest depth reached, in obtaining the marble, is about one hundred feet. Immense quantities have been taken out here within the last twenty years. A portion of the material used in the construction of Girard College was obtained at this place. One of the greatest difficulties in procuring the marble is the ingress of water. The depth made here could never have been reached without the aid of a number of pumps, propelled by steam. This is a serious obstacle to the successful working of marble quarries, and entails considerable expense. That there is an abundance of this beautiful material in this township there is no doubt, and it is believed as the demand for it increases this difficulty will be the easier surmounted. About half a mile from the King of Prussia, and near the Chester Valley railroad, is the quarry formerly worked by J. Brooke, but now in possession of Derr and Adams. There is here, also, a steam saw-mill. They employ about twelve men. These two are the only Marble quarries that have been worked. The census of 1840 states that in Upper Merion there was nine men employed in the business, producing marble to the amount of six thousand seven hundred and sixty dollars. A few yards above the mouth of Gulf Creek, on the Schuylkill, Henry Munson owns an extensive stone quarry. A large amount of building stone is taken from here to Philadelphia and other places by teams, canal and railroad. When we were here in August, 1858, the Navigation company were raising and repairing Plymouth dam, which is near this quarry, and stones were used in its construction which we are certain were over twelve feet in length and a foot and a half in thickness. This stone dresses easily and affords an excellent building material.

Upper Merion was first settled by the Welsh, and their descendants at this day probably constitute a majority of its population. A few years afterwards several Swedish families took up large tracts of the best land, which they settled upon, and are chiefly in possession of their descendants. At a later period several English families removed here. Within the past thirty years many Irish have settled here, through the encouragement given them as laborers in the lime, marble and iron business. This township, in 1741, contained fifty-two taxables; in 1828, three hundred and sixty; in 1849, nine hundred and thirty-five; and in 1857, nine hundred and two. The census of 1810 gives the total population at one thousand one hundred and fifty-six; in 1820, one thousand two hundred and eighty-five; in 1830, one thousand six hundred and eighteen; in 1840, two thousand eight hundred and four; and in 1850, three thousand and seventy-five. By the erection of Bridgeport into a borough, in 1851, the population was somewhat reduced. We should estimate it at this time to be about three thousand two hundred.

In the way of improvements this township is pretty well provided, and which have had a great tendency to develop further its resources. Besides the canal, the Reading railroad runs its entire length on the Schuylkill, a distance of nine miles. The Chester Valley railroad, which was finished in 1853, extends through its entire width, from east to west, about four miles. It commences at Bridgeport and connects with the Pennsylvania railroad at Downingtown. There are, besides, several short branches, erected by private enterprise, leading from mines and quarries to the Schuylkill, none of which, however, we believe are over a mile in length, and will be hereafter mentioned. A turnpike extends from Bridgeport to the King of Prussia, three miles, and was finished in 1853. The census of 1850 gave six hundred and twenty-four houses and one hundred and eight farms. According to the triennial assessment of 1856, the real estate of Upper Merion was valued at seven hundred and forty-nine thousand nine hundred and fifteen dollars; and the horses and cattle at twenty-six thousand four hundred and four dollars. In 1858 it contained three public houses, nine stores, three coal yards, four grist mills, three saw mills, three iron furnaces, two marble mills and seven or eight cotton and woolen factories. It will be seen by this that the inhabitants are extensively engaged in manufactures, independent of the lime and marble business. There are post offices at the villages of Port Kennedy, King of Prussia and Gulf Mills.

Upper Merion, for the school year ending with June 1st, 1857, had nine schools, which were open ten months, and employed seven male and three female teachers. The wages of the former was thirty dollars and of the latter twenty-five dollars per month. Five hundred and sixty-six scholars attended these schools during the year. The amount levied to defray the expenses was three thousand two hundred and sixty-nine dollars and ninety-seven cents. There is, we believe, but one library in the township, which is at the King of Prussia, and has been only recently started.

Port Kennedy, if not the largest village, is certainly the most extensive business place in the township. From the amount of materials we have relating to it, and its importance in the valley of the Schuylkill as a place of trade, we have concluded to defer a further account till in a separate article. Swedesburg is pleasantly situated on a bank of the Schuylkill adjoining the eastern line of Bridgeport. It contains about sixty houses, chiefly small two story frame, a church, school house, one or two stores, and a blacksmith and wheelwright shop. The census of 1850 gives it three hundred and eighty-eight inhabitants. This place has chiefly grown up within the last fifteen years, and owes much of its prosperity to the manufacturing business carried on in its neighborhood. The Reading railroad passes through the place. About half a mile below this village William B. Rambo carries on lime burning quite extensively. He has sixteen kilns and employs fifty hands in quarrying, burning and hauling the lime. He has a railroad laid from the quarries to the river, half a mile in length. Most of the lime is sent by the canal to New Jersey, Delaware and Maryland. Ballygomingo is a manufacturing village on the Gulf Creek, about half a mile from the Schuylkill. It contains about thirty houses, a Baptist church, a store, school house and several mechanic shops. Before the Revolution, George English erected a fulling mill here, which was afterwards owned by William Custer, who carried it on for a number of years. On his death, his son-in-law, Bethel Moore, the present owner, made valuable improvements and entered more extensively into the manufacture of woolen goods, especially sattinetts, giving employment to a considerable number of hands. The name of this village is given after a town in Ireland. A short distance above this George

Townsend has an extensive factory, altered from a grist mill, which formerly belonged to David Brooke. Matsunk is the name of a village that has chiefly grown up within the last twelve years, and is situated on a small stream of the same name, near the Schuylkill, and about a mile below Swedesburg. It contains nineteen dwelling houses, several of which are splendid residences, surrounded with fine shady lawns and gardens, and enclosed with iron railing. Abraham Supplee has here a manufactory of Kentucky jean, employing some twenty-five hands. The extensive works of the "Swede Iron Company" are also here, and comprise two large furnaces, a railroad leading from the mines to the river, nearly a mile in length, numerous out buildings, and about sixty acres of land, on which there is an abundance of iron ore and limestone of the best quality. The total cost to the company is said to be over two hundred thousand dollars. These works have not been in operation for some time. The firm of Potts & Jones, of Philadelphia, are said to be the principal stockholders. The land in the vicinity of Matsunk is of superior quality and among the best in the county. King of Prussia is situated near the centre of the township, at the intersection of the Gulf and State roads. This name was derived from an inn here more than a century ago. It contains a public house, store, post office, blacksmith shop, wheelwright shop and seven houses. Five roads centre here, one of which was turnpiked, in 1852, to Bridgeport, a distance of three miles. There is a stone bridge here, over Elliott's Run, built in 1835. The township elections are held here, which, on the formation of the county, in 1785, were held at the Court House, in Norristown, but which, we believe, since taken from there, have been continued at this place. Within a few years a library has been started, of which C. J. Elliott is librarian. The Chester Valley railroad passes to the south of this village, about a hundred yards. There is fertile land in this vicinity. About a mile south of this, at the head of Elliott's Run, and near the Chester county line, is the Croton factory and a saw-mill, belonging to William Hughes.

Bird-in-Hand is situated on the Gulf road, where it crosses Gulf Creek. It contains seven houses, one store, and blacksmith and wheelwright shop. Here was formerly a tavern, the sign of which has given a name to the place. The first post office in the township was located here, which was before 1827, and two years after its name was changed to its present one of Gulf Mills. Gulf Creek is here crossed by a venerable stone bridge. The Gulf Hill rises immediately on the south side of the creek quite steep and is wooded to the top. About a quarter of a mile above the "Bird," on the creek, George M'Farland has a large three story factory, for spinning wool and cotton and weaving jeans. There are here four houses. At Sandeman's marble mill, previously mentioned, there are some six houses. Near the intersection of the Gulf and Matson Ford road there are four or five houses, a grist mill, saw mill and school house. There is here, also, a one story stone meeting house, belonging to the Christian Baptists, or "Plummerites," built in 1835. The Matson Ford Road passes from Delaware county, by this place, to Conshehocken, and forms the boundary between Upper and Lower Merion The grist mill last mentioned is about a mile from the "Bird," and stands in a romantic situation, on the west side of the Gulf Road, and to the antiquary is an object of interest. It is now owned by Rebecca Thomas, and was built in 1747, and is known as the "Old Gulf Mill." This is probably the oldest mill now standing in Montgomery county, and excepting some of its machinery, it is believed to have undergone no alteration since its erection. It is built of stone and may yet with care stand for centuries. It was, no doubt, in its day, considered a great affair. On Wm. Scull's map of 1770, the "Gulf Forge" is marked as being in this vicinity. An account of the village of Valley Forge will be omitted at this place for a separate article.

There remain several objects of interest yet undescribed in this township, which are worth a visit from the lovers of the curious. As we have spoken of the name of Gulf being applied to a road, a creek, a hill, a mill, and a post office, it is perhaps time that we enlightened the reader what this word "Gulf" implies, or rather how it originated and why implied. What is understood to be the Gulf is where the Gulf Creek passes through the Gulf Hill, and for the purpose of a passage has cleft it to its base. The stream and the road by its side wind through it somewhat in the shape of an S, and at the narrowest part there is just room enough for both, the whole width not being more than forty feet. The hills on either side are pretty steep, and are covered with rocks, bushes and trees to their summits. The hill on the north side is about one hundred and fifty feet high, and on the west side not quite that elevation. Near the old Gulf Mill, on the south side of the entrance, a rock juts out at the road side to an elevation of about fifteen feet, which has sheltered people from the rain. As this hill runs a considerable distance west of the Schuylkill, and as the road through it is perfectly level, it will at once appear obvious that from the earliest period of the settlement above this passage was a great advantage in passing to and from the city. Hence its name is mentioned from an early date. To be in such a place in the dreary hour of midnight, with the roar of the troubled waters among the rocks, and the gloom of the wood-covered gorge, is enough to arouse in the solitary traveler feelings of an unusual kind.

From Bridgeport to Valley Forge is six miles, and few walks in Pennsylvania are more interesting than that along the tow-path by the river for this distance. The towns, villages, manufactories and scenery on each side, at every turn of the river, present something new and beautiful, which, were we to describe at length, would occupy too much of our space. About a mile above Bridgeport, by the tow-path, and not seven feet from the edge of the river, stands a noble beach tree, over eight feet in circumference and very high. It is still quite thrifty and shows no signs of decay. We observed quite a number of initials of names cut on its bark. It stood here, no doubt, some time before the white man settled in the vicinity, and is, very probably, the largest of the kind in Montgomery county. If this tree could speak what a history it might unfold! A quarter of a mile below the catfish dam, and three miles above Bridgeport, from the tow-path, is presented one of the most beautiful landscapes we remember seeing most any where. It is worth, as Thomas Jefferson has said, a voyage across the Atlantic to see the scenery of the Potomac at Harper's Ferry: then we say it is, at least, worth traveling from Norristown, on any fine day, to this spot, to view the scenery of the Schuylkill Valley. In standing at a certain point here and looking up the stream, the falls of the Catfish dam are seen extending across the Schuylkill, and about three-fourths of a mile beyond is seen, nestled in the hills, a portion of Port Kennedy, with its bridge; and still beyond, and for the back ground, in the centre, and as if springing from the river, the picturesque and fine wooded hill-tops of Valley Forge, four miles off—the whole forming such a combination of objects, so advantageously connected, as are seldom found in any one view. At the dam aforesaid, are two locks, placed side by side, which are called the Catfish locks. These, as well as the dam, were built by the Navigation Company.

Upper Merion contains four churches, which, with one exception, have been built within a recent time. The one to which we allude is Christ Church, at Swedesburg, and of which we have given a description in our article on the Swedes. It was originally built in 1760 and enlarged in 1837. Some of the tombstones go back to 1744–5 and 8, showing that a grave yard was here some time before the erection of a church. A great many are buried here, and in looking over the stones the following are found to be the most common names: Broades, Brooke, Holstein, Gartley, Supplee, Novioch, Custer, Ramsey, Thomas, Amies, Jones, Clay, Hughes, Munson, Learnard, Pastorious, Dehaven, Rambo, Engle, Coats, Roberts, Famous and Henderson.—Though the form of worship is Episcopalian, yet this church is not attached to the diocess, this right being reserved by its members. Of all the Swedish Lutheran churches in Pennsylvania, it is said this is now the only one not merged in the Episcopal diocess. Its present pastor is the Rev. William Henry Rees.

In regard to the early history of Upper Merion, we know, from Thomas Holmes' map of original surveys, commenced in 1682 and completed before 1695, that the upper half of the township was included in Letitia Penn's manor of Mount Joy, the middle portion to William Penn, jr., and the lower part adjoining Lower Merion, to John Pennington and company. The remaining portion of the manor of Mount Joy lay in the adjoining township of Tredyffrin, in Chester county, and included in all seven thousand eight hundred acres. The land belonging to John Pennington and company no doubt was a part of the Welsh tract, which we know extended through a part of the township, and extended into Chester county, comprising in the whole, forty thousand acres, and of which we have already made mention in the history of Lower Meron. It was chiefly through this last great purchase that the original settlers were Welsh, and who gave it the name of Merion, after the shire from whence they came. The Swedes came into the township about 1712, and settled on a large tract which they purchased from the Welsh. The names of these settlers were Mats Holstein, Gunner Rambo, Peter Rambo, Peter Yocum and John Matson, who each took up from eight hundred to one thousand acres of land, which lay from the present borough of Bridgeport down to the Lower Merion line, and back about two miles from the river. This tract, for fertility, is almost unequalled in Pennsylvania, and is still chiefly in the hands of their descendants and comprises nearly one third of the present area of the township. On this tract the names of Swedes' Ford, Swedes' Church, Swedesburg, Swedeland and Matson's Ford sufficiently indicate the presence of these settlers. As a pretty full account of the Swedes has already been given, further information is deemed unnecessary. A road was laid out from Whiteland, in Chester county, in 1723, to the Swedes' Ford by way of the present King of Prussia, thus showing that the travel at this early period must have been considerable in this direction. The following is a list of settlers living in Upper Merion in 1734, being thirty-two in number, copied from the list prepared for Thomas Penn. It will be observed that about one half are Welsh: Mathias Holstein, Hugh Hughs, Morris Edwards, Owen Thomas, Griffith Phillips, John Moor, Owen Jones, Thomas Jenkin, John David, Alexander Henderson, Mounce Rambo, John Rambo, Gabriel Rambo, Elias Rambo, Peter Yocum, Andrew Supplee, Hugh Williams, Benjamin Davis, John Sturges, Isaac Rees, Richard Bevan, David James, William Rees, Edward Roberts, Mathew Roberts, Wm. George, Thomas Rees, Harry Griffith, Hannah Jones, Griffith Rees, David Lewis and John Rees.

Hugh Hughs, we know, settled here some time before 1723. Edward Roberts was commissioned one of the justices of the Philadelphia County Courts in 1726, and was continued in the same, in 1741. Richard Bevan, in the aforesaid list, advertises in the Pennsylvania Gazette, of July 24th, 1751, that he has for sale, "near the Gulf Mill, a likely negro-man, about thirty years of age, fit for town or country business. Also a negro-girl, about fifteen years of age." No doubt, before the Revolution, there was a considerable number of slaves in the country. Even the census of 1790, it should be remembered, gives to Montgomery county one hundred and fourteen slaves, which, in 1830, had decreased to one solitary slave.

The Revolutionary history of this township is not without interest, for nearly all the leading events connected with the encampment at Valley Forge happened within its limits. This will be hereafter given in a separate article. But a few days after the defeat of Washington at Brandywine, he retired to Germantown, where he allowed his army one day for rest and refreshment; he then re-crossed the Schuylkill, September 15th, 1777, for the purpose of giving the enemy battle upon the field of his late defeat, if his camp yet remained there. Monseur Der Coudray, a French officer, who had been commissioned a Major General on the 11th of August, set off with a party of French gentlemen to overtake Washington. As he rode a young and spirited mare, which was placed in a flat-bottomed boat for the purpose of being transported across the river, scarcely had they started, when she backed to the extreme end of the boat and then into the river, with her rider on her back, and during the struggle both were drowned. Congress, on hearing of this occurrence the next day, ordered his corpse to be interred at the expense of the United States, and with the honors of war. His death happened in the vicinity of Matson's Ford, on the 16th of September. In November following, Lieutenant Colonel Lacey marched with a force of some three or four hundred men under his command from the encampment of the American army at Whitemarsh, to join General Potter's brigade on the west side of the Schuylkill. A position was taken by the united forces near the Gulf Mills on the main road leading to Philadelphia. The British having received information of this left the city about midnight, and arrived here early in the morning, when a severe attack was made. At the first fire two of Potter's regiments fled, but a portion under Lacey stood their ground until they were completely outnumbered, when they fell back to the brow of the hill where General Potter had stationed his second line. Here another struggle ensued, when the Americans again fell back and began to retreat. General Potter and Colonel Lacey used every effort to rally them, but in vain. Soon a general consternation prevailed, which resulted in a route. So rapid was the retreat that the British were soon all left behind but two dragoons, who followed at full speed. After a chase of some distance, the Americans were satisfied that the British army was no longer in pursuit, and probably thinking it too great disgrace for several regiments to be fleeing before two single horsemen, Colonel Lacey ordered the men to turn around and fire, which was instantly done, and both horses and riders fell to the ground, pierced by a hundred balls. Somewhat to the credit of the Americans engaged in this affair, it has been supposed that the horses of these dragoons became unmanageable, and thus forced their riders, however much against their will, to exhibit a courage from which, could they have avoided it, they would have gladly escaped. The loss of the Americans was one officer and seventeen men. General Potter now marched to Swedes' Ford, where, about the middle of December, he joined the main army under Washington, who were on the way to go into winter quarters at Valley Forge. At this place a court-martial was held by order of General Potter to try such men as threw away their arms and equipments for the purpose of facilitating their escape in the late attack. A number were sentenced to be publicly whipped, which sentence was carried into effect, and produced not a little excitement in the camp. Although Upper Merion lay at some distance from Philadelphia yet its citizens suffered considerable from the marauding expeditions of the British army. The assessor appointed to rate the damages committed by them placed them at £1517.

The Hon. Jonathan Roberts was a native and resident of this township, and died in July, 1854, at the advanced age of 83 years; and, at his request, was buried on a part of his place called "Red Hill," where he had appropriated two acres of land for the poor of the neighborhood to bury their dead free of charge. Mr. Roberts was elected a member of Congress in 1811, and in February, 1814, was chosen a member of the United States. Senate, which office he held till 1821.

BRIDGEPORT.

The borough of Bridgeport is of recent origin, having been incorporated by an act of Assembly passed the 27th of February, 1851. Its area is four hundred and sixty acres, and was wholly taken from the township of Upper Merion, in which it had been previously situated. In its form it is quite irregular, having somewhat the shape of a scalene triangle. It is bounded on the north and north-east by the Schuylkill, and on the south and west by Upper Merion. Few towns have a more beautiful and advantageous situation. It is opposite Norristown, and the land rises gradually from the river. The borough extends on the Schuylkill from the dam down to the out-let lock, a distance of a mile. DeKalb street, which was laid out in 1830, as the State road, extends across the bridge from Norristown, and is piked. Ford street extends from DeKalb street to the Swedes' Ford bridge. The nearest street running parallel with the river, is called Front street; next is Second, and so on to Tenth street, which forms the south-western boundary of the borough. DeKalb and Front are the principal streets and contain a number of elegant brick houses, several of which are occupied by persons of wealth and who have retired from business. According to the census of 1850, Bridgeport contained five hundred and seventy-two inhabitants, and in 1856, two hundred and forty-seven taxables. At this time the population is probably about thirteen hundred.

That Bridgeport is no inconsiderable business place is sufficiently proven from the number of stores and manufactories within its limits. In May, 1858, it contained three inns, one grocery, two merchandise, one drug, one shoe, one clothing, one clock, one variety and one confectionary store. There is a large cotton factory belonging to John Ogden, who employs about fifty hands in spinning and weaving. White and Brothers have a large straw-hat and bonnet factory, and employ nearly one hundred hands. Body and Jacobs have a woolen factory for sattinetts; Raysor and Templeton, a steam sash and door factory and planing mill; E. Potts and Co. carry on the manufacture of agricultural implements, and H. K. Stahl has an extensive coach and carriage manufactory. Besides these there are two flour mills, two lumber yards, two coal yards and one brick yard.

According to the triennial assessment of 1856 the real estate is valued at one hundred and ninety-seven thousand eight hundred and seventeen dollars, and the horses and cattle at two thousand four hundred and ninety-two dollars. The public school house was built in 1856, and is a large two story brick building with a cupola, on DeKalb street. For the school year ending with June 1st, 1857, three schools were kept in it, taught by one male and two female teachers, Mr. Huckins being the principal. These were open five months, and one hundred and ninety-three scholars attended, and one thousand one hundred and eighty-one dollars were levied to defray the expenses of the same. The Baptist church is the only house of worship in Bridgeport, and was built in 1849. It is a one story stone building with a basement. The Rev. C. J. Thompson is the present pastor. The Methodists, on Sundays, hold worship in the basement of the public school-house. A library company was organized in May 1858, and near the close of the year contained two hundred and fifty volumes, Dr. G. W. Holstein being librarian. The post office was established some time before 1855. That Bridgeport has rapidly increased within a recent time is sufficiently attested by an enumeration made in 1832, when it contained but one inn, a store, a mill and eight houses.

The various public improvements that either pass through or begin here contribute much to the prosperity and business advantages of the place. Among the first constructed was the Schuylkill navigation and canal. This great work is one hundred and eight miles in length, beginning at the Fairmount dam and extending to Port Carbon above Pottsville. It was commenced in 1816 and finished in 1824 for the passage of boats of sixty tons burden. To this place it was sufficiently completed in 1818 to admit the descent of a few boats. The whole line, in 1846, was enlarged, and boats of one hundred and eighty-six tons now pass and repass. When the navigation company had made the dam here in 1816–18, it was their intention to make the canal on the east side of the river, through Norristown, beginning at or near the present Swedes' Ford bridge to the dam. But as the people of Norristown were almost unanimously opposed to any such measure, they were induced, through the liberal offers of Elisha Evans, the owner of the land on the Bridgeport side, to locate it there. No doubt, at that early day, and when there was but two houses here Mr. Evans foresaw the advantages that would arise in the future from such an arrangement.

The bridge over Schuylkill, on DeKalb street, is eight hundred feet long, and with the abutments one thousand and fifty feet. It rests on three stone piers, and cost thirty-one thousand two hundred dollars. Of this amount the county subscribed ten thousand dollars, and the state six thousand dollars. It was erected by a joint stock company, chartered the sixth of April, 1830. It was begun in the spring of 1829, and by September of this year it was so far completed that foot passengers could cross on it. It was finished in 1830. For a number of years before the erection of this bridge efforts were made at different times to have one erected here, but always fell through for the want of sufficient capital. Even the Legislature chartered a company for this purpose as early as 1815. The Swedes' Ford bridge company was incorporated the 30th of March, 1848, but the bridge was not built till 1851. The Chester Valley railroad crosses it and forms a connection with the Philadelphia and Norristown railroad. This bridge is about half a mile below the Norristown bridge.

No sooner was the bridge built than efforts were made to have a State road laid out from New Hope, on the Delaware, by way of this place and West Chester to the Maryland line. To authorize this the Assembly passed an act at the same time the bridge was chartered. This road was laid out the 29th of December, 1830, and passes through Montgomery county a distance of sixteen miles. The court, on the 17th of August, 1831, directed it to be opened and cleared to the breadth of forty feet. It has since generally gone by the name of the State road. From this borough to the King of Prussia, a distance of three miles, this road was turnpiked a few years ago.

The Reading railroad company was chartered April 4th, 1833, and the next year the larger portion of the road was put under contract. On the 9th of December, 1839, the first locomotive and train of cars passed over it to Reading. It was not opened to Pottsville till early in 1842 when the event was celebrated with military display and an immense procession of seventy-five passenger cars, one thousand two hundred and fifty-five feet in length, containing two thousand one hundred and fifty persons, three bands of music, with one hundred and eighty tons of coal, part of which was mined the same morning, four hundred and twelve feet below the water level. In August, 1858, while standing near the railroad, in DeKalb street, we counted a train of ninety five cars passing with coal, drawn by a single locomotive. The depot and station is a commodious edifice, well calculated for the business and travel of the place. Near by the railroad company have also a building and reservoir, to supply the locomotives with water while stopping, which is elevated by means of water power furnished at the spring. The Chester Valley railroad at this place connects both with the Reading and Norristown railroads, and extends to Downingtown, where a connection is also made with the Pennsylvania railroad. It is twenty-one miles long. The first train of cars passed over this road on the 12th of September, 1853.

Although Bridgeport is of recent origin, as has been already stated, yet its history extends back to an early period. Swedes' Ford is within its limits, and around which cluster both colonial and revolutionary reminiscences. The history of the latter, we might add, terminates where the other begins. About the year 1712 Mats Holstein, with his wife Brita, moved into this neighborhood from the county below, accompanied by several other Swedish families. He purchased, from a Welshman, one thousand acres of land, upon which he settled and built a stone house in 1714, about one and a half miles from this borough. This tract had a front on the river of about a mile, and extended back into the country some two miles, including all the present territory of Bridgeport, which comprises less than half that area. The name of Swedes' Ford must have been applied to this place before 1723. For we know in November of this year application was made to the Governor and Council to have a road laid out from Whiteland, in Chester county, to this ford, which, in the spring of the following year, was confirmed, and ordered to "be with all convenient speed opened, cleared and made good." A portion of the old Swedes' Ford tavern, now owned by Col. Bush, was supposed, by the late Mathias Holstein, to have been built before 1730. He at one time kept it as a public house, and built an addition to it. Near by stood the "twin pines," so called from the fact of their growing from one butt and separating about four feet from the ground and thence growing in close proximity to a very great height, and serving as a land-mark to the country around. These trees were a remnant of the ancient forest, and on this account were preserved from violence and regarded with interest. One of them was blown down during the prevalence of a violent storm on Easter Sunday, 1822. The other continued to flourish till about 1842, when it began to show symptoms of decay, and by 1847 had so far *pined* away in stately grandeur, that as a matter of prudence it was cut down. It measured over two feet in diameter. Sherman Day, the distinguished author of the Historical Collections of Pennsylvania, and who was here in 1841, thus speaks of it: "A tall and solitary pine, a remnant of the ancien forest, still stands beside it, (the old Swedes Ford tavern,) like some faithful old sentinel; some years since it had a companion, and the two formed a beautiful head."

The battle of Brandywine was fought September the 11th, 1777. At twelve o'clock that night Washington wrote a despatch to Congress from Chester, in which he says: "This day's engagement resulted in our defeat." On the 13th he formed his head quarters at Germantown, with the determination of having another engagement before the fate of Philadelphia should be decided. From an original letter now in our possession, written in the city on the 11th, by Mrs. Margaret Stedman to Mrs. Ferguson, of Græme Park, is taken this extract: "General Washington and all his army are come over this side and marched up to the Falls, expecting the English will cross at the Swedes' Ford." General Armstrong, with a portion of the militia, was posted along the Schuylkill, to throw up redoubts at the different fords where the enemy would be most likely to cross, and which were to be occasionally occupied, while Washington moved with the main body of the army, on the other side, to make another attack. Apprehending that it would be very likely that the British would attempt to cross at Swedes' Ford, Chevelier Du Portail, a French engineer, constructed a number of redoubts on the east side of the river, upwards of half a mile in length, with the assistance of Armstrong's command. It is said that they had scarcely completed these works before the British made their appearance at the place, and that when they beheld the defence changed their purpose with the intention of crossing higher up, which they subsequently did at Fatland Ford, below Valley Forge. When Washington broke up his encampment at Whitemarsh, with the intention of going into winter quarters at Valley Forge, he crossed at this place, near the middle of December. Major Holstein, then a boy, witnessed the passage, and related that it was effected by making a bridge of wagons, all backed to each other. He also says that trees then abounded on the banks.

From the Pennsylvania Gazette of 1780, we learn that at that time there was "a great road leading from Coryell's ferry (now New Hope,) to the Swedes' Ford." On Reading Howell's map of Pennsylvania, published in 1792, Swedes' Ford is mentioned. More than a century ago there were three public houses in Upper Merion: one was at this place, one at the Bird-in-hand, and the other at the King of Prussia. These, from their situation, formed an exact equalateral triangle, being each three miles distant from the other. A respectable lady of this borough, now nearly eighty, remembers well, in her youth, when this was a favorite round with the young people in sleighing time. Before we drop the time-honored name of Swedes' Ford, it may be well in this place to mention its exact locality, so that it may be the more readily recognized. It extended a few yards below the present Swedes' Ford tavern, directly across the Schuylkill, where a large and venerable willow still stands to mark the spot, on the Norristown side. It is about one hundred yards above the present Swedes' Ford bridge. Except from some of the objects just mentioned, it would otherwise be difficult to recognize its locality from the great change made in the neighborhood by the improvements of the last forty years.

As Chevelier Du Portail was a resident of this place a further notice may not be amiss. While Dr. Franklin and Silas Deane were in Paris, they were instructed by Congress to procure for the American army four competent engineers, and who had served in this capacity in the French armies. They were accordingly selected and sent to this country. Among this number was Du Portail. It is said that he came over with La Fayette. As to this we cannot vouch. The first we know of his services is in the capacity of an engineer, along the Schuylkill, in September, 1777. On the following 17th of November, he was commissioned a Brigadier General in the army, and in the beginning of 1778 a colonel of engineers. He was at the siege of Yorktown, and for his services there was commended by Washington. The 16th of November, 1781, he was promoted to the rank of Major General. In consequence of the war coming to a close, he sailed for France the same month, and after a brief stay came back again. Being a man of wealth, and charmed with the beauty and fertility of this part of the country, while engaged in the capacity of an engineer, induced him to purchase, after the peace, the farm upon which the greater part of Bridgeport has since been erected. He continued to reside here until about the year 1800, when he sailed for France, but died on the passage. An aged and respectable friend informs us that he was a son-in-law of Count Pulaski, the Polish General. A portrait of Du Portail may now be seen in Independence Hall, Philadelphia, having formerly been in the Peale collection. Shortly after his death, the property, with about two hundred acres of land, was sold to Elisha Evans, who, in 1810, sold off forty acres to Robert Jones. With this exception, Mr. Evans retained the balance as farm land till his death, in 1830, when it came in possession of his son, Cadwallader Evans, who still resides in the borough.

At this time Bridgeport contained three dwelling houses, a tavern and a large three story stone mill, which is still standing near the canal, in DeKalb street, and was built in 1826. It was through the liberality of Elisha Evans that the canal was made through the whole length of his property. The erection of the Norristown bridge, in 1829, and the opening of the State road the year after, began to give the first impulse to improvement, which has not since been materially checked. In 1832, besides a store, the number of houses had increased to eight; in 1840, to fifty-three, and in 1849, to ninety-six. The number now is probably over two hundred.

After the incorporation of Bridgeport into a borough, in the winter of 1851, Perry M. Hunter, L. E. Corson, M. McGlathery and Alex. H. Supplee were appointed commissioners to lay out its territory from the township of Upper Merion. The following boundaries were then agreed upon: Beginning at low water mark of the river Schuylkill, in said township; thence on a line dividing lands of C. Evans and the Schuylkill Navigation Company, south twenty degrees and twenty minutes, west thirty-four perches and two-tenths of a perch to a point in a public road in the great valley; thence along the middle of said road, south sixty-five degrees and forty minutes, west one hundred and sixty five perches and five-tenths of a perch to a point in the middle of a road leading to Swedes' Ford road; thence along the same south twenty-six degrees thirty-five minutes, west one hundred and fifty-six perches to a point in lands of Henry Novioch; thence north sixty-six degrees east seventy-three perches to a point in a line between lands of John and Lindsay Coates; thence by lands of Samuel Coates south eighty-three degrees, east one hundred and forty-five perches and four-tenths of a perch to a point; thence by lands of said Samuel Coates, north sixty-three degrees thirty minutes, east two hundred and fifty-three perches to low water mark of the river Schuylkill aforesaid, and along and up said river the several courses thereof to the place of beginning.

PORT KENNEDY.

The village of Port Kennedy is situated on the south bank of the Schuylkill, in the township of Upper Merion, and is twenty-one miles from Philadelphia and four from Norristown. The country, in this vicinity, is rolling, and the soil fertile. It is noted for the vast quantities of lime burned here and exported to other places. Through this business it owes its chief prosperity. Thirty years ago it was almost a waste, with nothing on it to attract attention but a beautiful spring of excellent water. At this time it contains one hotel, two stores, a furnace, church, school house, blacksmith and wheelwright shop, and forty-two dwelling houses. The census of 1850 gives Port Kennedy four hundred and forty-nine inhabitants. If this enumeration was correct, we doubt whether at this time it contains that population. The number of houses is too small to warrant such a conclusion. From the hill, on the road to Valley Forge, a short distance from the village, there is a fine prospect of the place and surrounding country, as well as of the Schuylkill for several miles down its course.

The hotel, which is the only one in the place, is a large three story stone building, upwards of forty feet square. It has an elevated position on the river's bank, and the Reading railroad has a station near by. The furnace here belongs to Patterson & Co., of Philadelphia, and was built in 1855. It is a large establishment, and during the year 1857 gave employment to thirty hands and turned out from twelve to fifteen tons of pig iron per day. In August, 1858, when we were here, it was not in operation. It is called the Montgomery furnace, and is said to be constructed in the most substantial manner, and with the latest improvements in the art of smelting. The principal portion of the ore used was obtained in the vicinity. A considerable quantity was procured from the farm of Isaac Richardson, one mile off, in the same township—also, from William Roberts' farm and from near the White Horse, in Chester county, by means of the Chester Valley railroad. Ore was also obtained from Lake Champlain, some of which yielded seventy-five per cent. The Presbyterian church was built in 1845, and is a handsome stone building, in the east part of the village. The present pastor is the Rev. Henry S. Rodenbaugh, who resides in Lower Providence township. The Port Kennedy bridge company was incorporated by an act of Assembly passed March 9th, 1846. It is a frame covered bridge, resting on three stone piers, and is of sufficient width to admit two wagons passing. It was not completed till the close of the year 1849.

It is the lime business that has given this place its present importance, and probably in this respect is not exceeded by any other in the valley of the Schuylkill. The lime manufactured is of superior quality and most of it is shipped off by the canal to New Jersey, Delaware and Maryland; a considerable quantity is also sent to Philadelphia and New York. When we were here in August, 1858, three schooners, one sloop and a canal boat were loading at the wharves. One of these, a schooner, was a neat and beautiful craft, and so symmetrical in form that one might have supposed that it had been intended rather as a pleasure yacht than for the more useful purposes of trade. As the vessels, in order to reach this place from the city, have to pass under bridges, it becomes necessary for them to have falling masts, which are raised while loading. According to the census of 1840, Upper Merion produced lime to the amount of seventy-four thousand seven hundred and seventy-two dollars. At this time Port Kennedy alone produces twice that sum; thus showing that this business has greatly increased and will yet arise to much greater importance. The burning of lime is carried on here the most extensively by John Kennedy, Esq. His kilns are nearest the village, and are fourteen in number, some of the largest of which contain two thousand five hundred bushels. The quarry has been worked at some places to the depth of forty feet. He generally has from sixty to seventy men in his employ. Mr. Kennedy resides in a large and handsome mansion on an elevated situation, near the Presbyterian church. There is a large conservatory attached, containing a number of curious plants. David R. Kennedy, brother of the aforesaid, carries on the business extensively, about a quarter of a mile south west of the village. David Zook has also several kilns and carries on the business to some extent. Reeves, Buck & Co., have recently purchased a tract of land here, and keep a large number of men engaged in quarrying, hauling and boating the stone for the use of their extensive furnaces at Phœnixville, six miles distant.

As great houses are built from small bricks so great fortunes are often made from small beginnings. As an example we might mention Alexander Kennedy, the founder of this place, and after whom it was called. He was a native of Ireland and came to this country poor, and was first employed by a person of wealth in this vicinity. Through his industry and business qualifications he accumulated, in the course of years, a handsome fortune. The property on which this village is located belonged to Mordecai Moore, who died in 1803, at an advanced age. It was then purchased by Mr. Kennedy, who moved on it in the spring of 1805. He continued to reside here till in the fall of 1824, when he died at the age of about sixty-three years, and was interred at the Great Valley Presbyterian church. He was a highly respected and useful man, and his loss was lamented by a large circle of friends. He has four sons still surviving. John and David R. Kennedy reside here, and are the principal property holders of this village and vicinity. William resides in Kent county, Maryland, and Alexander, in East Pikeland, Chester county. Before this village had attained near its present size it was called by the less dignified name of "Kennedy's Hollow;" but time, the changer of all things, has transformed this uncouthness into its present more euphonious name.

Not many years ago, in working in the limestone quarries here, an extensive cavern was reached, which had an area fully equal to many of our largest public buildings. It contained a considerable number of stalactites of calcareous matter, some of which extended to the floor and formed several conical arches, with borders of variegated colors—also pyramidal columns of various sizes. This cavern, from the singularity of its chambers, was an object of considerable curiosity during the brief period it was open to visitors. A concert was held in one of its largest *saloons*, on the 4th July, 1846, at which several hundred persons were present. Its existence has now become only a matter of the past, for it has been quarried away these several years. How singular that a cave in the solid rock should be burned up by man and not a particle left remaining! No doubt it lay here concealed for ages, even before the creation of man himself, and which his industry has only lately revealed and destroyed, for the more beneficial purposes of enriching his fields.

VALLEY FORGE.

Dear to every lover of freedom must be this spot, consecrated as it has been by the devotion and sufferings of that patriot band. No where in the wide world but here, during the winter of 1777–8, did liberty dare to raise her arm against oppression. Truly may it be said that at that time whatever portion of mankind may have longed for a brighter era, here their hopes must have been centered. Cold and piercing as were the blasts of that winter on these hills, there was still enough warmth remaining in those bosoms, in spite of their scanty covering, to sustain them through the terrible trial. As the antiquary or traveler rambles in its vicinity, and gazes on the remaining relics of that encampment and reflects on their sufferings, he cannot but think where are now the men that composed that army, and where is now that noble chief who endured with them? Gone, yes, forever gone, as they all are, from the theatre of action on this earth; yet they still live in the hearts of their countrymen—in the hearts of the great and good of other nations. The example lives—and though tyranny may flourish her sceptre and justice be wronged, it cannot long survive such recollections as Valley Forge presents. It is this that ennobles history and makes the historian the champion of the rights of man and a benefactor of his race.

The village of Valley Forge is situated on the south bank of the Schuylkill, at the mouth of the East Valley creek. It is distant twenty-three and a half miles from Philadelphia and six above Norristown. That portion of it comprised within the limits of Upper Merion contains Charles H. Rogers' cotton factory, a grist mill, store, hotel and ten houses. On the Chester county side is Thropp's cotton factory, a store, post office and fifteen houses. The Reading railroad, which has a station here, crosses the creek, near its mouth, by a bridge some thirty feet above the water, and from which a beautiful view is offered by looking up the creek. Among the interesting objects seen are the falls of the dams belonging to the grist mill and cotton factory, a short distance above each other, and of the venerable stone bridge crossing it a hundred yards above. These, with the deep gorge of the stream and the high and rugged hills rising on either side, which hem in the village near by, form an interesting sight—a picture, we might add, to be properly appreciated should be seen. Description cannot do it justice. Stolid, indeed, must the person be who has the recollections of the past stirring within him that can gaze on such a scene unmoved.

The cotton factory belonging to Mr. Rogers is a large and extensive establishment and employs nearly one hundred hands. Near by he has a splendid residence surrounded by fine lawns and shrubbery. Isaiah Thropp's factory of Kentucky jean also gives employment to a number of hands. Through the liberality of Mr. Rogers an observatory was erected on his lands, on the hill, about two hundred yards south-east of the village. It is not situated quite on the most elevated part of the hill, but still a splendid view is offered of the surrounding country. It is approached by a path through the fields, and its site points out the spot where Washington's marquee was planted on the day of his arrival here. The observatory is of an octagonal form and about forty feet high, and is ascended by a spiral staircase. From the open gallery, on its top, can be seen Norristown, Phœnixville, Pawling's Bridge, Edge Hill, Barren Hill, Methacton Hill, and a number of other places. We were here on the 17th of August, 1858. The day was beautiful but warm. We observed that the highest and steepest hill here is on the Chester county side, and are satisfied, from its peculiar appearance, that it can be seen from an elevation near the Willow Grove, twenty-four miles distant. The hills, on both sides of Valley creek, are generally steep, rugged and wooded to their summits, and present an unusually wild appearance, more so than one might expect from the populousness of the surrounding country. At the close of this article an account will be given of the house still standing in the village in which Washington had his head quarters, also of the existing remains of the encampment, besides notices of a number of relics in the possession of persons in the vicinity.

In reverting to the early history of this neighborhood, we learn, from Holmes' map of original surveys, made between the years 1682 and 1695, that the manor of Mount Joy comprised all of the upper portion of Upper Merion, as well as a portion of the adjoining township of Tredyffrin, in Chester county, and contained about seven thousand eight hundred acres, which belonged to Letitia, the daughter of William Penn. There is a tradition that William Penn, who, on a visit in this vicinity, got lost on the high hill on the Chester county side, and that he did not know where he was till he got on the hill this side of the stream, on which the observatory is, when by a glimpse of the Schuylkill and the country to the southward, he regained his way, and in consequence named the former hill Mount Misery and the latter Mount Pleasant, which they respectively bear to this day. The name of

Valley Forge is derived from a forge erected here by Isaac Potts, a son of John Potts, after whom Pottstown was called, and who was an early settler and extensive landholder there. How early the forge was erected here we cannot say, but it is marked on William Scull's map of Pennsylvania, published in 1770. Some time after the revolution it was torn down and the spot is now occupied by Mr. Rogers' cotton factory. Mr. Potts was also the proprietor of a large tract of land in this vicinity. There is now no forge or furnace in this vicinity, but iron ore is still dug in considerable quantities on the farm of Richard Marten, about a quarter of a mile from the village, on the road to the King of Prussia. The house of Isaac Potts stood a short distance below the forge, near the mouth of the creek, and was used as the residence and head-quarters of Washington during the encampment.

The battle of Brandywine was fought the 11th of September, 1777, and resulted disastrously to the Americans. Washington immediately crossed the Schuylkill, with the intention, if the British attempted to cross it, to make another attack, and thus, at least, by one more effort, try to save Philadelphia. He, however, shortly afterwards returned to have another engagement near the scene of the late struggle. On the 17th the two armies met near the Warren tavern, on the Lancaster road. Preparations were made to attack the left wing of the enemy, and an engagement was about to take place near the Goshen meeting house, when a violent storm of rain came on and suddenly wet the powder of both parties and prevented a conflict. The storm continued all night, and before dawn the enemy left their position and moved down the road leading to Swedes' Ford. When they there beheld the defence or breastworks on the opposite side of the river they wheeled around and proceeded in the vicinity of this place. In the meantime Washington crossed the Schuylkill at Parker's Ford, hoping to be able to confront them while on their passage of the river. A detachment of the British army arrived at the Forge and burned the mansion house of Colonel Dewees and the iron works, leaving the grist mill uninjured. On the 19th they encamped on the hills of this vicinity. In the meantime Washington arrived near Pottsgrove, supposing Howe's design to be either to turn the right of his army, or to get possession of the American stores deposited at Reading. The movement of the British appears to have been to deceive Washington, for as soon as they ascertained that his army was near Pottsgrove, they crossed the Schuylkill at Fatland Ford, about half a mile below Valley Forge, on the night of the 22d of September, and proceeded leisurely towards Philadelphia, which they did not enter till the 26th, spending three days in a March of twenty-three miles. Immediately on learning that the British had crossed the Schuylkill, and were on their march to Philadelphia, Washington wrote a letter to Congress, at Lancaster, from his camp, near Pottsgrove, in which he says: "The enemy, by a variety of perplexing manœuvres, through a country from which I could not derive the least intelligence, (being to a man disaffected) contrived to pass the Schuylkill last night at the Fatland and other fords in the neighborhood of it. They immediately marched towards Philadelphia, and I imagine their advanced parties will be near the city to-night. They had so far got the start before I received certain intelligence that any considerable number had crossed, that I found it in vain to think of overtaking their rear with troops harrassed as ours have been with constant marching since the battle of Brandywine."

The British had now full possession of Philadelphia, and for winter quarters were comfortably situated. The battles of Brandywine and Germantown were fought, and had resulted to the Americans with a loss of two thousand soldiers. The autumn had now nearly passed, and Washington and his army still lay at Whitemarsh, with nothing but tents to shelter them from the inclemencies of the weather. The question now arose, where and how were they to spend the winter? Should they disband and leave the country unprotected, and to the ravages of a foreign soldiery, or should they enter into winter quarters, somewhere convenient to the city, where, by taking a strong position they might both secure themselves and the country from any attacks? The latter alternative seemed the most effective, and at the same time the most feasible. Had they disbanded for the winter it perhaps would have occasioned such a dissolution in the army that might have been fatal to its re-organization in the spring.

Both Washington and his officers were satisfied that Whitemarsh was not the proper place for a winter encampment. The former, therefore, requested his general officers to communicate to him, in writing, their sentiments respecting the most eligible site for that purpose. A council of war was held on the 30th of November, at which a wide difference of opinion prevailed as to the locality and the best manner of cantoning the troops. So various and contradictory were the opinions and councils, that unanimity could not be hoped for, and it was necessary for Washington to act according to his own judgment and upon his own responsibility. He decided to form an encampment at Valley Forge, where he might be near enough to the British army to watch its movements—keep its foraging parties in check, and protect the country from the depredations of the enemy.

On the 11th of December, the patriot army left Whitemarsh and crossed the Schuylkill at Swedes' Ford the same day, by making a bridge of their wagons, all backed to each other. Here they were joined by General Potter and his brigade, who had marched from a strong position on the Gulf Hill. At what exact time they arrived in the vicinity of Valley Forge is not known, but, very probably, about the 16th. The next day Washington issued a proclamation to the army, in which he gives his reasons for the course he had pursued. This is an interesting document and breathes the language of devoted patriotism throughout, while at the same time it evinces the cool determination to conduct the war to a happy close.

"HEAD QUARTERS ON SCHUYLKILL, Dec. 17, 1777.

"General Orders. The Commander-in-Chief, with the highest satisfaction, expresses his thanks to the officers and soldiers for the fortitude and patience with which they have sustained the fatigues of the campaign. Although in some instances we have unfortunately failed, yet, upon the whole, Heaven has smiled upon our arms, and crowned them with signal success; and we may, on the best grounds, conclude that, by a spirited continuance in the measures necessary for our defence, we shall finally obtain the end of our warfare—*Independence, Liberty and Peace.* These are blessings worth contending for at every hazard; but we hazard nothing—the power of America alone, duly exerted, would have nothing to dread from the force of Britain. Yet we stand not wholly upon our own ground. France yields us every aid, and there are reasons to believe the period is not very distant when we will take a more active part, by declaring war against the British crown. Every motive, therefore, irresistibly urges us, nay, commands us, to a firm and manly perseverance in our opposition to our cruel oppressors—to slight difficulty, endure hardships, and continue every danger. The General ardently wishes it were now in his power to conduct the troops into the best winter quarters; but where are they to be found? Should we retire to the interior of the State, we should find them crowded with virtuous citizens, who, sacrificing their all, have left Philadelphia and fled hither for protection; to their distresses, humanity forbids us to add. This is not all!—We should leave a vast extent of fertile country to be despoiled and ravaged by the enemy, from which they would draw vast supplies, and where many of our firm friends would be exposed to all the miseries of an insulting and wanton depredation. A train of evils might be renumerated, but these will suffice. These considerations make it indispensably necessary for the army to take such a position as will enable it most effectually to prevent distress, and give the most extensive security; and in that position we must make ourselves the best shelter in our power. With alacrity and diligence, huts may be erected that will be warm and day. In these the troops will be compact, more secure against surprises than if in a divided state, and at hand to protect the country. These cogent reasons have determined the General to take the post in the neighborhood of this camp, and influenced by them, he pursuades himself that the officers and soldiers, with one heart and one mind, will resolve to surmount every difficulty with a fortitude and patience becoming their profession, and the sacred cause in which they are engaged. He himself will share the hardships and partake of every inconvenience."

The army did not reach the valley till about the 18th, and it is said that in their march to this place from Whitemarsh, they might have been tracked by the blood of their feet over the hard frozen ground, as many were compelled to travel barefooted for the want of shoes. According to a recommendation of Congress, the whole army engaged in religious services, and observed the day with public thanksgiving and praise. On the morning of the 19th, as

Mr. Lossing observes in his Field Book of the Revolution, they spread over the hills of Valley Forge and began the work of hutting All was activity among those who were sufficiently clad to allow them to work in the open air. Some cut down trees, others fashioned them, and in a few days the barracks, erected upon the plan of a regular city, were completed. The whole number of men was eleven thousand and ninety-eight when the encampment commenced. Of this number two thousand eight hundred and ninety-eight were unfit for duty. The British army, at the same time, contained thirty-three thousand seven hundred and fifty-six men, of which nineteen thousand five hundred and thirty were stationed in Philadelphia. This latter number, alone, it will be observed, was nearly double that of Washington's command. The wonder is at this day, after holding possession of the city for about nine months, how such an army of men should have remained so inactive and effected so little.

"Washington gave explicit directions for constructing the huts. He ordered the colonels or commanding officers of regiments, to cause their men to be divided into parties of twelve, and to see that each party had its proportion of tools, to commence a hut for that number; and as an encouragement to industry and art, the General promised to reward the party in each regiment which finished its hut in the quickest and most workmanlike manner, with a present of twelve dollars. He also offered a reward of one hundred dollars to the officer or soldier who should substitute a covering for the huts cheaper and more quickly made than boards. The following were the dimensions and style of the huts, as given in Washington's Orderly Book: "Fourteen by sixteen feet, each, the sides, ends and roofs made with logs; the roofs made tight with split slabs, or some other way; the sides made tight with clay; a fire-place made of wood and secured with clay on the inside eighteen inches thick; this fire-place to be on the rear of the huts; the door to be in the end next the street; the door to be made of split oak slabs, unless boards can be procured; the side walls to be six feet and a half high. The officers' huts are to form a line in the rear of the troops, one hut to be allowed each general officer; one to the staff of each brigade: one to the field officer of each regiment, and one to every twelve non-commissioned officers and soldiers." Until his soldiers were thus comfortably lodged, Washington occupied his cheerless marquee, after which he made his quarters at the house of Mr. Potts.

"Near Washington's quarters, on a gentle elevation by the river, were stationed his body or life guard, under the command of Charles Gibbs, of Rhode Island. A little to the right of the guard was the brigade of General McIntosh; and further up the hills were the brigades of Huntington, Conway and Maxwell. Between these and McIntosh's brigade were a redoubt and slight intrenchments; and directly in front of them was a line of *abates*. Nearer the Schuylkill, and on the top of the hill, was the brigade of General Varnum, near a star redoubt. At a distance of about a mile, and forming a line from the Schuylkill to Valley creek, was the main portion of the army, under Brigadiers Muhlenburg, Weedon, Paterson, Learned, Glover, Poor, Wayne, Scott and Woodford, with a line of intrenchments in front. The artificers of the army were on the north side of the creek, opposite the General's quarters; and near the cotton factory was the army bake-house. There was also an irregular line of intrenchments along the brow of the hill, on the south side of the creek. Not far southward of Roger's observatory was a redoubt, and near it was Knox's artillery. The remains of this redoubt are yet very prominent in the woods, on the right side of the road leading from Valley Forge to Paoli; also, the redoubt on the left wing of the encampment, (now near the Reading railroad) is well preserved, the forest protecting it from demolition." A temporary bridge was thrown across the river, to facilitate communications with the surrounding country. While the huts were building, General Potter was stationed some distance off, to cover the main army, in case of any attack, as well as to watch the motions of the enemy.

"Here, after an arduous campaign of four months, during which neither party obtained a decided advantage, other than good winter quarters at Philadelphia, on the part of the enemy, the shattered remains of the American army vainly sought repose. They had marched and counter-marched, day and night, in endeavoring to baffle the designs of a powerful enemy to their country and its liberties; now they were called upon, in the midst of comparative inaction to war with enemies more insidious, implacable and personal. Hunger and nakedness assailed that dreary winter camp with all their progeny of disease and woe. Thither, as we have seen, the soldiers came with naked, bleeding feet, and there they sat down where destitution held court and ruled with an icy sceptre. The prevalence of Toryism in the vicinity, the avaricious peculations of some unprincipled commissioners—the tardy movements of Congress in supplying provisions, and the close proximity of a powerful enemy, combined to make the procurement of provisions absolutely impracticable without a resort to force. But few horses were in camp, and such was the deficiency in this respect, for the ordinary as well as the extraordinary occasions of the army, that the men, in many instances, cheerfully yoked themselves to vehicles of their own construction, for carrying wood and provisions when procured, while others performed the duty of pack-horses, and carried heavy burdens of fuel upon their backs."

Though the army had been but a few days in camp, the soldiers began to suffer for the want of straw for lodging, which could not be had because the farmers of the surrounding country would not thresh their grain. To put a stop to this evasion, the following order was issued with the intention of remedying this inconvenience:—

By His Excellency, George Washington, Esquire, General and Commander-in-chief of the forces of the United States of America.

By virtue of the power and direction to me especially given, I hereby enjoin and require all persons residing within seventy miles of my head quarters, to thresh one half of their grain by the first day of March next, ensuing, on pain, in case of failure, of having all that shall remain *in sheaves* after that period above mentioned, seized by the commissaries and quarter-masters of the army, and paid for as *straw*. Given under my hand, at head quarters, near the Valley Forge, in Philadelphia county, this 20th day of December, 1787.

(Signed) G. WASHINGTON.

Robert H. Harrison, Secretary.

December had now but a few days left, and the soldiers were too illy clothed to be exposed any longer to the inclemency of the season. For up to this time, it should be remembered, they had only been sheltered like their commander-in chief, under mere tents. Besides the want of straw, blankets and clothing, their sufferings were increased by the want of provisions for the commissary's department, which, through the neglect of Congress, had been badly managed. An opinion of their condition and appearance may be formed from the following letter, written by General Wayne to the late Judge Peters of Philadelphia, under date of December 30th, 1777: "We are busy in forming a city. My people will be covered in a few days. I mean as to huts, but half naked as to clothing; they are, in this respect, in a worse condition than Fallstaff's recruits, for they have not one whole shirt to a brigade—he had more than one to a company."

At what time Washington left his cheerless marquee for the house of Isaac Potts is not exactly known to us, but it was either on or a few days previous to the 2nd of January, 1778. Here, for the remainder of the encampment, was his head-quarters. He now set about devising some plan, in connection with his officers, for reforming some of the present abuses in the army, and to secure the future welfare of the soldiers. He made strong appeals to Congress on the subject, and on the 10th of January that body appointed a committee, consisting of Messrs. Dana, Reed, Folsom, Carroll and Gouverneur Morris, to proceed to Valley Forge. Washington there laid before them a communication extending to fifty folio pages, containing the sentiments of himself and officers. This formed the basis of a report the committee made to Congress, after remaining nearly three months in the camp. This report was in the main adopted.

As the winter advanced, as might have been expected under the circumstances, their sufferings increased. "At no period of the war," says Chief Justice Marshall, the historian, "had the American army been reduced to a situation of greater peril than during the winter at Valley Forge. More than once they were absolutely without food. Even while their condition was less desperate in this respect, their stock of provisions was so scanty that there was seldom at any time in the stores a quantity sufficient for the use of the troops for one week. Consequently had the enemy moved out in force, the American army could not have continued in camp. The want of provisions would have forced them out of it; and their deplorable condition, with respect to clothes, disabled them from keeping the field in the winter. The returns of the first of February exhibit the as tonishing number of 3,989 men in camp unfit for duty for want of clothes. Of this number, scarcely a man had a pair of shoes. Even among those returned capable of doing duty, very many were so badly clad that exposure to the colds of the season must have destroyed them. Although the total of the army exceeded 17,000 men, the present effective rank and file amounted to only 5,012. The returns throughout the winter do not essentially vary from that which has just been particularly stated." The situation of the camp is such, wrote General Varnum to General Green, on the 12th of February, "that in all human probability the army must dissolve. Many of the troops are destitute of meat, and are several days in arrears. The horses are dying for want of forage. The country in the vicinity of the camp is exhausted. There can not be a moral certainty of bettering our condition while we remain here. What consequences have we rationally to expect?" On the 16th Washington wrote to Governor Clinton: "For some days past there has been little less than a famine in camp A part of the army has been a week without any kind of flesh, and the rest three or four days. Naked and starved as they are, we cannot enough admire the incomparable patience and fidelity of the soldiery, that they have not been, ere this, excited by their sufferings to a general mutiny and desertion." "It was with great difficulty," says Dr. Thatcher, in his Military Journal, "that men enough could be found in a condition fit to discharge the military camp duties from day to day, and, for this purpose, those who were naked borrowed of those who had clothes. The army, indeed, was not without consolation, for his excellency, the commander-in-chief, whom every soldier venerates and loves, manifested a fatherly concern and fellow-feeling for their sufferings, and made every exertion in his power to remedy the evil and to administer the much desired relief."

"Yet, amid all this suffering, day after day," as Mr. Lossing remarks, "surrounded by frost and snow, (for it was a winter of great severity,) patriotism was still warm and hopeful in the hearts of the soldiers, and the love of self was merged into the one holy sentiment, *love of country*. Although a few feeble notes of discontent were heard, and symtoms of intentions to abandon the cause were visible, yet the great body of that suffering phalanx were content to wait for the budding spring, and be ready to enter anew upon the fields of strife for the cause of freedom. It was one of the most trying scenes in the life of Washington, but a cloud of doubt seldom darkened the serene atmosphere of his hopes He knew that the cause was just and holy, and his faith and confidence in God as a defender and helper of right, were as steady in their ministrations of vigor to his soul, as were the pulsations of his heart to his active limbs. In perfect reliance upon Divine aid, he moved in the midst of crushed hopes, and planned brilliant schemes for the future." Isaac Potts, at whose house Washington was quartered, relates that one day, while the Americans were encamped at Valley Forge, he strolled up the creek, when, not far from his dam, he heard a solemn voice. He walked quietly in the direction of it and saw Washington's horse tied to a sapling. In a thicket near by was the beloved chief upon his knees in prayer, his cheeks suffused with tears. Like Moses at the Bush, Isaac felt that he was upon holy ground, and withdrew unobserved. He was much agitated, and on entering the room where his wife was he burst into tears. On her inquiring the cause he informed her what he had seen, and added: "If there is any on this earth whom the Lord will listen to it is George Washington; and I feel a presentiment that under such a commander there can be no doubt of our eventually establishing our independence, and that God in his providence has willed it so." A distinguished foreign officer related to Mr. Thatcher "that, at one time, he was walking with General Washington among the huts, when he heard many voices echoing through the open crevices between the logs, '*No pay, no clothes, no provisions, no rum!*' And when a miserable wretch was seen flitting from one hut to another, his nakedness was only covered by a dirty blanket. Then he despaired of independence for America."

Shortly after the battle of Brandywine, and when the British began to approach the Schuylkill, Congress was in session in Philadelphia, but in consequence adjourned to Lancaster, where they assembled on the 27th of September. They then adjourned the same day to York, where they met on the 30th, and continued their sittings there until the British evacuated the city the following summer. Washington, in a letter to Congress, dated February 27th, says: "Baron Steuben has arrived at camp. He appears to be much of a gentleman, and, as far as I have had an opportunity of judging, a man of military knowledge and acquainted with the world." This is the earliest information we possess, of an official character, of this distinguished soldier's arrival here, who was afterwards to play a conspicuous part in the drama of the revolution.

"Before the opening of spring," says Mr. Woodman, in his manuscript History of the Valley Forge, "the fuel necessary for the purpose of keeping the half-clad and famished soldiers warm, was so far exhausted that a further supply had to be obtained from a distance, and such was the scarcity of the means of conveyance that it had to be brought to the camp by means of manual labor. Often have I heard people who remembered the time, (especially my mother,) mention of their having seen the soldiers, particularly those from the Eastern States and some of the subordinate officers, who could best endure the rigor of the winter, yoke themselves like oxen, and on temporary sleds, formed for the occasion, haul fuel in this way, some of it a distance of more than two miles, eight, nine, ten, or more, forming a team and using grape vines to draw them with instead of ropes. And when provisions and other necessaries became, in like manner, exhausted, requisitions had to be made from people living more remote from the same, and foraging parties had to be sent to scour various sections of country in order to obtain and secure sustenance for the famishing army, and when thus obtained the conveyance of them to the place was attended with a great deal of inconvenience."

It may be great to lead a powerful army on to victory, but surely it was greater, in Washington, to preserve the shattered remnants of this discouraged band together, when we might say the enemy was trampling over them—when Congress could do but little for them—when starving families at home were weeping for their return, and when there seemed scarcely any other prospect before them but miserable defeats. It was, indeed, an arduous task to keep together and supply with provisions this army of suffering men, but the character of Washington stood nobly forth—night and day his efforts were almost unceasing for their comfort and convenience. As a last resort, he compelled those who had withheld provisions to furnish them forthwith. Their necessity obliged him, in this instance, to treat the American tories with as little consideration as the English soldiers. In obedience to a resolution of Congress, he had issued the proclamation already given, requiring all the farmers within seventy miles of the camp to thresh out half their grain by the first of March, under the penalty of having the whole seized as straw. Many farmers refused, defending their grain and cattle, and in some instances burning what they could not defend. On the other hand, the British paid in gold, (which was very scarce in those paper money days,) for every thing they wanted in Philadelphia, and that at high prices, which induced many, in spite of the penalties, to incur the risk. Amongst them were many young men who had fled from their homes, either to escape from serving in the army or of save their fines. They usually carried poultry, meat, eggs, flour and grain; and brought back calico, tea, coffee, and, what was of great importance, salt. Many were arrested, found guilty, and publicly whipped, and their things forfeited to the captors. The horses taken, when fit for draught or dragoon service, were required to be sent to the quarter-master general of the camp, who paid the full value for them.

Amidst this gloomy prospect the time was not allowed to pass altogether away without being occasionally enlivened by a joke. The following anecdote was related by Col. Allen M'Lean, who was in service here during the whole period of the encampment. It was told to John F. Watson, the annalist, and was published in the Collections of the Pennsylvania Historical Society. On the morning of the 17th of March, being St. Patrick's day, some of the Pennsylvania Germans made a Paddy, and placed it at a conspicuous place in camp, to the great indignation of the Irish. They assembled in large bodies under arms, swearing for vengeance against the New England troops there, saying they had got up the insult. The affair threatened a very serious issue; none of the officers could appease them. At this time Washington, having ascertained the entire innocence of the New England troops, rode up to the Irish and kindly and feelingly argued with them; and then, as if highly incensed against the perpetrators, requested the Irish to show the offenders and he would see them punished. They could not designate any one. "Well," said Washington, with great promptness, "I too am a lover of St. Patrick's day, and must settle the affair by making all the army keep the day." He, therefore, ordered extra drink to every man of his command, and they all made merry and were good friends. Thus, for many years afterwards, St. Patrick's day at Valley Forge formed a subject of conversation among the soldiers whenever they met and was not soon forgotten among the rather monotonous duties of the camp.

From the Orderly Book of Adjutant Irvine, under date of April 29th, the following extract is taken: "Complaint having been made by Mr. Dewees, proprietor of the Valley Forge, that the soldiers pull down the houses and break up the timbers of the buildings which is called Valley Forge, the commander-in-chief strictly forbids all persons from damaging the said buildings and works, which he hopes will be particularly attended to, especially when they consider the great loss that Mr. Dewees has already suffered, and the great waste our army has been under the necessity of committing upon the wood and other improvements."

Washington, in a letter to Congress, from camp, dated the 30th of April, says: "Baron Steuben's length of service in the first military school in Europe, and his former rank, pointed him out as a person peculiarly qualified to be at the head of this department. This appeared the least exceptionable way of introducing him into the army, and one that would give him the most ready opportunity of displaying his talents. I therefore proposed to him to undertake the office of inspector-general, which he agreed to do with the greatest cheerfulness, and has performed the duties of it with a zeal and intelligence equal to our wishes." So satisfactory were the services of Steuben that through the recommendation of Washington, Congress appointed him a major-general, on the following 5th of May. So eager was he to serve in the American army that he at first joined as a volunteer, but he was not long in this position before his knowledge of military tactics showed itself. As is well known he was one of the most thorough disciplinarians in Europe, and it was through his talents and instructions that our men acquired a facility and precision in drill, which soon after enabled them to carry the Revolution to a glorious termination. Mr. Headly gives the following interesting sketch of Steuben, at Valley Forge: "A more sorry introduction to our army, for one who had served in Europe, could not well be conceived. He had found our cities in possession of a powerful enemy, and when he came to look for the force that was to retake them he saw only a few thousand famished, half-naked men, looking more like beggars than soldiers—cooped up in miserable log huts, dragging out a desolate winter amid the straw. As the doors of these hovels opened he beheld men destitute of clothing, wrapping themselves up in blankets, and muttering complaints against Congress, which could treat them with such injustice and inhumanity. He was astonished, and declared that no European army could be kept together under such sufferings. All discipline was gone, and the troops were no better than a ragged horde, with scarcely the energy to struggle for self-preservation. There was hardly any cavalry, but slender artillery, while the guns and accoutrements—a large portion of them—were unfit for use. Our army had never before been in such a state, and a more unpropitious time for Steuben to enter on his work could not have been selected. Nothing daunted, however, and with all the sympathies of his noble nature roused in our behalf, he began, as soon as spring opened, to instruct both officers and men. His ignorance of our language crippled him at first very much; while the awkwardness of our militia, who, gathered as they were from every quarters, scarcely knew the manual exercise, irritated him beyond measure. Still the soldiers loved him, for he was mindful of their sufferings, and often his manly form was seen stooping through the doors of their hovels, to minister to their wants and relieve their distresses. It was his practice to rise at three o'clock in the morning, and dress his hair, smoke, and take his cup of coffee, and at sunrise to be in the saddle. By that time, also, if it was a pleasant day, he had the men marching to the field for their morning drill. First he would place them in a line, then pass along in front, carefully examining their guns and accoutrements, and inquiring into the conduct of the subordinate officers. The fruit of this labor soon appeared in the improved condition of his men, and Washington was very much impressed with the value of his services. Owing to his recommendation he was made inspector-general. This branch of the service now received the attention it deserved, and discipline before irregular, or practiced only under particular leaders, was introduced into every portion. All the arrangements, even to the minutest, were planned and perfected by Steuben, and the vast machinery of our army began to move in harmony and order. He had one company, which he drilled to the highest point of discipline, as a model to instruct the others. The result of all this was seen in the very next campaign, at the battle of Monmouth. Washington there rallied his men when in full retreat, and brought them into action under the very blaze of the enemy's guns. They wheeled like veteran troops into their places and then moved steadily on the foe."

Winter had disappeared and spring was now here and with it had brought the 1st of May. Washington, in consequence, was now beginning to make preparations for his men to take the field for the summer's campaign. On this day he issued more stringent orders relative to delinquent officers—also in regard to keeping more regular returns and more correct accounts of the actual state of the army—the number of men on duty—the number of sick, in hospitals and absent on furlough, and also reiterating the orders to the officers to have their men clean dressed on parade, and other matters in common with the regulations of the camp, and directed that thes eorders were to be posted up, with strict injunctions that they should not be removed.

By the help of the important success of the surrender of General Burgoyne at Saratoga, Dr. Franklin negotiated a treaty of alliance with France, February 6th, 1778; by which that government duly acknowledged our independence. Intelligence of this event did not reach the camp till the 1st of May, over two and a half months from the time the treaty was signed. On hearing news so auspicious, Washington, on the 7th, issued the following general order :—

"It having pleased the Almighty Ruler of the universe, to defend the cause of the United American States, and finally to raise up a powerful friend among the princes of the earth, to establish our liberty and independence upon a lasting foundation, it becomes us to set apart a day, for gratefully acknowledging the divine goodness, and celebrating the important event, which we owe to his divine interposition. The several brigades are to be assembled for this purpose at nine o'clock to-morrow morning, when their chaplains will communicate the intelligence, contained in the postscript of the Pennsylvania *Gazette*, of the 2d instant, and offer up a thanksgiving, and deliver a discourse suitable to the occasion. At half past ten o'clock a cannon will be fired, which is to be a signal for the men to be under arms; the brigade inspectors will then inspect their dress and arms, and form the battalions according to the instructions given them, and announce to the commanding officers of the brigade that the battalions are formed. The commanders of brigades will then appoint the field officer to the battalions, after which each battalion will be ordered to load and ground their arms. At half past eleven a second cannon will be fired as a signal for the march; upon which the several brigades will begin their march by wheeling to the right by platoons, and proceed by the nearest way to the left of their ground by the new position. This will be pointed out by the brigade inspectors. A third signal will then be given, on which there will be a discharge of thirteen cannon; after which a running fire of the infantry will begin on the left of the second line and continue to the right. Upon a signal given the whole army will huzza, "*Long live the King of France!*" The artillery then begins again and fires thirteen rounds; this will be succeeded by a second general discharge of musketry in a running fire, and huzza, "*Long live the friendly European Powers!*" The last discharge of thirteen pieces of artillery will be given, followed by a general al running fire and huzza 'The American States!'"

On this day Washington, with his lady and suite, Lord Stirling and his lady, with other general officers and ladies, attended the religious services of the Jersey brigade, when the Rev. Mr. Hunter delivered a discourse. Afterwards all the officers of the army assembled and partook of a collation provided by the commander-in chief. When he took his leave there was universal huzzaing, "*Long live General Washington!*"

As an act of clemency worthy the occasion, Washington issued the following: "The Commander-in Chief, in season of general joy, takes occasion to proclaim pardon and releasement to all persons now in confinement, whether in the provost or in any other places. This he is induced to do that the influence of prosperity may be as extensive as possible. Even those that merit punishment rather than favour, should not be excluded the benefit of an event so interesting to mankind as that which has lately appeared to the affairs of America. He hopes the indulgence will not be abused, but excite gratitude and produce a change of conduct and an allowance of every practice inconsistant with the duty they owe to their country." He also remarked the satisfaction it afforded him to see the improvement in the discipline and arrangements of the camp, and presents his thanks to the Baron Steuben and the gentlemen acting under him for their indefatigable exertions in the discharge of their offices, the good effects of which were so evident.

In this season of general joy the enemy endeavored to injure the American cause by preventing enlistments. Washington on hearing this published a reply on the 23d of the month, from which the following is an extract: "A most scandalous report has made its appearance in the Philadelphia *Evening Post*, of the 3d of this month, having all the appearance of a genuine act of Congress, setting forth that those brave men who have enlisted or have been drafted to serve in the continental army for a limited time are nevertheless to be detained during the war between the United States and Great Britain. The Commander-in-Chief assures the army that this publication is as false as it is wicked, and is intended to induce those who have already enlisted, or have been drafted, to desert, or to intimidate others from engaging into the service of their country. Our enemy finding themselves unable to reduce us by the force of their arms are now practising every insidious art to gain time and disunite us."

During the spring a number of discharged soldiers and vagrants, taking advantage of the distresses of the army, went about intimidating the country people. No sooner did Washington hear of the outrages and impositions which were practiced, than he issued, on the 29th, the following: "The Commander-in-Chief has been informed that it is a common practice for soldiers to go about the country and make use of his name to extort from the inhabitants by way of sale or gift any necessaries they may want for themselves or others. He strictly enjoins it upon all officers to take the most effectual measures to stop a practice so daring and infamous, and assures all concerned that if any person shall be detected in the commission of it they will be punished with every mark of disgrace and severity."

On the 17th of May, Sir Henry Clinton succeeded Sir William Howe in the command of the British army, in Philadelphia, the latter having returned to England. The ministry, in their instructions to the former, ordered him to evacuate the city. He had resolved to do so as early as the 23rd of the month, and proceed, by water, to New York; but fearing both a blockade of the Delaware, by the French, and a delay from head-winds, which, in either event, might lead to the capture of New York by Washington, he, in consequence, changed his plan with great secrecy, to cross the Delaware below Philadelphia, and to proceed direct by land with his army to New York. In the meantime, Washington, informed of the evident intention of the enemy to evacuate Philadelphia, placed his army in a condition to march immediately at the beating of the drum. By a resolution of Congress, Washington was directed to administer the oath of allegiance to the officers of the army, before leaving Valley Forge. The army was now in good condition, both as respects equipage, dress and discipline, and numbered about 15,000 men fit for service. The late news from France, besides, had made the soldiers cheerful, as they looked to the future with bright anticipations. The gloom that had settled over the suffering band at Valley Forge in the winter had now disappeared. The calm and majestic countenance of Washington alone remained unchanged. Bright and beautiful June, the month of roses, was here, and the cold and piercing blasts of the past winter were forgotten amid the preparations to be in readiness to move at a moment's warning.

Washington was awaiting their departure with considerable interest, and in a letter to Congress, on the 15th, thus expresses himself on this matter: "Our expectations that Philadelphia will be evacuated in the course of a few days are again up. The information received yesterday, through various channels, and in a pretty direct way, would seem to place the matter almost on the footing of certainty." When the British landed in the fall to march to Philadelphia, their army numbered upwards of 18,000 men, and though their loss in battle was small, and their comfortable quarters had kept them unusually healthy, yet, chiefly through desertion they were actually reduced to less than

11,000 at their departure. Immediately on hearing of the evacuation, Washington wrote a letter to Congress, on the 18th of June, informing them of the event. It appears by this that, down to the very moment the troops were put in motion, he was puzzled as to what route the enemy would take, and even of his destination.

"I have the pleasure to inform Congress that I was this morning advised by Mr. Roberts that the enemy evacuated the city early this morning. He was down at the middle ferry, on this side, when he received the intelligence from a number of citizens, who were on the opposite shore. They told him that about three thousand of the troops had embarked on board transports. The destruction of the bridge prevented him crossing. I expect every moment official accounts on the subject. I have put six brigades in motion; and the rest of the army is preparing to follow with all possible despatch. We shall proceed towards Jersey, and govern ourselves according to circumstances. As yet, I am not fully aware of the enemy's destination; nor are there wanting a variety of opinions as to the route they will pursue, whether it will be by land or sea, admitting it to be to New York. Some think it probable, in such case, that the part of their army which crossed the Delaware will march down the Jersey shore some distance and then embark. There is other intelligence corroborating Mr. Roberts, but none official is yet come."

Major General Charles Lee, with six brigades, on the evening of the 20th, crossed the Delaware, at Coryell's Ferry. Washington, with the main body of the army, at the same time, was at Doylestown, where he stayed over night. Though, in this march, the weather was very rainy, they still pushed on, and on the evening of the 22d had all crossed the Delaware, and the 28th found them engaged with the enemy in the memorable battle of Monmouth. Thus it will be seen, by the breaking up of the encampment, that the army was exactly six months at Valley Forge, having come there December 19th, 1777, and leaving the following 18th of June. We believe, through all the revolutionary war, at no other place had the Americans so great a number of men together, and for so great a length of time, as here.

The arrival, trials, sufferings and departure of the American army at Valley Forge have been given; but there yet remain in our collections a number of facts which, for the want of a proper connection, are deferred for the close of this article.

In no period of the Revolution was the character and reputation of Washington more sorely tried than while here. The troubles that have already been detailed would have been sufficient—yes, more than sufficient—for any ordinary man to bear. It is believed that not one commander in a thousand, if placed under similar circumstances, could have effected what Washington did; for few men could have secured the influence, nay, the devoted affections, of the soldiery, which was so essential to success, amid such trying scenes. What we now particularly mean, and to which no allusion has yet been made, is the attempted conspiracy to supplant Washington as commander-in-chief for some other more designing person. The plot was conceived amidst the most trying times of the camp. In this combination were General Conway, General Gates and General Lee, all three foreigners, and who were believed to be at the head of the movement. In connection with them were several members of Congress, whose names it has been difficult to ascertain, as the affair was conducted with great secrecy. But it is known that General Mifflin, of Pennsylvania, and Samuel Adams, of Massachusetts, besides two or three others in the New England delegation and one from Virginia, were of the number. Their intention, it is believed, was to place General Gates to the supreme command on account of the laurels he had won at Saratoga. It is supposed that Conway was the most active among the secret enemies of Washington. He was an Irishman by birth, but received his military education in the French service. He was appointed Inspector-General in May, 1777, and through the recommendation of Washington, Steuben, shortly after, became his successor. During the battle of Germantown, he was discovered by General Reed and General Cadwallader, in a farmhouse instead of being in the action. Shortly afterwards, when he sought promotion from Congress for Major General, this circumstance was mentioned by Cadwallader, which led to a challenge from Conway. The result was a duel with Cadwallader, on the 4th of July, 1778, by which the former was wounded in the face. Believing his end near, he sent an apologetic letter from Philadelphia, on the 23rd of the month. He recovered, however, and some time after went to France. Conway was a person of some literary acquirements, and it is known that he was the author of several anonymous letters in disparagement of Washington, several of which were signed De Lisle. Mr. Lossing, in speaking of this conspiracy makes the following judicious remarks: "The first important movement in this conspiracy, was the sending of anonymous letters to the President of Congress, and to Patrick Henry, then Governor of Virginia. These letters were filled with complaints, insinuations, and exaggerated statements, ascribing the misfortunes of the army to the incapacity or ill-timed policy of the commander-in-chief. Similar letters were sent to different members of Congress, and, it is believed, to some of the presiding officers of some of the State Legislatures. Washington was early apprised of these secret machinations, but a patriotic jealousy of the public good made him suffer in silence. 'My enemies,' he said, in a letter to the President of Congress, when the matter became the subject of correspondence, 'take an ungenerous advantage of me. They know the delicacy of my situation, and that motives of policy deprive me of the defense I might otherwise make against their insidious attacks. They know I cannot combat their insinuations, however injurious, without disclosing secrets which it is of the utmost moment to conceal.'" Charles Thomson, who was secretary of Congress for fifteen consecutive years, in speaking of the Congress that sat at York, while the British had possession of Philadelphia, and among whom was the faction that was opposed to Washington, as a body of weak men, compared to former delegations. "Happily for America," says a distinguished writer, "there was in the character of Washington something which enabled him, notwithstanding the discordant materials of which his army was composed, to attach both his officers and soldiers so strongly to his person, that no distress could weaken their affections, nor impair the respect and veneration in which he was held by them To this is to be attributed the preservation of a respectable military force under circumstances but too well calculated for its dissolution."

During the time that the army lay at Valley Forge, no engagements took place, except with foraging parties at some distance, who were then scouring the country in search of necessaries for the support of their respective forces. These occasional skirmishes had the effect of producing much fear and consternation among the inhabitants of the neighborhood. It is believed that there was but one person executed at the camp. This was a man who had come from Philadelphia in the character of a spy.

It is gratifying to our pride that one of the most important commands at Valley Forge was given by Washington to General Peter Muhlenberg, a native of this county. Never was high trust placed in better hands. The portion under his charge lay nearest the city, and was protected by intrenchments, and had at any time an attack been made, this would have very probably, from its situation, felt the first effects. While General Muhlenberg was here he was in the occasional practice of visiting his aged father at the Trappe, eight miles distant. For this purpose, he would generally start in the evening and return early next morning. Presuming that these visits would be repeated, the enemy made several attempts to capture him, and on one occasion he was only saved by the fleetness of his horse.

In the latter part of the summer of 1796, and after his second term as President of the United States had nearly expired, and was therefore about to retire to the shades of private life, Washington concluded to see Valley Forge once more, the scene of so many toils and struggles. For the information respecting this visit I am indebted to my friend Henry Woodman, who derived it from his father, who at the time was engaged in plowing on his farm in the vicinity of the encampment. It was in the afternoon that he observed an elderly man, of dignified appearance, on horseback, dressed in a plain suit of black, accompanied by a colored servant, ride to a place in the road nearly opposite, when he alighted from his horse and came into the field and cordially took his hand. He told him he had called to make some inquiry concerning the owners and occupants of the different places about there, and also, in regard to the system of farming practised in that part of the country—the kinds of grain and vegetables raised—the time of sowing and planting—the best method of tilling the ground, and numerous other questions relating to agriculture. He also made inquiry after certain families in the neighborhood. As answers were given he noted them down in a book. Mr. Woodman informed him that he could not give as correct answers as he wished, for he had not been brought up to farming, and besides had only moved in the vicinity since the war, though he had been in the army while it was encamped here. This gave a new turn to the conversation. The stranger informed him that he had also been in the army and at the camp, and that as he expected to leave the city in a few months, with the prospect of never returning, he had taken this journey to visit the place which had been the scene of so much suffering and distress, and see how far the inhabitants had recovered from its effects. On being informed that his name was George Washington, he told him that his appearance was so altered that he did not recognize him, or else he would have paid more respect to his late commander and now the chief magistrate of the nation. He replied that to see the people happy, and the desolate fields recovering from the disasters they had experienced, and to meet with any of his old companions, now peaceably engaged in the most useful of all employments, afforded him more satisfaction than all the homage that could be paid to his person or station. He then said that pressing engagements rendered it necessary for him to be in the city that night, and taking him by the hand bade him an affectionate farewell. Such, dear reader, was Washington's last visit to Valley Forge.

The house occupied by Washington as his head-quarters is still standing, having undergone but little alteration since that time. It was owned in the revolution by Isaac Potts, the proprietor of the Forge. It is a two story stone building, situated near the Reading railroad. The main portion of it has a front of about twenty-four feet and thirty-three in depth. The outside front is of dressed stone, pointed. The interior wood work is still in a good state of preservation, and with care this building may be made to last for centuries, as its walls appear to be as durable as when first built. No one familiar with our revolutionary history can enter the room which served the great chief for nearly half a year, both as a reception room and bed chamber, and where he wrote many important despatches, without feelings of the deepest emotions. In the sill of the east window of this room, and out of which can be seen a considerable portion of the camping ground, is still pointed out a small rough box, as having contained his papers and writing material. We gazed at this depository and other objects around with considerable interest, hallowed as they are by so many associations of the times that "tried men's souls." Adjoining is a wing one and a-half stories high and about twenty-four feet in length, which has been built since the war, but it occupies the site of a smaller structure that was erected for the accommodation of Mrs. Washington. In a letter to a friend this lady says: "The General's apartment is very small: he has had a log cabin built to dine in, which has made our quarters much more tolerable than they were at first." This property is at present owned by Hannah Ogden.

There are various remains of the encampment still visible. On the road to Port Kennedy is a portion of ground unenclosed, belonging to William Henry, Esq. On this tract the foundations of the hut occupied by Baron Steuben are still visible, and the ground undisturbed where he used to drill his soldiers. Several extensive redoubts and breastworks on the south-eastern side of the hill are still pointed out. These consist of large embankments of earth, arranged one after the other along the slope of the hill. The redoubts now lie in the depths of the forest, and their outlines as well as the foundations of many of the huts are still easily recognized. On the property now owned by Jacob Massey is a fort in a good state of preservation. Its outlines are those of an equalateral triangle, forty yards in length and about five feet high. As most of the land on which the encampment was is still in a state of nature and has therefore generally remained unmolested, it has been the means of preserving the greater part of the remains to this day, though upwards of eighty years have rolled away since that eventful period.

Relics are still occasionally found by persons living in the vicinity. William Henry, Jr., has a number, found on his father's farm, which he recently exhibited to us. Among them were several pewter buttons, with the figures 7, 8 and 10 on them; no doubt intending to show the regiment or brigade to which they belonged. Also, spoons, bayonets and fragments of musket locks, looking considerably time-worn, besides a variety of musket balls, some of which were of a large size. William R. Kennedy, in the spring of 1857, turned up with the plow, on his farm, several twelve and sixteen pound balls and several hatchets. The latter were about the usual size, but shaped precisely like a chopping ax

IX.

SPRINGFIELD.

The township of Springfield is bounded on the north and north-east by Upper Dublin, east by Cheltenham, south and south-west by Philadelphia, and west and north-west by Whitemarsh. Its central distance is about seven miles from Norristown. Its greatest length is six, and greatest breadth two and a-half miles, with an area of four thousand one hundred and seventy-three acres. No township in the county, and probably in the State, is so remarkably irregular in its form. Its outline on the county map justly excites the wonder of a stranger, being a narrow belt extending to the Schuylkill of only one-third of a mile in width and three and a quarter in length. The reason why it was laid out in this manner is given near the close of this article.

The surface of Springfield is agreeably diversified with hill and dale, and the soil is naturally fertile, containing excellent limestone. Edge Hill is the most considerable elevation and extends nearly through the centre of the township for a distance of about two miles in a north-east and south-west direction and crosses the Bethlehem turnpike south of Hendricksdale. Church Hill begins in the north corner of the township, near the Upper Dublin line, and after a distance of about three fourths of a mile, extends into Whitemarsh. Besides limestone, Springfield contains mineral wealth. Iron ore, at this time, is extensively dug on the farm of Jacob Server, about a quarter of a mile north-west of Hendricksdale, and keeps a number of teams employed in hauling it to the furnaces. A mile and a quarter north-east of this village ore was also dug in considerable quantities, but within a recent time has not been worked.

Immediately on the banks of the Schuylkill, in Philadelphia, but adjoining this township, is an extensive soapstone quarry, which is deserving of notice. It formerly belonged to the Hon. John Freedley, of Norristown, but since his decease has come in possession of Samuel F. Prince, his nephew, who resides near by. It is leased and worked by Joseph Davis, who generally has from seven to eight hands employed in quarrying and loading. The stones are remarkable for withstanding the effects of fire, and in which consists their chief value, and are therefore extensively used in puddling furnaces of iron works, rolling mills and lime-kilns. After being quarried, they are generally dressed here on the spot into large square blocks so as to answer for immediate use in walls. As it lies but a few yards from the canal and railroad, it possesses great advantages for sending the stones to market. When we were here, in August, 1858, a canal boat was loading with them, and we were informed that no inconsiderable quantity was annually shipped to England. A few yards below this quarry the railroad has a station called Soapstone, where there is also a batteau ferry for passengers across the Schuylkill. The landing place on the opposite side is a few yards above the mouth of Mill Creek, in Lower Merion township.

The Wissahickon Creek flows nearly through the centre of Springfield, but only for half a mile, in which distance it propels a grist-mill. The next considerable stream is Sandy Run, flowing near its northern corner, which also propels a grist-mill. A small stream flows for some distance through the centre of the township, and, like Sandy Run, is a branch of the Wissahickon. These are all steady, constant streams.

Springfield, both in area and population, is the smallest township in the county. In 1734, it contained 16 landholders; in 1741, 29 taxables; in 1828, 166; in 1849, 205; and in 1858, 258. According to the census of 1810, it contained 550 inhabitants; in 1820, 639; in 1830, 368; in 1840, 695; and in 1850, 743. From its proximity to the city the population has considerably increased within the last six years, and may probably be at this time 1300.

This township is well improved. The North Pennsylvania Railroad passes through the entire width of Springfield, a distance of two miles in a northwest direction, close to the Upper Dublin line. This road was completed in 1856 to Gwynedd, and in 1857 to the Lehigh River. The Chestnut Hill and Springhouse turnpike passes through the township upwards of one and a-half miles. The Ridge and the Germantown and Perkiomen pikes pass only a short distance through the narrow belt. An account of these roads is given in our article on Whitemarsh. The Wissahickon turnpike begins at Flourtown and runs direct to the Ridge pike, a distance of two and a-half miles, and for nearly two miles is on the line between Springfield and Philadelphia. It was finished in 1855, and crosses the Wissahickon creek by a covered frame bridge one hundred and thirty-three feet long. The Schuylkill Navigation passes on its southwest extremity. According to the census of 1850, Springfield contained one hundred and fourteen houses and sixty-five farms. In the vicinity of Chestnut Hill, and built within the last six years, are several splendid country-seats, owned chiefly by Philadelphians, and occupied as summer residences. It contained, in May, 1858, five inns and two stores. According to the triennial assessment of 1858, the real estate was valued at $354,312, and the horses and neat cattle $18,650. Education is not neglected in Springfield, and for the school year ending June 1st, 1857, four schools were open eight months, attended by three hundred and forty-nine scholars, and $1,031 were levied to defray the expenses of the same.

Flourtown is the largest village in the township, and is situated on the Chestnut Hill and Springhouse turnpike, twelve miles north of Philadelphia. It contains four inns, two stores, a church, a blacksmith and wheelwright shop, and forty-two houses, which are mostly scattered along the pike for the distance of three-quarters of a mile to the Whitemarsh line. A turnpike leads from here to the Ridge pike, two and a-half miles. The Presbyterian church was built in 1857, and is a handsome two-story stone building, and has several acres of ground attached. Its front yard is laid out in neat walks, and none had been buried here up to August, 1858. This was the first, and up to the present time, the only church in the township. This village is an ancient settlement. Before 1719 there was a mill in the neighborhood on the Wissahickon, but in Whitemarsh, to which the people came a great distance for flour. It was from this circumstance that afterwards, when the population had increased, it received the name of Flourtown. We know, from the Pennsylvania Archives, that it bore this name in 1781. Scott, in his Gazetteer of 1795, speaks of Flourtown as being "a village containing sixteen or seventeen dwellings." Gordon, in his Gazetteer of Pennsylvania, published in 1832, mentions it as then containing twenty dwellings.

Hendricksdale is also situated on the Chestnut Hill and Springhouse turnpike, and is a mile below Flourtown, and the same distance above Chestnut Hill. It contains one inn, a steam saw-mill, a carpenter, blacksmith and wheelwright shop, and twelve houses. It is ten and a-half miles from Philadelphia. Several handsome residences have been erected here within the last few years.

At the extremity of the long narrow strip on the Schuylkill, three stone houses have been built within a few years past. It has a front of about one-third of a mile on the river, and rises here in a rocky elevation.

Springfield no doubt received its name from a parish in Essex, England. There are also two villages so called in Scotland. On Holmes' map of original surveys, made between 1682 and 1695, this township is marked as "Gulielma Maria Penn's Manor of Springfield" At this day it has the same singular outline as given in the aforesaid map. At the time it was laid out for this lady, she requested that a strip should be attached to it leading to the Schuylkill, so that forever afterwards both her and her successors would have the privilege, whenever they desired, to reach the river by their own land. This will explain the origin of this singular belt.

Some account of this lady may not be amiss. She was the daughter of Sir William Springett, of Darlington, in Sussex, who was killed in the civil wars, at the siege of Bamber. Mention is made, in English history, of Herbert Springett, of Broyle, in Sussex, who was made a baronet by Charles II, in 1659. This was probably the father of the aforesaid. After his first religious visit to the continent and in the 28th year of his age, William Penn married Gulielma Maria Springett, who possessed principles similar to his own. She died in 1694, leaving him a widower for several years, when he subsequently married Hannah Callowhill. It is a singular circumstance in the life of Penn, that both his father and his wife's father were military men by profession.

Springfield, in 1734, had sixteen landholders residing within its limits. The following is a a list of their names: Harman Greathouse,

John Greathouse, Samuel Adams, Joshua Harmer, William Nice, Thomas Silance, Job Howell, Thomas Hicks, Christopher Ottinger, George Gantz, Alm Forster, Henry Snyder, Adam Read, Hugh Boyd, Michael Clime and George Douat.

Thomas Penn, in 1738, owned sixteen hundred acres of land in this township, which was valued at seventy-five pounds per hundred acres, which, according to our present currency, would be three thousand two hundred dollars for the whole tract. The aforesaid was the last surviving son of William Penn, and died the 21st of March, 1775, when he had just completed the seventy-fourth year of his age. Lady Juliana, his widow, survived him many years.

X.

WHITEMARSH.

The township of Whitemarsh is bounded on the north-east by Upper Dublin, south-east by Springfield, south-west by the Schuylkill and Conshehocken, west by Plymouth, and north west by Whitpain. Its length is six and a-half miles by two and a-half in breadth, and contains an area of eight thousand six hundred and ninety-seven acres, having been reduced three hundred and twenty acres by the erection of the borough of Conshehocken, in 1850.

The surface of the country is rolling and the soil is generally of a superior quality, being a rich loam, with an abundance of excellent limestone. Edge Hill extends through this township a distance of two and a-half miles, and crosses the Schuylkill below Spring Mill. It is a singular circumstance that no limestone, iron or marble is found anywhere on the south side of this hill. Barren Hill and Camp Hill are well known elevations that figure in our revolutionary history, but do not extend to any length.

Whitemarsh possesses several fine lasting streams of water. The Wissahickon Creek rises by two branches in Montgomery township, and then flows through Gwynedd, Whitpain, Upper Dublin, Whitemarsh and Springfield townships, and empties into the Schuylkill nearly a mile below Manayunk. Its total length is about nineteen miles, of which thirteen are in this county and three and a-half in this township. It is an excellent mill stream, being steady, copious and rapid in its current. Its principal branches are Valley Run and Sandy Run. At a very early period the Wissahickon was used for mill purposes, a grist mill having been erected at the present village of Whitemarsh before 1719. On Holmes' map of original surveys made between the years 1682 and 1695, it is called "Whitpaine's Creek," after Richard Whitpain, a large landholder on this stream, in the present township of Whitpain, after whom it was named. Wissahickon is an Indian name, and in their language, according to Heckewelder, signifies the catfish stream or the stream of yellow water.

Not many townships in Pennsylvania exceed Whitemarsh in the value of the products of its mines and quarries. In the quality of its lime, marble and iron it is not surpassed in the State. The excellence of "Whitemarsh lime" is known over the Union. In October, 1848, the author of this work was travelling in the interior of Orange county, New York, and at a country store his attention was arrested by a sign with "Whitemarsh Lime for Sale Here." This trifling circumstance begat thoughts of home, and curiosity led us to inquire how they sold it. The reply was, fifty cents per peck; and that it was used only as a whitewash. From the Colonial Records we learn that lime was burned in this township before 1698. According to the census of 1840, Whitemarsh produced lime to the value of $51,457. No doubt at the present time twice this amount is produced. Lime-burning is carried on the most extensively at Whitemarsh village and near Plymouth and Lancasterville.

The marble of Whitemarsh is of different qualities and colors. A superior white marble is produced, of which great quantities have been sent to Philadelphia and Norristown, and used in many public and private edifices. There is also much produced annually of a dark blue and variegated color. Much of the marble used in the city, not only for buildings, but for many ornamental purposes, came from here. The dark and blue marble is heavier than the white. According to the census of 1840, this township produced marble to the value of $30,640, and gave employment to fifty-one men. In consequence of the extensive use of this beautiful material for building purposes, the business of late years has, of course, much increased. Daniel O. Hitner has the most extensive quarry, having been worked to the depth of two hundred and twenty-five feet. The seam of marble, on the surface, is fifteen feet thick, but at the greatest depth narrows down to six feet. It is inclosed in limestone, and it has been ascertained that the deeper it is procured the better is its quality. It could never have been worked to this great depth without the aid of candle-light, and steam to pump out the water. The marble and limetone is raised to the surface by ponderous hoisting-machines and tackle, three horses being sufficient to draw up the largest sized blocks, some of which have weighed twelve tons. This quarry lies open to the depth of one hundred feet, and to walk near its edge and look down requires some degree of courage. A considerable portion of the marble used in Girard College was obtained from here. Mr. Hitner has at his quarry an extensive steam mill for sawing marble, propelled by a twenty-nine horse power engine, which also pumps the water from the quarry. In consequence of the business being dull when we were here in August, 1858, this mill was not in operation. Mr. Hitner works also the adjoining marble quarry, belonging to John Wentz. About a mile from Conshehocken, near Harmanville, are two extensive quarries and a saw-mill. What was formerly Dager's marble quarry is now worked by Potts and Hallowell, who employ thirty hands. Near by is the quarry of Major Peter Fritz, of Philadelphia, which, when we were here, was not in operation. We have since learned that in November, 1858, he had fifteen hands employed, and that he contemplates building a saw-mill. This quarry was commenced in the year 1800, and has been worked to the depth of one hundred and seventy-five feet.

Iron ore is dug on the farm of Henry Hitner, at Marble Hall, and by the aid of a steam engine, which raises both the ore and water from the mine, he has been enabled to reach the depth of ninety-five feet perpendicular, which is forty five feet below water level. The ore is sent to the William Penn furnaces, at Spring Mill, of which Mr Hitner is a proprietor. On the farm of Charles Williams, about half a mile northeast of Barren Hill, ore has lately been discovered, which is now extensively worked and is said to be abundant. Several pits have also been recently opened near Harmanville, on the Plymouth line, where it appears there is an immense bed of it

After Lower and Upper Merion, Whitemarsh is the most populous township in the county. In 1741, it contained 89 taxables; in 1828, 379; in 1849, 639; and in 1858, 659. The population, according to the census of 1810, was 1328; in 1820, 1601; in 1830, 1924; in 1840, 2079; and in 1850, 2408 It is supposed to contain, at this time, over 3100 inhabitants.

As might be expected from the advantages of its situation, the fertility of its soil and its extensive mineral deposits, Whitemarsh contains a number of valuable improvements. By the census of 1850, it contained three hundred and ninety-eight houses and one hundred and forty-nine farms. In May, 1858, it contained ten inns, fifteen stores, six flour mills, three furnaces, two marble mills, one paper mill, two coal yards, one plaster mill and an auger factory. According to the tri-ennial assessment of 1858, the real estate was valued at $797,565, and the horses and neat cattle, $39,674. Some of the finest farms in the county are to be found in Whitemarsh. Among these might be mentioned those formerly owned by the late Hon. Morris Longstreth and George Sheaff, Esq., whose reputation as skillful farmers was widely known. Besides the common roads, which are numerous, there are five turnpike roads, which traverse the township. The first of these is the Germantown and Perkiomen pike, which was incorporated by an act of Assembly, passed February 12th, 1801, and begins in the city and passes through the townships of Springfield, Whitemarsh, Plymouth, Norriton, Worcester, Perkiomen and Lower Providence, to the Perkiomen bridge. It was built wholly by individual subscription and cost $285,000, or $11,287 per mile, the original price of shares being $100. This road traverses the township about two and three quarters of a mile, and runs parallel to the Ridge pike, being only from three fourths to a quarter of a mile apart in this distance. The Chestnut Hill and Springhouse turnpike was incorporated by an act of March 5th, 1804, and extends through Springfield, Whitemarsh and Upper Dublin to the Springhouse tavern in Gwynedd. This road was begun in 1804, was completed the following year, and is eight miles in length. It was built wholly by individual subscription, and cost $70,000, or $8,750 per mile. The Ridge turnpike was incorporated by an act of March 30th, 1811, and commences at Philadelphia and passes through Norristown to the Perkiomen Bridge, and is twenty-four miles in length. It was commenced in 1812 and finished in 1816, and cost $7500 per mile, the State taking $25,000 of its stock. This road traverses the township about two and a-half miles. A turnpike passes along the entire northwest line of Whitemarsh, from Conshohocken, a distance of six and a-half miles, and has only been completed within the last four years. A turnpike has also been completed, within a few years, from Whitemarsh village to Skippack. Besides the Philadelphia and Norristown railroad and the Schuylkill navigation, the North Pennsylvania railroad passes through the east corner of the township about a mile, close to the Upper Dublin line. This improvement extends from Philadelphia to the Lehigh River, a distance of sixty-eight miles, and cost $6,106,280. It was commenced in 1854 and finished in 1857.

For the school year ending with June 1st, 1857, Whitemarsh had eight schools, which were open ten months, and attended by four hundred and thirty-eight scholars. These were taught by five male and three female teachers, the former receiving thirty dollars and the latter twenty dollars per month for their services. The sum of $3,142 was levied to defray the expenses of the same. There is a parochial school attached to St. Thomas' Episcopal Church, under the charge of the pastor. Post offices are established at Barren Hill, Whitemarsh, Broad Axe and Plymouth Meeting House, the two latter being on the township line.

Before the Revolution, the electors, not only of this township, but of the whole county, gave their votes at the inn opposite the State-house, in Chestnut street, Philadelphia. By an act passed June 14th, 1777, the elections of this and all the adjoining townships were required to be held at the public house of Jacob Coleman, in Germantown. After the erection of Montgomery county, an act of Assembly was passed September 13th, 1785, which divided the county into three districts, and the freemen of the townships of Whitemarsh, Springfield, Cheltenham, Abington, Mooreland, Horsham, Upper Dublin, Gwynedd, Montgomery, Towamencin, Hatfield, Lower Salford and Franconia were required to hold their elections at the tavern of George Eckhart, in the present village of Whitemarsh. By an act of March 31, 1797, the number of districts was increased to five, and the number of townships reduced to Whitemarsh, Springfield, Upper Dublin and Horsham, which continued to hold their elections at the same place for a number of years afterwards. The elections of the township are now held at Barren Hill.

Spring Mill is the largest village in the township, and is situated on the east side of the Schuylkill, twelve miles from Philadelphia. It contains two inns, two stores, three furnaces, a grist mill, school house, a smith shop, and fifty dwelling houses. The boats of the Schuylkill navigation pass directly in front of the place, and the cars of the Philadelphia and Norristown railroad stop here. The William Penn furnaces are two in number, and belong to D. O. Hitner, Cresson and Company. When we were here, in August, 1858, there was but one in operation, giving employment to ten or twelve men. The ore used here is chiefly from Marble Hall, Flourtown and Chester Valley, near Downingtown. Furnace Number Two was built in 1853; the other was built some time previously. Mr. Hitner now resides here. The Spring Mill furnace is now worked by Reeves, Buck and Company, of Phœnixville, and, we have recently learned, has resumed operations. The grist mill here does also merchant work, and is one of the most ancient structures of the kind we came across. It has no date, but no doubt it has been built considerably over a century. At the upper end of the village, near the railroad, are the pottery and terra cotta works of Macintire and Scharff. They manufacture chimney tops, drains, flue pipes, stone ware and statuary. They exhibited to us some very beautiful specimens of their handicraft. They employ four or five hands, and have been established here since 1856. Spring Mill has received its name from several large springs of water near the village. The principal ones are five or six in number, and gush out with considerable force. They are all situated within an area of half an acre, and empty into one stream, which, after a course of a quarter of a mile, empties into the Schuylkill. In this distance it has sufficient power to propel, the whole year round, the grist mill just alluded to. At these springs about two acres of ground are enclosed in which is a grove of ancient buttonwood and oak trees. As this spot is visited sometimes by pleasure parties and pic-nics, a platform has been erected, covered with canvass, and a small building adjacent for refreshments and music. In addition, there are several seats scattered around for the accommodation of visitors. Taken as a whole, we were greatly disappointed in this place; instead of a pleasure ground, as we had expected, it is an undrained swamp, which has never been cultivated and is rank with various kinds of weeds, without gravel walks, or even an attempt at it, and the ground is as rude and as rough as when first discovered. No village on the Schuylkill has a better location for a town than Spring Mill. The land is elevated and recedes gradually from the river, with the advantages of excellent water and of easy access from the back country, and must yet become a place of considerable importance. Just below the William Penn furnaces, Edge Hill crosses the Schuylkill and continues up the other side of the river to opposite Conshehocken, when it turns to the southwest. The river is quite narrow where it flows through Edge Hill, which rises on either side to an elevation of upwards of one hundred and fifty feet, and imparts a great deal of beauty to the scenery. An act was passed by the Assembly, September 8th, 1787, empowering Peter Le Gaux to establish and keep a ferry here. He was a native of Lorraine, in France, where he was born in 1743, was a counsellor by profession, came to America in 1785, and shortly after settled at this place, where he died in 1828. He appears to have been a man of education and wealth, but exceedingly eccentric. His will, which may be seen in the Register's office, at Norristown, is quite lengthy and may be regarded as one of the curiosities of literature.

Barron Hill has a high location on an eminence of the same name, which is a spur of Edge Hill and affords a fine view of the surrounding country. The Chestnut Hill and Perkiomen turnpike and Ridge turnpike approach here within a quarter of a mile of each other, between which the village is chiefly situated. It contains three inns, three stores, two wheelwright shops, two blacksmith shops, a mill, church, school house, post office, and thirty-three houses. This place has considerably improved during the last few years, within which time several handsome buildings have been erected. A steam grist mill was built in 1858. The school house is a large two-story stone building. The post office was established before 1827. St. Peter's Lùtheran church is a handsome edifice, founded in 1761 and of which a further account will be given. In the Revolution it is said to have contained, besides the church, a school house and four or five houses.

The village of Whitemarsh is situated on the Spring House turnpike, fourteen miles from Philadelphia. It contains two large grist and merchant mills, propelled by the Wissahickon creek, two inns, two churches, a store, post office, school house and seventeen dwellings. A considerable quantity of lime is burned here, annually, in kilns belonging to the estate of Jacob Wentz. A further account of the Episcopal and Union churches will be hereafter given. This village is, without a doubt, one of the oldest settlements in the township. The Episcopal church was built in 1710, and on Lewis Evans' map of 1749, "Whitemarsh" is marked as being situated at the forks of the roads leading to Bethlehem and Skippack. In 1785 the elections of thirteen townships were ordered to be held here till 1797, when the number was reduced to four townships. The post office was established before 1827. The road from here to Skippack was turnpiked a few years ago. There is some excellent land in this vicinity.

Marble Hall is situated on the Germantown and Perkiomen turnpike, and extends nearly to Barren Hill. It contains two stores, a marble mill, wheelwright and blacksmith shop, and forty-two houses. Within the last eight years a number of brick houses have been erected here. Henry S. Hitner procures considerable iron ore from his farm for the Spring Mill furnaces, and the marble quarry of Daniel O. Hitner is also here. As both the iron mine and marble quarry have already been described it is needless for us to give any thing additional. Daniel Hitner, father of the aforesaid, and who was the founder of the place, died March 3d, 1841, aged nearly seventy-six years. He is buried at the Barren Hill church, where a beautiful monument marks the spot. Daniel O. Hitner, who formerly resided here, but is now a resident of Spring Mill, is still a considerable property holder in the village, where he owns two hundred and thirty-five acres of excellent land. Henry S. Hitner's farm contains two hundred and seventy acres.

Lancasterville contains an inn, store, Methodist church, school house and seven or eight houses. It is situated two miles south of

Whitemarsh village, and in traveling this distance we were surprised at the wildness of the country, especially from the Skippack pike to this place. The distance is about a mile and a-half, and the greater part of the way is by woods with but few houses. Fort Washington is a station of the North Pennsylvania railroad, and is situated at the intersection of the Spring House turnpike road. It contains a large new hotel, a store, coal yard and several houses. LaFayette is the name of a station on the Norristown railroad, near the Schuylkill. There is an extensive paper mill here which was built in 1856, and is owned by Mr. Cope, of Germantown, who employs about forty hands. There are, besides, five dwellings and the ruins of a grist mill, burned a few years ago. An account of Plymouth and Harmanville is given in our article on Plymouth township.

St. Thomas' Episcopal church, at the village of Whitemarsh, has an elevated situation on Church Hill, near the Spring House turnpike, and its spire, which rises to the height of a hundred feet, serves as a land mark for many miles around. It is built of stone and is in the Gothic style of architecture. From the churchyard can be seen Flourtown, Chestnut Hill, Barren Hill, Camp Hill, Fort Washington, and for some distance the romantic valley of the Wissahickon. Small as the graveyard is we were informed that the church records show that upwards of two thousand persons have been actually buried here. On the tombstones the most common family names are those of Burke, Shay, Houpt, Ingleman, Barge, Wells, Cleaver, Bisbing, Robison, Nash, Acuff, Donatt, Taylor, Allison, Farmer, Woolen, Brant and White. The most ancient inscription we found is the following: "Here lyeth the body of James Allison, who departed this life October the 2, 1727, aged 45 years." This was nearly one of the first Episcopal churches erected in Pennsylvania, and was founded in 1710. The land on which it stands was given for this purpose by Edward Farmer, a conspicuous man in the colony and a resident of the vicinity, and of whom a biographical sketch is given in the appendix of this work. The society for propagating the gospel in foreign parts in 1718 appointed the Rev. Mr. Wayman their missionary at Oxford and Radnor. He came to this country and entered upon his ministry with diligence and made his residence at Oxford. He shortly afterwards informed the society "that there is a congregation at Whitemarsh, about ten miles distant from Oxford, who are desirous of a minister, and have, for the decent performance of divine worship, erected a goodly stone building." The Rev. Eneas Ross came over from London in June, 1741, and shortly after became the pastor of Christ church, Philadelphia, when he resigned in July, 1743, to take charge of the churches at Oxford and Whitemarsh. It is said that when the British came out to attack Washington, in December, 1777, they mutilated a number of the tombstones in this graveyard. The old church building stood originally near the centre of the present graveyard, but having been destroyed by fire was rebuilt in 1817, on its present site. The tower was built at the same time, but the spire was not added till a few years ago. The present pastor is the Rev. D. C. Millett, who has also in charge a parochial school.

St. Peter's Lutheran church, at Barren Hill, is one of the handsomest houses of worship in the county, outside of the boroughs. It is built of stone, in the Gothic style, two stories high, with buttresses and stained glass windows. Its dimensions are about seventy by forty-eight feet, with a tower and spire one hundred feet high. The graveyard contains several acres of ground and is surrounded by a handsome iron railing and wall. The most common names on the tombstones are those of Mitchell, Hiltner, Bisbing, Kolp, Lentz, Freas, Wampole, Bartle, Dager, Fie, Rupell, Haas, Hitner, Streeper, Snyder, Schlatter, Staley, Hagy, Steer, Harman, Hallman, Rex, Faust, Thompson, Clay, Cressman, Gilmar, Woolf, Stull, Katz and Scheetz. There are a great number of tombstones and many hundreds must be buried here. The steeple of this church from its high situation is seen for many miles around. From the churchyard a splendid prospect is obtained, particularly in a north-east direction. The present pastor is the Rev. Mr. Sentman, who has recently succeeded the Rev. William Baum. This church owes its origin to a division in the Germantown congregation, and was built in 1761. The Rev. Henry M. Muhlenberg laid the corner-stone and gave towards it out of a certain legacy twenty-four pounds, and preached in it before it was roofed, in which state it had cost five hundred pounds, and on its completion cost upwards of five hundred pounds more. It appears that the congregation had subscribed but very little towards its building, for they were in debt upwards of one thousand pounds ($2,666 66,) when the church was finished. Hearing of the pecuniary embarrassment of this church the chaplain of the King of England authorized Mr. Muhlenberg to draw on him for one hundred pounds sterling After the most clamorous of the creditors were paid off, the church, schoolhouse and lot were, by indenture, conveyed to the German Lutheran congregation of Philadelphia. But what principally enabled the sureties to meet their engagements was a legacy of thirteen thousand guldin, ($5,200) from the Count of Roedelshiem, in Germany, which he bequeathed to the German Lutheran congregations of Pennsylvania; three thousand ($1,200) of which was expressly given towards the payment of the indebtedness of this church. Having become much in want of repair the congregation objected to making it, unless the church was again restored to them by the Philadelphia congregation, which was accordingly done under an act of Assembly, passed February 25th, 1801. In June, 1760, Rev. John Frederick Schmidt accepted the charge of the Germantown congregation, and preached every other Sunday in the parochial churches of Frankford and Whitpain, and occasionally at Barren Hill, in which church divine service had been previously held every other Sunday by the Germantown ministers, during the time of pastors Kurtz, Voight and Buskirk. Not long after Mr. Schmidt's election to Germantown, the Rev. Daniel Schrœder had the charge of this congregation. During the Revolution this church received considerable injury, having been by turns occupied by the contending armies and used as a battery and stable. The Rev. Henry M. Muhlenberg, in his journal, under date of November 4th, 1777, says, "that it was used as a stable for horses, by a portion of the American army, encamped in the vicinity," and farther mentions that a short time previous the British army had been here, and taken from the people their horses, oxen, cows, sheep and hogs. LaFayette, as a point of observation, quartered in this church during his brief tarry on the hill, in the middle of May, 1778, and came near being captured by General Grant, with a strong detachment of the British army. After the war, as may well be supposed, it was almost a ruin, full of rubbish and dirt, and its members from being pillaged were miserably impoverished and destitute of even the necessaries of life. The present splendid building stands on the same spot where the old one stood, and was built in the summer of 1849.

The Union church, as it is called, from being held in common by the Lutheran and German Reformed, is situated in the lower part of the village of Whitemarsh on the turnpike and was built in 1818. Its present pastors are the Rev. George Wagner and the Rev. Mr. Hippy. The most common family names on the tombstones are Kramer, Cox, Shaffer, Fisher, Stover, Keyser, Gotchalk, Stout, Wolf, Wentz, Blyler, Nace, Scheetz, Gilbert, Dager and Francis. A handsome monument is erected here to the memory of Gen. Henry Scheetz, who died September 4th, 1848, aged nearly eighty-four years. Mr. Scheetz was a man that figured considerably in public life, and at the close of the last century was one of the commissioners of the county, and in 1830 was appointed one of the viewers of the State road leading from New Hope by way of Norristown to the Maryland line. There was a Justice Scheetz Sheriff of the county from 1816 to 1819.

The name of Whitemarsh, we believe, is original, no other place to our knowledge having previously borne it. Both its origin and application has puzzled us, and it was not till on a visit to the springs near Spring Mill, that the idea occurred how it may have originated. The springs there rise from a marsh of white earth and sand, resembling pewter sand, and the name of Whitemarsh would not have been inapplicable to the spot, which afterwards may have been applied to the township.

According to Thomas Holmes' map of original surveys, made between the years 1682 and 1695, we learn that "Major Jasper Farmer" owned all the land in the present township south of the Skippack or Church road, which is an original road. North of this tract all the land in the township was owned by John Green and Samuel Rolls. The township line road, leading from the Schuylkill, at Conshehocken, and running the whole length of Whitemarsh, is also an original road, and is marked on the aforesaid map. Jasper Farmer arrived here the 10th of 9th month, 1685, in the Bristol Merchant, John Stephens commander, with his family, consisting of Mary, Edward, Jasper, Sarah, John, Robert, Catharine and Charles

Farmer. His tract here must have contained about seven or eight thousand acres. From the Colonial Records we learn that he had a number of servants residing on this tract, and that John Scull was his overseer. We regret that we are not at present able to give more particulars concerning this purchase. Both John and Nicholas Scull came over with him. Biographical sketches of Nicholas Scull and his son Edward Farmer, are given in the appendix. A road upon the petition of Nicholas Scull, was ordered to be laid out by the Council the 19th of May, 1698, for the purpose of hauling lime from the kilns to the city, and that it was to form a connection with the Plymouth road near Cresheim, or the upper part of Germantown. This road, it is believed, is the present one leading from Whitemarsh village to Chesnut Hill. From the records of the Friends' meeting, at Plymouth, we learn that before the year 1703 John Rhoads, Abraham Davis and David Williams settled in this township in that vicinity. William Trotter was also an early settler, and in his 21st year became a minister of Plymouth meeting. He died in 1794, aged fifty-three years.

The following is a list of thirty-seven landholders and tenants residing in this township, in the year 1734: Edward Farmer, Jonathan Robinson, Edith Davis, John Klinky, Henry Bartenstal, Marchant Maulsby, Nicholas Stiglitz, Benjamin Charlesworth, John Morris, Jonathan Potts, Samuel Gilkey, Josiah White, David Davis, John Petty, Margaret Nichols, Francis Cawly, David Harry, William Williams, Frederick Stone, Joseph Williams, Adam Kitler, Lodwick Knoos, Walter Gahone, Casper Simms, Jacob Coltman, Isaac Morris, William Trotter, James Stroud, John Anderson, Joseph Woolen, Evan Jones, John Scull, John Parker, Henry Rinkard, John Ramsey, Jr., Edward Stroud, John Ramsey, John Campbell, Henry Steward, Thomas Shepherd, William English, Jenken Davis, John Patterson, Joseph Fareis, John Coulson, Handle Hansell and Mathias Ignorance.

That popular preacher, the Rev. George Whitefield, in his visit to America, thus relates in his Journal, published in London, in 1756, the following account of a trip to this township: "Set out, April 18th, 1740, about nine o'clock, for White Marsh, about twelve miles from Philadelphia. Had near forty horse in company before we reached the place. Preached to upwards of two thousand people, and perceived great numbers of them much melted down, and brought under convictions, when I made free to them of Jesus and his benefits, if they would believe on him; took a little refreshment at a Quaker's, baptized two children belonging to the church of England, at his house; returned back to and preached at Germantown, with much of the Divine Presence to near four thousand hearers."

Whitemarsh is rich in revolutionary associations, and on its hills are still to be seen the remains of redoubts and entrenchments erected in that memorable struggle. The information that we have collected on that period we have concluded, from its length, to place in a separate article.

An allusion has been made to the farm of George Sheaff, Esq., which is situated about a mile northwest of Whitemarsh village, near the Skippack turnpike. He had formerly been a merchant in Philadelphia, and having accumulated a considerable fortune, purchased this property, on which he made extensive improvements. Mr. Downing, in his work on Landscape Gardening, thus speaks of a visit he made here in 1848: "Among the sylvan features here most interesting are also the handsome evergreens, chiefly Balsam or Balm of Gilead firs, some of which are now much higher than the mansion. These trees were planted by Mr. Sheaff twenty-two years ago, and were then so small that they were brought by him from Philadelphia, at various times, in his carriage. This whole establishment is a striking example of science, skill and taste, applied to a country-seat, and there are few in the Union, taken as a whole, superior to it. The farm is three hundred acres in extent, and, in the time of De Witt Clinton, was pronounced by him the model farm of the United States. At the present time we know nothing superior to it; and Capt. Barclay, in his agricultural tour, says it was the only instance of regular scientific system of husbandry in the English manner, he saw in America. Indeed, the large and regular fields, filled with luxuriant crops, everywhere of an exact evenness of growth, and everywhere free from weeds of any sort; the perfect system of manuring and culture; the simple and complete fences; the fine stock; the very spacious barns, every season newly whitewashed internally and externally, paved with wood, with stalls to fatten ninety head of cattle;

these, and the masterly way in which the whole is managed, both as regards culture and profit, render this estate one of no common interest in an agricultural, as well as ornamental point of view." Since the decease of Mr. Sheaff, the greater portion of the farm has been sold, but his family still occupy the mansion.

The extensive farm called Valley Green, and owned by the late Morris Longstreth, is situated on the Springhouse turnpike, below Whitemarsh village, adjacent to the Springfield line. The commodious buildings and ample grounds, planted with various kinds of trees, still bear witness to his taste. In November, 1849, he wrote an "Answer to the Queries of the State Agricultural Society of South Carolina," which bears evidence of his knowledge of practical farming. It is quite full and interesting, and at the time was published in a number of papers, both in South Carolina and Pennsylvania. It is said that he went to the city a poor lad, and by attention and industry he arose to be one of the prominent merchants of Philadelphia. He subsequently retired from business, and spent the remainder of his days on his farm. He was a man of sterling integrity and decidedly republican principles. He was, for some years, an associate judge of Montgomery county, and was afterwards elected canal commissioner of the State. In 1848 he ran as the democratic candidate for governor, but was defeated by William F. Johnston by a very small majority. He died a few years ago, and was interred in the Cathedral cemetery, over Schuylkill. Valley Green is still in possession of Mr. Longstreth's family.

From the collision of two trains on the North Pennsylvania railroad an awful accident happened in this township, about half a mile below the Fort Washington station, on the 17th of July, 1856, by which forty persons were killed instantly, and twenty died subsequently. The wounded numbered nearly sixty. This accident arose in consequence of the up train being heavily laden with a Sunday School excursion on a visit to Fort Washington, and being a few minutes behind time, the down-train, not awaiting their arrival, as it should, dashed on, and the result followed. Had that train waited but two minutes all would have been right. Not long since, in being at this spot, we could not help but reflect what pleasant anticipations that party must have had but a few moments previously, when Fort Washington, the object of their journey, was almost in sight.

XI.

WHITEMARSH;

ITS REVOLUTIONARY HISTORY.

The battle of Brandywine was fought September 11th, 1777, and resulted disastrously to the Americans. Washington retreated that night to Chester, and the next day crossed over the Schuylkill, resolved to give them another battle. On the 17th he made an attack at Goshen, in Chester county, but a violent storm accompanied by torrents of rain stopped its further progress and rendered it impossible for either army to keep the field. Washington concluded to replenish his ammunition and therefore retired with the main army up the Schuylkill and crossed at Parker's Ferry on the 19th, and on the 23d was near Pottsgrove. Sir William Howe, early on the morning of the 21st, decamped from the Great Valley, and crossed the Schuylkill at Fatland Ford, and by easy march continued his route to Philadelphia, which he entered on the 26th without opposition, at the head of a detachment of British and Hessian grenadiers. The remainder of his army encamped at Germantown.

Washington, after several days' rest, broke up his camp near Pottsgrove, with a view of placing his army in a strong position and within a convenient distance from the British, encamped on the Skippack road, about sixteen miles from Germantown. The American army at this time was in a wretched condition, particularly as respects clothing and shoes. Upwards of one thousand men were actually barefooted and performed their marches in this condition. Not disparaged, however, with these difficulties, early on the morning of October 4th, Washington led his little band through the mist and fog and made an attack on the enemy's outpost at Germantown. In the beginning every thing appeared favorable to the American cause, but through several mistakes the tide turned and they had to leave the field in possession of those who had previously occupied it. Washington, that same night, marched his men to Pennypacker's mill, on the Perkiomen, twenty-six miles from Philadelphia, and two miles above the present Skippackville. Here they remained till the 9th, if not longer, to recover from their fatigues and attend to their wounded and dying.

News having reached the camp of a signal victory having been gained by General Gates over General Burgoyne, on the 7th, at Saratoga, a *feu de joy* on the 15th was ordered in honor of the event. On the 16th the army encamped at Peter Wentz's in Towamencin township, twenty miles from Philadelphia, and on the same grounds they had occupied on the morning of the 4th, when the attack was made on Germantown. The army occupied this position till the 21st, when the line of march was taken for the vicinity of the present village of Whitemarsh, where they pitched their tents on the neighboring hills. The whole British army under Burgoyne having surrendered on the 18th, strong reinforcements were shortly after sent by General Gates, and on this accession Washington's army numbered eleven thousand men, of whom three thousand were unfit for duty, "being barefooted and otherwise naked." In a letter to Congress, then at York, Pennsylvania, dated Whitemarsh, October 21st, Washington says: "It gives me great concern to inform Congress, that after all my exertions we are still in a distressed situation for want of blankets and shoes. At this time no inconsiderable part of our force are incapable of acting through the deficiency of the latter, and I fear, without we can be relieved, it will be the case with two-thirds of the army in the course of a few days."

Washington selected a strong position for his army at Whitemarsh, being on a range of hills, since called Camp Hill, then covered with timber and commanding the road leading from Bethlehem to the city. Around the brow of the hill a line of entrenchments were thrown up mounted with cannon, and redoubts erected here and there for the greater security of the camp. While the army lay here, Washington established his head-quarters at the large and hospitable mansion of Mr. Elmar, near by, which is still standing. Howe, about this time, withdrew his troops from Germantown, probably fearing another attack, and concentrated his force in the city and its immediate vicinity for greater security. The British had not long been in possession of the city before they made excursions into the country for the purpose of plundering. At the same time parties of soldiers were sent from the army at Whitemarsh, to search all places for fire-arms, grain and cattle, which they took forcibly for the use of the army, and likewise to prevent their falling into the hands of the enemy. Whatever was taken they left orders for, to be paid by the Quarter Master-General. The consequences were great pains were taken in those troublesome times by the country people to conceal, in partitions, garrets, ceilings, and other places, their most valuable effects and such as were likely to be wanted by the army. Tea, coffee, salt and cotton goods became very high and scarce, owing mostly to the obstructions existing between the city and country by the patrolling parties of both armies. Men and boys were impressed into the service by the British as well as Americans.

From the Journal of the Rev. H. M. Muhlenberg, of the Trappe, we learn that in the latter part of October of this year, a bushel of salt brought £15, or $40 of our present currency. Under date of November 4th, he says: "All young men of eighteen years must go into the field with the militia; those under eighteen are exempt, but must show proof of their age." Washington, in a letter to Congress, of November 11th, in speaking of these matters, makes the following remarks: "The condition of the army for the want of clothes and blankets, and the little prospect we have of obtaining relief according to the information I have received from the board of war, occasion me to trouble you at this time. The mode of seizing and forcing supplies from the inhabitants, I fear, would prove very inadequate to the demands, while it would certainly embitter the minds of the people, and excite perhaps a hurtful jealousy against the army. I have had officers out for the purpose of purchasing and making voluntary collections of necessaries: and, in a few instances, more coercive measures have been exercised: but all these have proven of little avail; our distresses still continue, and are becoming greater. I would, therefore, humbly submit it to the consideration of Congress whether it may not be expedient for them to address the several legislative and executive powers of the States on this subject as early as possible, and in the most urgent terms."

In consequence of the late victory achieved by General Gates over Burgoyne, at Saratoga, and the two successive repulses of Washington, at Brandywine and Germantown, there were men at this time, both in and out of Congress, who were desirous of a change in the supreme command of the army, and wished to substitute General Gates in Washington's position. This faction was not strong, but they were sufficiently active for some of their proceedings to reach Washington. On this matter, in a letter to Congress, on the 17th, he says: "I am informed that it is a matter of amazement, and that reflections have been thrown out against this army for not being more active and enterprising than, in the opinion of some, they ought to have been. If the charge is just, the best way to account for it will be to refer you to the returns of our strength, and those I can produce of the enemy, and the enclosed abstract of the clothing now actually wanting for the army; and then, I think, the wonder will be, how they keep the field at all in tents, at this season of the year. What stock the clothier-general has to supply this demand, or what are his prospects, he himself will inform you, as I have directed him to go to York to lay these matters before Congress."

We shall shortly introduce to the reader's acquaintance Daniel Morgan and his brave riflemen, in actual engagement with General Howe's army on the fields of Whitemarsh and vicinity; but, before doing so, we wish to make a few remarks on this effective corps, which may be necessary for a better understanding of the subject. In the beginning of June last, through the recommendation of Washington, a regiment of riflemen was authorized by Congress, and of which Colonel Morgan received the command; Richards of Pennsylvania was appointed lieutenant-colonel and Morris, of New Jersey, major. This regiment was divided into eight companies and on Morgan was conferred the power to select the captains. It was particularly at Saratoga that this regiment of sharp-shooters rendered conspicuous service to the American cause, and it is believed, in that affair, that Morgan and his men did more to bring about the victory than any other portion of the army. It appears that General Gates always unwillingly acknowledged the merits of Morgan and his men in that triumph.

General Burgoyne having surrendered on the 18th of October, Colonel Morgan and his regiment were sent on with all possible despatch. He marched to Albany, where, having embarked his men and baggage in a number of sloops, he arrived, in a few days, at Peekskill. From this point he advanced without delay, and arrived at Whitemarsh about the 18th of November. No men in the American army were held in greater dread by the British than these sharpshooters; and on every occasion, where they possibly could, would show them but little mercy. The Rev. H. M. Muhlenberg, in his Journal, gives the following interesting account of one of the means they used to accomplish this object: "Several Hessian prisoners have been brought to Philadelphia. One of them accidentally met a settler who was his first cousin, who asked him what induced him to come to America to injure his own flesh and blood. The prisoner answered that he was dragged out of his bed from his wife and children, and forced into service. Others were asked why they attacked the Americans on Long Island so violently, and treated them with such barbarity? He said the English officers had made them believe that the Americans were savages and cannibals, in particular those with fringe on their dress, who were especially to be put out of the way as fast as possible, if they were not desirous of being tortured and eaten while still living. These very riflemen are mostly native-born, of English or German descent; and in this way the Hessians were especially set on their own people and blood; for the cunning Englishmen would rather fill the ditches of a fortified line with purchased foreign fascines than with their own domineering bodies."

Not long after the arrival of Morgan's regiment, General Greene, with all the troops that were with him, also came in, except Huntingdon's brigade, which did not arrive until the 1st of December, which now made Washington's strength about eleven thousand men. Scarcely had a few days passed, when it became known to Washington that General Howe meditated an attack upon the American camp. It appears that this information was obtained in the following manner: Opposite General Howe's head-quarters, in Second street, below Spruce, lived William and Lydia Darrah, members of the Society of Friends. A superior officer of the British army, believed to be the Adjutant General, fixed upon one of their chambers, a back room, for private conference, and two or three of them frequently met there in close consultation. About the 2d of December, the

Adjutant General told Lydia that they would be in the room at seven o'clock, and remain late, and that they wished the family to retire to bed; adding that when they were going away, they would call her to let them out and extinguish the fire and candles. She accordingly sent all her family to bed: but, as the officer had been so particular, her curiosity was excited. She took off her shoes, and putting her ear to the key-hole, overheard an order read for the British troops to march out late in the evening of the 5th and attack General Washington's army. On hearing this she returned to her chamber and laid down. Some time afterwards the officers knocked at her door, but she rose only on the third summons, having feigned herself asleep. Her mind was so much agitated that she could not eat nor sleep; supposing it to be in her power to save the lives of thousands of her fellow countrymen, but being unable to convey the information to General Washington, not daring to confide the secret to her husband. The time left, however, was short. She quickly determined to make her way, as soon as possible, to the American outposts. She informed her family that as she was in want of flour she would go to Frankford for some. She got access to General Howe, and solicited, what he readily granted, a pass through the British troops on the lines. Leaving her bag at the mill, she hastened towards the American lines, and encountered on the way an American, Lieutenant Colonel Craig, of the light horse, who, with some of his men, was on the look-out for information. He knew her and inquired where she was going. To him she disclosed her secret, after having obtained from him a solemn promise never to betray her individuality, as her life might be at stake with the British. He conducted her to a house near at hand, directed something for her to eat, and hastened to headquarters, when he made General Washington acquainted with all he heard. As Washington speaks of having had "a variety of intelligence" of this meditated attack, it appears he also got information from other sources. The American General, as may well be expected, made all due preparations to prevent surprise.

It was not, however, till Thursday night, the 5th, that General Howe moved from Philadelphia with all his force, amounting to upwards of twelve thousand men, excepting a very inconsiderable portion, which was left in his lines and redoubts. Captain McLane, who had been sent forward with one hundred chosen light horsemen to watch the enemy, discovered them on the advance, at Three Mile Run, a short distance below the Rising Sun, on the Germantown road, and compelled their front division to change their line of march. They passed forward, however, and lay near Chestnut Hill over night. On this morning the Americans were all under arms and everything prepared for battle. Brigadier General Irvine, with six hundred Pennsylvania militia, was sent forward by Washington to skirmish with their light advanced parties on Chestnut Hill, but unfortunately fell in with them before he got there, at the foot of the hill. A sharp conflict ensued, but his people soon gave way, leaving him wounded with the loss of three fingers and a bad contusion of the head. Four or five others were also wounded and taken prisoners. The enemy lost about twelve in killed and wounded, among them a Sir James Murray. Nothing more occurred on this day. In the night, the British changed their ground, moving towards the northeast, within a mile of the American line, where they remained quietly and advantageously posted during the whole of the next day. On Sunday, the 8th, they inclined still further in the direction of the village of Abington, and from every appearance there was reason to apprehend that they were determined on an action. In this movement their advanced and flanking parties were warmly attacked by Colonel Morgan and his corps, and also by the Maryland militia, under Colonel Gist. They were also supported by General Potter's brigade and Colonel Webb's regiment. Near where the Susquehanna Street road crosses Edge Hill, Morgan met the British and a short but severe conflict ensued. The British concentrating their forces, Morgan and the militia withdrew on account of superior numbers. The enemy now filed off, and by two or three routes made a hasty retreat to Philadelphia. By this engagement twenty-seven men were either killed or wounded in Morgan's regiment, among the latter, but beyond all hope of recovery, was the noble-hearted and intrepid Major Morris, who left a wife and children to mourn his loss. Among the Maryland militia there were sixteen or seventeen wounded. It is said, on the return of the enemy to the city, they lost, in this excursion, three hundred and fifty in killed and wounded.

The principal design the British commander had in this expedition was, by means of demonstrations, to get Washington to quit his strong position, in order to bring on a general engagement, which he prudently declined. By his retreat to Philadelphia he had to acknowledge that he did not dare to risk an attack, (though he had come out with some such intention,) notwithstanding he outnumbered the Americans. Washington, in his official account of this affair to Congress, speaks thus on the subject: "I sincerely wish they had made an attack, as the issue, in all probability, from the disposition of our troops and the strong situation of our camp, would have been fortunate and happy. At the same time, I must add that reason, prudence and every principle of policy, forbade us quitting our post to attack them. Nothing but success would have justified the measere; and this could not be expected from their position."

In February, 1856, there was still living in Hempstead, in his ninety-seventh year, Zachariah Greene, who served as a soldier in this encampment and by request furnished a relation of his services while here. The following is an extract, and gives some additional light on the subject: "I was also in the battle of Whitemarsh, about fifteen miles above Philadelphia, where the British were robbing the people of their cattle, horses, corn, wheat, hay, &c. I marched with the troops that were ordered to march in haste, without change of clothes, to their relief. We reached the field of battle the 7th of December, 1777, in the afternoon. I was on the right flank of the advanced guard, my brother on the left flank, and we were both wounded. My wound was dressed in one of General Washington's rooms, and then myself and others left the house to make room for others, and took up our lodging in a horse-shed, without a blanket or an overcoat, and lay on buckwheat straw—rather coarse and damp substitute for feathers. The night was sleepless, the cold distressing, and it is difficult to describe the anguish I endured in my shattered bones, but it was for American freedom. The next morning, General Greene procured rooms for myself and brother, where my wound and his were dressed by the young ladies of the family."

Winter was now approaching and the soldiers were still only sheltered from its inclemencies by tents; besides they were too poorly clothed to be enabled much longer to withstand exposure, and their sufferings were also increased by a want of blankets and shoes. Notwithstanding the tardiness of Congress in supplying their wants, the time was at hand when something had to be done, and that quickly, too, for delays had already been practised to such an extent that poor human nature could not be expected to impose much more for suffering to endure. What was to be done in this dilemma? It was decided by the officers of the army that Whitemarsh was not a proper place for a winter encampment. A council of war was held on the 30th of November, at which a wide difference of opinion prevailed as to the locality and the manner of cantoning the troops for the winter. Washington was satisfied from the great diversity of opinion that prevailed on these subjects that unanimity could not be hoped for. He therefore fixed upon Valley Forge as the most suitable place for a winter encampment, and that it possessed the advantages of strength and distance from the enemy, so as to be enabled to watch his movements and keep his foraging parties in check and protect the country from depredations. The distance from Whitemarsh encampment to Valley Forge was about thirteen miles, and on the 11th of December the patriot army started on the march and crossed the Schuylkill at Swedes' Ford. Of this body no less than two thousand eight hundred and ninety-eight were unfit for duty, and so scarce were shoes among the soldiers that they might have been tracked by the blood of their feet in marching barefooted over the hard frozen ground.

During the encampment, which was from October 21st to December 11th, a period of seven weeks, several important events transpired in our revolutionary history. The court marshal for the trial of Brigadier General Wayne was held here on the 25th, 26th, 27th and 30th of October, for his conduct on the 20th of September, at Paoli. General Sullivan was President of the board, and after a patient and impartial investigation they unanimously decided that on that occasion he had done every thing that could be expected from an active, brave and efficient officer, and therefore acquitted him with the highest honor.

The house used by Washington, as his headquarters, is situated about two hundred yards east of the North Pennsylvania railroad, in

Upper Dublin township, but only a few yards from the Whitemarsh line, and fourteen miles from the city. Sandy Run flows near by, in front, and Camp Hill is directly in the rear, on which the principal part of the army were posted. This house is of stone and about eighty feet in length by twenty-seven in width, two stories high, and had a hipped roof which was modernized in 1854. Even now it is considered of large size, but certainly when it was built, which was some time before the revolution, it must have been great. We were here several years ago, before any alterations had been made, and could still see some traces of its former elegance. Through the centre from the main entrance was a hall fifteen feet wide, leading to the rooms on either side, which had been occupied by Washington. This was approached by a flight of ancient looking, but well finished steps, wrought out of soapstone. The hospitality of Mr. Elmar, its wealthy owner, still lives in the traditions of the neighborhood, and which have been corroborated by Mr. Greene. In our visit here in 1854, a sketch was made of this mansion which we hold in our possession. There is still attached to this place an extensive farm which belonged to John Fitzwater, but after his decease was sold in 1857 to its owner, Mr. Charles Amen.

Camp Hill, on which the principal part of the army was posted, as already stated, is immediately in the rear of the house used by Washington as his head-quarters. Here the army took a strong position and added extensive field works. On the 26th of May, 1857, we were on this hill and were delighted with the splendid view which it affords of the surrounding country. Its summit is still covered with woods, and innumerable violets and honeysuckles were then in full bloom, among which warbled sweetly the thrush, the cat-bird and the wood robin. Ah! thought we, how changed, after the lapse of eighty years!—the scene once so warlike now so peaceful. The remains of entrenchments on the brow of the hill are still discernable, running parallel with the road leading to the city.

What is popularly known as Fort Washington is nothing more than a redoubt erected on an eminence of the same name, by the army during the Revolution. Of all the works once on this hill this alone, we believe, has been spared by man. It is in the form of a square or diamond, with the upper side on the hill open. Its dimensions are seventeen steps on the north west side, or sixty-six steps around it on the top. These remains are elevated from six to ten feet above the surface of the ground on the outside. There are several cherry and cedar trees growing on it—some we presume forty years old. It commands the roads below for some distance. The Spring House pike approaches within one hundred and fifty yards of these works, and we suppose it is elevated perpendicularly above it about sixty feet. It is not quite on the highest part of the hill. A resident in the neighborhood informed us that even down to thirty years ago there were still considerable remains of entrenchments, which, by the cultivation of the land, have since become obliterated. Fort Washington is now owned by Jacob Haines, residing near by. This hill is situated upwards of half a mile west of Camp Hill, and is a continuation of the same range, but is separated from it by Sandy Run. On both of these hills muskets and cannon balls are yet occasionally found. We were told that a few years ago, in ploughing a field, there was discovered various relics, such as pewter plates, broken swords, bayonets, musket locks, &c.

While the American army lay at Valley Forge Washington received intelligence that the British contemplated to evacuate the city, and accordingly sent La Fayette with two thousand one hundred troops and five pieces of cannon, on the 18th of May, 1778, across the Schuylkill, to take post at Barren Hill. The principal object of this expedition was to cut off any foraging parties of the enemy that might be in the vicinity, as well as to restrain these depredations and to obtain, as far as possible, correct information of their movements, and in case of a departure to fall on their rear and harrass their march. As soon as he arrived at the place, he fixed his quarters a short distance west of the church, and made the requisite arrangements to prevent any surprise. The same day a tory in the neighborhood sent a messenger to Sir Henry Clinton, who was now in the command of the British army at Philadelphia, informing him of La Fayette's position and strength. A plan was immediately formed by Clinton for a surprise. On the night of the 19th, five thousand men were sent out under the command of General Grant, assisted by Sir William Erskine, who marched by way of Frankford and the present village of

Whitemarsh to a position in the rear of La Fayette. Another strong force, under General Grey, went up the Schuylkill and took a position about three miles below Barren Hill, while Sir Henry Clinton led in person a third division through Germantown, and before daylight halted at Chestnut Hill. The situation of La Fayette was now critical and he was nearly surrounded by a greatly superior force before he was aware of his situation. The first intelligence the Americans had was from an officer who was sent to reconnoitre, who observed the scarlet coats of the enemy through the trees about a mile distant, on the road leading from Whitemarsh to Swedes' Ford. La Fayette immediately conceived the danger of his position and stationed a considerable force within the churchyard, around which there was a strong stone wall. Being satisfied that he could not retreat with safety to Swedes' Ford, he accordingly moved in the direction of Matson's Ford, now Conshehocken, the road leading nearly all the way through the woods. At intervals in this distance he ordered several small parties in the rear to show themselves occasionally at different points so as to deceive General Grant, who halted to prepare himself for an attack, while at the same time he was awaiting the approach of the other divisions. While this delay occurred the Americans made a quick march to the ford where they crossed safely with all their artillery and took a position on the high ground opposite. General Grant, in the meantime, marched to Barren Hill and instead of meeting the Americans there, as he had expected, found the division under Clinton awaiting his arrival. They then marched as far as the ford, but finding it difficult to pass over wheeled round, disappointed and chagrined, to Philadelphia. In conveying their artillery across the river the Americans were fired at by an advance party, by which they lost nine men, either killed or taken prisoners. Of the enemy two horsemen were killed and several wounded. On arriving at Valley Forge, La Fayette and his men were greeted with the most enthusiastic huzzas. General Poor and Captain M'Lane were the principal American officers engaged in this expedition.

The damages that the people of Whitemarsh sustained from the British during the Revolution were estimated, by an assessor appointed for the purpose, at six hundred and sixty-one pounds, or one thousand seven hundred and sixty-two dollars and sixty-two cents of our present currency.

XII.

CONSHEHOCKEN.

The borough of Conshehocken is situated on the east bank of the Schuylkill, four miles below Norristown and thirteen from Philadelphia. It is bounded on the north and northwest by Plymouth, east and southeast by Whitemarsh, and south and southwest by the Schuylkill. In its territorial extent it is exactly one mile square, and therefore contains six hundred and forty acres, one-half of which was taken from Plymouth and the remainder from Whitemarsh. Its front on the river is also one mile. The land on which the borough is situated rises gradually from the Schuylkill for the distance of a quarter of a mile, when it attains a perpendicular height of about one hundred feet, after which it extends level. Just below the borough, and along the Schuylkill, is an extensive flat extending nearly to Spring Mill.

Though of recent origin, Conshehocken is quite an interesting and important place, particularly in the variety and number of its manufacturing establishments. According to the census of 1850, it contained within its limits seven hundred and twenty-seven inhabitants, one hundred and twenty-five houses and eight farms. Of late years, this place has rapidly increased, and its population at this time is probably over two thousand. According to the triennial assessment of 1858, the real estate was valued at $260,795, and the horses and neat cattle $5,228. In May, 1858, it contained four inns and the following stores: seven merchandise, two feed, one drug, one clothing, two shoe, three confectionary, one stove, one dry goods, two groceries, one tobacco and one trimmings; besides a lumber yard, coal yard, an Odd Fellows' hall and a post office.

The manufactories here are all extensive, and when in full blast give employment to a great number of hands. The Plymouth furnace, belonging to Stephen Colwell and Company, is one of the largest establishments of the kind in the State. Great quantities of pig iron is made from the ore in the vicinity. An extensive business is also carried on in casting various kinds of machinery and iron pipes for conduits. Of the latter, immense quantities have been made here. We were informed that in November, 1858, three hundred hands were employed in and around the works. When in full operation, we learn, more than four hundred hands are required. It has been stated on reliable authority that as early as 1848 three thousand tons of pipes were made here annually. This quantity, no doubt, has since been considerably increased. The ore used here is chiefly obtained in Plymouth township, principally in the vicinity of Harmanville. John Wood and Brother have an extensive rolling mill, and employ about thirty hands. Allan Wood and Company have also a rolling mill and employ twenty hands. It is said that no establishments in this country equal these in the superior excellence of their sheet-iron, being only surpassed by the celebrated Russia sheet-iron. It appears that in 1832 the only manufactories in the place was a rolling mill and a grist mill. Besides the aforesaid, Stanley Lee and Brother have a cotton factory; James and Lawrence Ogden, a woolen factory; Walter Cresson and Brother, a saw factory; Jacoby and Company, a marble saw mill, and near the mouth of Plymouth creek a saw mill for lumber. The manufacture of bricks is also carried on. The abundance of excellent iron ore, marble and limestone found in the neighborhood gives great advantages for this to become a large manufacturing town which is still in embryo.

The first improvement by the place, and which laid the foundation for its prosperity, was the Schuylkill Navigation, which extends from Philadelphia to Port Carbon, one hundred and eight miles. It was begun in 1816 and was sufficiently completed in 1818 for the descent of a few boats of six tons burthen, but was not finished till 1824. In 1846 it was enlarged for boats of one hundred and eighty-six tons burthen. It was the water-power of the dam here, which propels a rolling mill, saw factory and the marble saw mill, that caused the birth of this manufacturing town. The bridge over the Schuylkill was incorporated in 1832, and is called the Matson's Ford bridge. The Reading railroad crosses it by two tracks, and forms a connection with the Norristown railroad. On the night of September 2d, 1850, this bridge was swept away by a high freshet, but was shortly after built again. At its west end is the village of West Conshehocken, containing about thirty houses and a station of the Reading railroad. The Philadelphia, Germantown and Norristown railroad was finished through this place in August. 1835, when the first locomotive and train of cars passed over the road to Norristown. The Plymouth railroad, which was incorporated in 1836, is nearly four miles in length, and leads from the limekilns above Plymouth meeting house to this borough, where it connects with the Norristown railroad. The road that leads to the Broad Axe, and forms the line between Plymouth and Whitemarsh townships, is an original road which was turnpiked, in 1849, to Plymouth meeting house, a distance of two and a-half miles. It has since been continued beyond the village of Three Tons, where it strikes the Lime Kiln pike, seven and a-half miles further on.

Conshehocken has three public schools, which, for the school year ending with June 1st, 1857, were open ten months and attended by two hundred and thirty-two scholars. The sum of $1,375 was levied by tax to defray the expenses of the same. These schools are kept in a large two-story building, erected for this purpose in 1855, which is situated on the top of the hill, on the north side of the Plymouth pike or Fayette street. The elections for the borough are held in it. There is also a private school in the place, but, we believe, no public library. There are three churches in the borough. The first was erected by the Presbyterians, in 1848, of which the Rev. Joseph Nesbitt, of Norristown, is pastor. St. Matthew's Catholic church was built in 1850, and is under the charge of the Rev. Mr. Maginnes. The Methodist church was erected in the summer of 1857. These are all stone edifices.

Conshehocken is of Indian origin and was the name by which they called Edge Hill. We have the proof of this by the deeds of purchase from them by William Penn, July 14th, 1683, and of July 30th, 1685, where it is distinctly mentioned. This hill still retains this name on the west side of the Schuylkill, and from thence has been applied to this place. The reader will see an account of the aforesaid deeds in our article on the Indians, in the beginning of this work; further comment is therefore unnecessary. This place, before it bore its present name, was called Matson's Ford, which we know was given to it some time before the Revolution. It appears as early as 1712, John Matson took up a large tract of land on the opposite side of the river and as the population increased, roads were laid out to this place, and thus became known to the country around as Matson's Ford. However, it was not supplanted till about 1830, when the town was laid out as "Conshehocken."

During the revolution the American army crossed the Schuylkill at this place several times. On the 19th of May, 1778, while La Fayette was stationed with a detachment of two thousand one hundred men at Barren Hill, three and a half miles from here, the British attempted to surprise him with a greatly superior force divided into three divisions. One was led by General Grant and the others by Sir Henry Clinton and General Grey. When the division under Grant had approached within a mile of his rear, through an officer who had been sent early in the morning to reconnoitre, La Fayette received the first intelligence of their presence. Apprehending his situation critical he withdrew in haste to this ford, and as the last division of his command were crossing with the artillery, the enemy's advanced parties made their appearance on the banks and fired a volley after them, when a skirmish ensued in which the Americans lost nine men in killed and taken. The British loss was two light-horsemen killed and several wounded. La Fayette proceeded to the high ground opposite and formed in the order of battle, when the divisions under Grant and Clinton made their appearance, but who, not deeming it safe to cross, though they had more than four times the number of men, wheeled round and marched disappointed and chagrined to the city. In consequence of this affair the old road which led to the ford and on which this retreat was effected, has been called Fayette street.

On the hill, in this borough, a number of years ago, lived an aged black man by the name of Hector, who had been a team driver for the soldiers in the Revolution. It appears that the good people of the town have appreciated his services, for in laying out the streets of the borough, in 1850, they honored one with the name of "Hector Street." That Conshehocken has improved rapidly is shown by the fact that in 1833 it contained but one store, one tavern, a rolling mill, grist mill and six dwelling houses. By the year 1849 the place had sufficiently increased that its inhabitants petitioned for the rights and privileges of a borough. It was incorporated by an act of Assembly, passed the 15th of May, 1850. By its charter its bounds were fixed as follows:—

Beginning in the township of Plymouth at low water mark of the river Schuylkill, at the distance of half a mile, measured on a direct line at right angles from the middle of the Whitemarsh and Plymouth turnpike road, which is on the township line between said townships; thence north forty degrees forty-five minutes, east parallel to said turnpike road over lands of Cadwallader Foulke, John Stemple, Evan Davis and others, to a point where the continuation of a certain public road line which now leads into said turnpike at the eastern corner of the farm of James Cresson, and which road is nearly at right angles with said turnpike, if continued north-westerly would intersect said parallel line first mentioned as running north forty-three degrees, east then from said point, south easterly the course of said road and crossing said turnpike and continuing its course in Whitemarsh, up over lands late of Daniel Harry, deceased, and Isaac Jones' land, one mile to a point on the land of said Isaac Jones; thence on his said land south forty degrees forty-five minutes west to the river Schuylkill aforesaid, and along up said river the several courses thereof to the place of beginning.

The commissioners appointed for laying out the borough according to the act of incorporation were Isaac Roberts, Joseph Crawford, John M. Jones and L. E. Corson. The following names were given to the streets running parallel with and beginning at the river: Canal, Elm, and then comes Front Avenue, and so on to Twelfth, which is the last. Running east and west the streets are Freedley, Wood, Maple, Forest, Fayette, Harry, Hallowell, Jones and Richter. On the south side of Spring Mill Avenue to the river, are Hector, Elm and Washington streets. They are all out at right angles except those south of Spring Mill Avenue. Few towns or boroughs in the State are laid out so regular in streets and boundaries as this borough. At the upper end of the town, on Fayette street, are a number of beautiful private residences surrounded with beautiful lawns.

In August, 1858, while on a visit here, collecting information, we found a respectable old gentleman sitting by the steps of a private house, engaged in conversation with several children. Though a perfect stranger, and taking him to be one of the borough fathers, we approached and took a seat beside him, and, after some remarks on the weather, we got into a sage discourse on the past. We found him intelligent and communicative, and some of the information contained in this article was obtained from him. By and by, we spoke of the rapid increase of the place and the rise and value of real estate, when we obtained the following additional particulars: that he was then eighty-five years of age and lived at the south-east end of the town, on a farm of one hundred and fifty acres, wholly within the borough limits, which contains some of the most beautiful land for building purposes in the place. It had, down to a few years ago, contained two hundred acres, but by selling off fifty was reduced to its present area. He told us that he was a native of Delaware county, but had lived for a number of years here. Isaac Jones, for that is his name, is still a hale and hearty man for his age, and may live to see many a brick house yet spring up around him.

XIII.

PLYMOUTH.

The township of Plymouth is bounded on the north by Whitpain, east by Whitemarsh, south by the Schuylkill and the borough of Conshehocken, and west by the borough of Norristown and Norriton township. Its greatest length is three and a-half miles, and width two and a-half. It had contained an area of five thousand six hundred and thirty-one acres, but by the erection of Conshehocken into a borough, in 1850, three hundred and twenty acres were taken off; also, a long, narrow strip of one hundred and twenty-eight perches wide, on the Schuylkill, of about one hundred and fifty-eight acres by the enlargement of the borough of Norristown, in 1853—thus leaving its present area five thousand one hundred and fifty-three acres. Previously, from the years 1780 to 1850, it had not undergone any alterations in its territorial extent.

The surface of Plymouth is gently undulating and there are no elevations scarcely deserving the name of hills. Along the Schuylkill at several places the limestone assumes a rocky appearance, but nowhere rises above fifty or sixty feet perpendicular. In proportion to its extent we have no hesitation in saying that no township in the county equals it for the natural fertility of its soil. As to waste or unproductive land comparatively little can be found. In proportion to its size it also excels in the quantity of its limestone, the great source of its fertility. On the other hand it is not a well watered township, for it contains no streams that afford water-power. The largest is Plymouth Creek, which rises half a-mile east of Hickorytown, and after a course of four miles empties into the Schuylkill at Conshehocken. Saw Mill Run rises in Whitpain and after a course of a little over a mile through this township turns into Norriton. A small stream empties into the Schuylkill a short distance below Mogee's lime-kilns.

About two-thirds of Plymouth is underlaid with limestone, which, at some places, is on or near the surface, and again at other places lies deep. Nearly the whole distance of this township on the Schuylkill is a bluff of limestone, and few places are more favored for burning lime, both from the convenience of the material and the advantages of sending it to market. The limestone has a general dip to the south of about forty-five degrees, and varies in color from a dark blue to nearly a white. The greater portion of it makes lime of the very best quality. According to the census of 1840 the lime produced in this township was valued at forty-five thousand two hundred and eighteen dollars. We have not a doubt that its annual product at this time is near two hundred and sixty thousand dollars, which is a great increase. We counted in this township, in August last, seventy-five kilns, of which over three-fourths were in operation, which will show the extensiveness of the business. William Mogee & Co. have twenty-three kilns a short distance below Norristown, near the Schuylkill. We have been informed that they burned in fourteen months previous to June 1st, 1858, one million twenty-three thousand bushels of lime, in the manufacture of which they consumed seven thousand six hundred tons of coal. For the year ending with April 1st, 1858, the average number of hands employed was one hundred and nineteen. They had, also, engaged in the business, thirteen boats and thirty-three horses and mules. It is said that they used in one year two thousand kegs of powder. They have a wharf on the Schuylkill four hundred and ten feet long, and a railroad of seven hundred feet in length. When we were here, last summer, the schooners Diamond State and William Penn, both of Wilmington, Delaware, and two canal boats, were loading. At the head of the railroad, above Plymouth Meeting House, and on or near the turnpike, George Mulvany has three kilns. There are here, also, several old kilns, which have not been used for some time. Near by Hiram Blee & Co. have six kilns, which are owned by Daniel Mulvany, Esq., of Norristown. Opposite the former kilns but in Whitemarsh township, George Corson has five kilns. A short distance down the railroad are several that belonged to the late John Freedley. These, we believe, constitute all in this vicinity. Following the Schuylkill up from Conshehocken about a mile, the first kilns we arrive at are those of Elwood Norney and Brother, four in number. They have a track to the Norristown railroad about three hundred yards long. The limestone here shows its stratification and has a dip of forty-five degrees. The next are those of Jesse W. Ramsey, who has eight kilns. Next, Charles Earnest & Co. have eight kilns. Their quarries show that a great quantity of limestone has been taken from them. Then we come again to Elwood Norney's; he has here seven coal and five wood kilns. Much limestone has also been quarried here. Next, Corson & Wells have eight kilns about a quarter of a mile up a small stream from the river, to which they have a single track that connects with the Norristown railroad. These kilns are about a quarter of a mile from Mogee's, already mentioned. These constitute about all the kilns in the township. Marble, we believe, is not quarried.

Iron ore is now obtained in great abundance, while forty years ago it was but little known. In that part of the township which lies between the Plymouth railroad and the Whitemarsh line, from Conshehocken to Plymouth Meeting House, appears, from recent discoveries, to be one immense bed of ore. On the aforesaid tract, south of the Ridge pike, ore has been dug on the farms of Robert Potts, William Wells, Samuel Pippitt, and others; on the north side it is obtained from lands of Reuben Lukens, Jacob Albertson and David Karns. At these pits, in August last, upwards of sixty hands were employed. The ore is generally raised by horse and windlass, and on Albertson's property is brought up from a depth of seventy-five feet. The ore obtained is chiefly sent to the Plymouth furnace, at Conshehocken, and the Swede furnaces in Upper Merion.

The inhabitants of Plymouth are principally the descendants of English and Welsh Friends, who were the first settlers. Of late years, through the lime business, a considerable number of Irish have emigrated hither. This township contained, in 1741, forty-six taxables; in 1828, two hundred and twenty-eight; in 1849, four hundred and forty-eight, and in 1858, four hundred and five. According to the census of 1810 it contained eight hundred and ninety-five inhabitants; in 1820, nine hundred and twenty-eight; in 1830, one thousand and ninety-one; in 1840, one thousand four hundred and seventeen, and in 1850, one thousand three hundred and eighty-three. The erection of Conshehocken in the beginning of 1850, and the extension of Norristown in 1853, has been the means of reducing its population. We are satisfied that Plymouth has rapidly increased within the last few years. This is especially observable from the number of new houses which have been recently erected in its villages.

In May, 1858, Plymouth contained three inns, five stores, one steam grist mill, one powder mill, two coal yards and a brick kiln. According to the census of 1850 it contained two hundred and twenty houses and ninety-one farms. By the triennial assessment of 1858 the real estate was valued at three hundred and fifty-nine thousand one hundred and fifty dollars, and the horses and neat cattle at eighteen thousand nine hundred and ninety-eight dollars. The Ridge turnpike traverses the township two and a-half miles, and the Germantown and Perkiomen pike about three miles. The turnpike leading from Conshehocken to the Broad Axe forms the entire southeast boundary of Plymouth, a distance of three and a quarter miles, and separates it from Whitemarsh. The Norristown railroad passes through the south west side of the township, along the Schuylkill, over two miles. The Plymouth railroad is about three miles and three-quarters in length, and commences at the lime-kilns and quarries on the Whitemarsh line, above Plymouth Meeting House, and follows Plymouth Creek to Colwell's furnace, at Conshehocken, where it connects with the Norristown railroad. It consists of a single track and the cars on it are drawn by horses. Lime is chiefly taken down on it and coal and wood brought back. The company to whom it belongs was incorporated by act of Assembly passed the 18th of March, 1836.

Education is encouraged in Plymouth. For the year ending with June 1st, 1857, it contained within its limits six schools, which were open ten months and attended by three hundred and forty-one scholars. The amount taxed to defray the expenses of the same was two thousand and sixty eight dollars. At this place there is also a post office, and another at Hickorytown. Plymouth Meeting is the only house of worship in the township.

The village of Hickorytown is situated on the Germantown and Perkiomen turnpike, three miles south east of Norristown, and fourteen from Philadelphia. It contains an inn, store, school house, a blacksmith and wheelwright shop and twenty-nine houses. A number of the houses have been built within the past few years. The post office was established in May, 1857. The elections of the township are held here. In 1832 this village contained ten houses.

Harmanville is situated on the line of Whitemarsh township at the intersection of the Ridge and Plymouth turnpikes, one and a-half miles from Conshehocken. It contains a store, a wheelwright and blacksmith shop, and about thirty-five houses. R. R. Ellis also carries on the coachmaking business extensively. About one-half of this village is situated in Whitemarsh. It has chiefly grown up within the last eight years and bids fair to become a rising town. The iron ore and marble procured in the vicinity is what has given an impulse to its prosperity.

Plymouth Meeting House is the name of a village situated at the intersection of the Perkiomen and Plymouth turnpikes, on the township line. On this side is the meeting house, school house and four houses, and in Whitemarsh two stores, a blacksmith and wheelwright shop, post office and twenty-four houses. The houses in this village are chiefly situated along the Perkiomen or Reading pike, nearly adjoining one another, and being of stone, neatly white washed, with shady yards in front, present to the stranger an agreeable appearance. In the basement of the Library building the Methodists hold worship. This is an ancient settlement, whose history dates back nearly to the arrival of Penn, and is marked as a village on Lewis Evans' map of 1749. For some information respecting this place the reader is referred to the account of the meeting house. The post office was established here before 1827. In 1832 there were but ten houses here.

Plymouth is the name of a village at the head of the Plymouth railroad, on the township line, about a mile above Plymouth Meeting House. It contains a store and five houses in this township, and on the Whitemarsh side are seventeen houses and a Baptist church. The church was built in 1841 and is situated on an eminence, from the door of which a fine view is obtained of the surrounding country for some distance, especially in a southern direction. The Rev. Mr. Trotter is its pastor and resides in the village.

The Seven Stars is a small place two miles from Norristown, on the Ridge pike, where the Plymouth creek and railroad cross it, and contains one inn and three houses. The old "Seven Stars" inn, now kept by Samuel Pippitt, is nearly one of the most ancient in the county, and is marked on Scull's map of Pennsylvania, published in 1770. The turnpike bridge here was built in 1796.

At Mogee's Lime Works, adjacent the borough line and between the Ridge pike and the Schuylkill, a village has grown up chiefly within the last six years, which contains a store, several mechanic shops and thirty-four houses. Of these eight were built in the summer of 1858. There is a rope ferry here across the Schuylkill, for transporting the horses and mules attached to the boats, the navigation from here up being on the opposite side. About half a-mile east of Norristown is another village extending from the Ridge pike to the river. Here is an inn, toll gate, brick-kiln, powder mill, a blacksmith and wheelwright shop and twenty houses. The lime kilns of Corson and Wells are also here. This place has chiefly grown up within the last eight years.

The Plymouth meeting house is a very ancient stone structure, one story high, and in the summer of 1858 was repaired and a gallery placed in the east end. It is surrounded by an ample, shady yard, in which are several old and venerable looking buttonwood trees. The graveyard is large, and as is usual among

Friends, no ancient stones with inscriptions on them show who may repose here. On the house itself no date or inscription is found to indicate when or by whom it was built. With all these disadvantages, fortunately we have nearly sufficient material in our collections to give what we desire. About the year 1685 the township of Plymouth was originally purchased and settled by James Fox, Richard Gove, Francis Rawle, John Chelson and some other Friends who came from Plymouth, in Devonshire, England, who lived here for a time and kept meetings for worship at the house of the said James Fox, but being most of them tradesmen, and not used to a country life, they removed to Philadelphia, by which means the place became vacant. Not long afterwards, however, it was re-purchased and settled again. Among a number of others were David Meredith, Edmund Cartlege, Thomas Owen, Isaac Price, Ellis Pugh and Hugh Jones, nearly all Friends. In the immediate vicinity, but in Whitemarsh, settled about the same time, John Rhoads, Abraham Davis and David Williams. It appears they were sufficiently numerous here to receive the consideration of William Penn, who, in a letter from England to Thomas Lloyd, dated the 14th of 4th month, 1691, among other things says: "Salute me to the Welsh Friends and the Plimouth Friends, indeed to all of them." The aforesaid members, in the year 1703, by the consent of Haverford monthly meeting, to which they had joined themselves, continued to hold their meetings at the same house which had now come in the possession of Hugh Jones, where it remained for a number of years, and then by consent was removed to the house of John Cartledge, where it continued for some time. Through the increase of population it was agreed to build a meeting house for their better accommodation, which was accordingly done at the present spot, which for some time previous had been used as a burying ground. With the consent of the Haverford monthly meeting and the Philadelphia Quarterly meeting, the Friends of Plymouth and Gwynedd were permitted to hold a monthly meeting for business. Their first monthly meeting was held at Gwynedd meeting house, the 22d of 12th month, 1714–5. It cannot be ascertained from the records at what exact time this meeting house was built, but there is reason to believe that it could not have been many years previous to the last date. John Rees was appointed the 25th of 12th month, 1723, to keep the records of the births and burials of the meeting.

Plymouth derived its name from a seaport town in Devonshire, England, from which a number of the early settlers of this township originally came, as has been related in our account of the meeting house. On Surveyor-General Thomas Holmes' map of original surveys, made between the years 1682 and 1695, "The Plymouth township," as it is called, is laid out at that early period with the same boundaries it had down to 1850. Owing to a petition from James Fox and other early settlers, the Council gave a permit the 5th of 2d month, 1687, to lay out a "cart road" from Philadelphia to this township, which was shortly done. This is the same road leading from the meeting house to the city, now better known as the Germantown and Perkiomen turnpike, which was begun in 1801 and finished in 1804, at a cost of eleven thousand two hundred and eighty-seven dollars per mile.

After having advanced so far in this work, it is with pleasure that we bring before the reader the first literary attempt, to our knowledge, ever made in this county. Ellis Pugh, whom we have already mentioned as one of the early settlers of this township, was a native of Dolgelle, in Wales, where he was born in 1656. In his 18th year he became a member of the society of Friends through the influence of John Ap John, a celebrated preacher. At the age of twenty-four he came forth in the ministry. He arrived in Pennsylvania in 1687, and shortly after settled in Plymouth. In the year 1707, he went on a religious visit to the inhabitants of his native country and shortly after returned. About this time he wrote a religious work in the Welsh language with the following curious title: "A Salutation to the Britains to call them from many things, to the one thing needful, for the saving of their souls; especially to the poor, unarmed traveler, plowmen, shepherds and those that are of low degree like myself. This is in order to direct you to know God and Christ, the only wise God, which is life eternal, and to learn of him, that you may become wiser than their teachers." He died in the year 1718, at the age of sixty-two years. This work was translated by his friend Rowland Ellis, of Gwynedd, and revised by David Lloyd, of Philadelphia, where it was printed by S. Keimer, in 1727. It is a small octavo volume of two hundred and twenty-two pages, and, of course, rare. It is particularly interesting as an early specimen of Pennsylvania typography.

The following were residents and landholders of Plymouth, in 1734: Eleanor Meredith, Rice Williams, Benjamin Dickenson, John Hamer, John Davis, Joshua Dickenson, John Redwitzer, Peter Croll, Thomas Davis, Isaac Price, Joseph Jones, Mary Davis, Jonathan Rumford, Henry Bell, Philip John and John Holton. Of some of the aforesaid we have the following information: By the Abington records we learn that in 1695, Isaac Price was married to Susannah Shoemaker. David Meredith, the husband of Eleanor, had settled here, we know, before 1703. John Redwitzer was a native of Germany, and settled at Germantown before 1700. In 1709 he was naturalized with the privilege to enjoy lands. We have, also, some account of Jacob Ritter, who died in Plymouth, in 1841, which is given in the appendix.

During the Revolution, and while the British held possession of Philadelphia, Zebulon Potts lived in this township, about half a-mile from Conshehocken. He was an ardent whig, and through spies the British became informed of his opposition to their cause. They several times sent parties out to his house to capture him, and once they prosecuted their search so close as almost to find him. For his services in the American cause the citizens elected him the first Sheriff of the county, namely, from 1784 to 1787.

XIV.

NORRISTOWN.

The borough of Norristown is situated on the Schuylkill river, about sixteen miles northwest of Philadelphia, and is the seat of justice for Montgomery county. By its extended limits in 1853, it is nearly two miles square, and contains an area of about two thousand three hundred acres. Its front on the river is fully two miles and extends back from the same a distance of from one and a-half to two miles, and is bounded on the north, northeast and northwest by Norriton township, southeast by Plymouth, and on the south and southwest by the Schuylkill. It was erected into a borough in 1812, with an area of five hundred and twenty acres, and all its territory has been taken from Norriton, with the exception of about one hundred and fifty-eight acres from Plymouth by its recent enlargement.

Its surface is rolling, and that part on which the town is principally situated enjoys an elevated site, from the rear of which an extensive view is obtained of the fine scenery of the Schuylkill valley. Both adjacent and in the vicinity of the town the soil is excellent. Norristown combines, from its situation, great advantages, and in this respect few towns are so favored. It is remarkably healthy, its location beautiful, its water excellent, and its neighborhood unsurpassed in the quality and abundance of its marble, iron and limestone. Within the limits of the borough two streams enter the Schuylkill. The larger is Stony creek, which has its source in Whitpain township and is seven miles in length, two of which are in the borough. This stream, with its branches, propels six grist mills, two saw mills, besides several manufactories. Saw Mill run rises also in Whitpain, and is four miles in length, of which two are in the borough, and in its course propels a clover, grist and saw mill; besides several manufacturing establishments.

As may be well expected from a town so advantageously situated, and, above all, having an enterprising population, it has rapidly increased. According to the census of 1820, it contained 827 inhabitants; in 1830, 1089; in 1840, 2937; and in 1850, 6024. Its present population is estimated at nearly 11,000. In 1850 its colored population was two hundred and sixteen out of eight hundred and fifty-seven in the county. In 1828 it contained 231 taxables; in 1849, 989; and in 1858, 1954. In 1790 it contained eighteen houses; in 1832, one hundred and fifty-one; and in 1850, one thousand and six. The following is the amount of valuation made by the triennial assessment of 1858:—

	Real Estate.	*Horses and Cattle.*
Upper Ward,	$712,427	$10,040
Middle Ward,	558,675	3,425
Lower Ward,	550,679	4,330
Total,	$1,821,781	$17,795

In May, 1858, the borough contained nine hotels, and one hundred and eight stores, as follows: seventeen grocery, twelve dry goods, nine merchandise, eleven confectionery, four trimmings, three book and stationery, five tobacco, eight boot and shoe, three stove, three clothing and hat, seven clothing, four drug, three furniture, two hat, five jewelry, two leather, four provision, one hardware, one gun, one agricultural, two shoe findings, and one soap and candle store. The census of 1840 gave but fourteen dry goods, grocery and other stores. It also contains four lumber and eight coal and wood yards.

Norristown has attained considerable importance as a manufacturing town. William and Samuel Jamison have a very extensive cotton manufactory; also, Mr. Ewing, (late B. McCredy's,) and Mr. Hurst a smaller one. Gen. William Schall has the Lucinda furnace and a rolling mill and nail factory; James Hooven a rolling mill; Thomas Saurman an iron foundry; and Thomas, Corson & West lately the manufacture of steam engines and boilers. Arthur McCarter & Brother have a machine establishment, and Bolton, Christman & Co., Fluck & Guest, and Samuel F. Groff, have steam planing mills and sash, door and blind manufactories. In addition to the aforesaid, there are two large merchant flour mills, one saw mill, two marble yards, two brick yards, and gas and water works. In the place are also two market houses, two fire engines, and two hose companies.

The various improvements leading to or by this borough have contributed much to its prosperity. In the order of time the first that may be mentioned is the Ridge turnpike, leading from Philadelphia to Perkiomen bridge, twenty-four miles in length, and passing through the borough two miles on Main or Egypt street. It was commenced in 1812 and finished in 1816, and cost $7,000 per mile. The Schuylkill Navigation was commenced in 1816 and was sufficiently completed in 1818 to admit of the descent of a few boats; but it was not until about 1826 that the whole line went into operation. This work did much to advance the prosperity of the place. The company constructed a dam here of nine hundred feet in width, between the abutments, which, in 1830, was raised to its present height and is the means of furnishing valuable water power to several manufacturing establishments. Boats of one hundred and eighty-six tons burthen pass on it and unload coal, grain and lumber in the place. The bridge over the Schuylkill, at DeKalb street, was commenced in the spring of 1829, and by September was so far completed as to admit foot-passengers to pass over. It was built by an incorporated company and was finished in 1830, at a cost of $31,200. It is eight hundred feet in length, or, with the abutments, one thousand and fifty feet. The State road—in the borough called DeKalb street—was laid out in 1830, of forty feet in width, from New Hope, through this place and Bridgeport to West Chester, and from thence to the Maryland line, pursuant to an act of Assembly. The Philadelphia, Germantown and Norristown railroad company was incorporated by an act of Assembly, passed the 17th of February, 1831. It was commenced that year and was opened from the city to Germantown on the 6th of June, 1832, in what would now be considered a very novel manner, namely—by nine cars, or rather carriages, each drawn by one horse in shafts, and containing twenty passengers inside and sixteen outside, making in all three hundred and twenty-four guests, who had been particularly favored for the excursion. Here was in reality a passenger railway twenty-six years ago, about which, within two years past, there has been almost a mania of introducing. What is equally singular, the road was similarly opened with considerable display to Manayunk, October 18th, 1834. Saturday, August 15th (anniversary of Napoleon's birth-day), 1835, was a great day in Norristown. The road was now completed, and its opening was to be duly celebrated. Two trains of cars, each drawn by a *locomotive*, started from the depot, corner of Ninth and Green streets, at twelve o'clock, well laden with invited guests. The locomotives were gaily dressed with flags, and a band of music enlivened the way, and the only stoppage was made at Manayunk. On the approach to Norristown, as well as the entire way, was one continued triumph. Cheers and shouts of welcome were heard in all directions, while the waving of handkerchiefs expressed the congratulations of the fair. Thousands collected together to behold for the first time the iron horses, and gazed on them with wonder. No doubt there were then to be seen here and there knots of wise men (in their estimation) who looked down on the whole with contempt, thinking that a little time would prove it a failure—but, alas! grievously mistaken. For this occasion, the company erected a large tent in the borough, near the river's bank, where three hundred and fifty guests sat down to a sumptuous banquet. This road, with its branch to Germantown, is twenty-one miles in length, and cost $1,811,000. Within the last three years, from the increase of its business, the company has built a large depot in this borough, and laid the entire road with a double track. This improvement extends through Montgomery county something over seven miles. The Reading railroad extends, on the opposite side of the river, from the city to Pottsville, and was opened this whole distance in 1842. The Swedes' Ford bridge company was incorporated the 30th of March, 1848, and was completed in 1851. The Chester Valley railroad crosses this bridge and forms a connection with the Norristown railroad, and with the Pennsylvania railroad at Downingtown. Where Main street and the turnpike cross Stoney creek, a broad and substantial stone bridge was built in 1854, by contributions from the borough, turnpike company and several citizens. For a fuller account of several of the above-mentioned improvements, the reader is referred to our articles on the Schuylkill, Bridgeport and Whitemarsh.

The schools of Norristown, both public and private, have a high reputation ; and the County Superintendent assures us that they are not excelled by those of any other borough in the State. Its inhabitants, from an early period, have bestowed considerable attention to the matter, and the result has been a continual progress in their condition. Schools, particularly in towns, perform a more important part in the affairs and duties of life than is generally accredited to them. By this we mean, more especially, their influence on order and morals. What would be the condition of any town of this size, if its schools were all closed for one year ? We have no hesitation in believing, if this experiment were tried, that some of the most clamorous and unwilling in paying their taxes would be the first to wish them opened. In this borough, about one-fifth of its whole population attends school; if this number, instead of being there preparing for future usefulness, should be let loose on the streets, its character would soon change. The condition of things that would ensue can be better imagined than described, and it is, therefore, useless for us to dwell upon it. The author can aver, from a brief residence, that he has found few places where better order and decorum is observed, especially amongits juvenile population.

For the school year ending with June 1, 1857, this borough had twenty public schools, in which were employed two male and eighteen female teachers, and were attended by two thousand and ninety-one scholars. The amount levied to defray the expenses of the same was $11,609 14. These schools are kept in three large and convenient buildings, erected expressly for this purpose. The principal building, and in which the Grammar school is held, is three stories in height and stands within a square, containing an area of several acres, planted with trees. It was built in 1849, and Rev. G. D. Wolff is principal. In addition to the aforesaid, there is a frame one story school house for colored children. In 1842 there was but one private seminary, which was for boys, in the place, while at present there are no less than three. The Oakland Female Institute, of which the Rev. J. Grier Ralston is principal, is one of the largest buildings in the county devoted to the purposes of education. Within the past few years, a number of young ladies have been educated here. The Tremount Seminary, of which the Rev. Samuel Aaron is principal, consists of two large three-story stone buildings, and has also educated, for some time, a number of young men and boys. The Adelphian Institute, by the Misses Bush, is an excellent school, deserving encouragement. In taking a glimpse at the educational establishments of the past, the old Academy should not be forgotten ; for within its time-honored walls many now on the stage of action received their education. From application made for the purpose, the Legislature passed an act the 29th of March, 1804, to empower certain persons, as trustees, to sell a lot of ground and a school house for the purpose of building an academy in its stead. In the year 1805, the "Norristown Academy" was accordingly erected, thirty by forty feet, two stories high, and of brick. In the order of time, it was the tenth incorporated in Pennsylvania. The State, the same year, appropriated $2,000 towards its completion. This building stood till 1849, when the spirit of improvement razed its walls to the ground, and DeKalb street now passes over the spot. In 1832, there were but two primary schools in the place.

The Norristown Library company was founded in May, 1796. The price of shares is $5 00, with an annual payment of $1 00. In 1832, it had increased to about eleven hundred volumes. In 1835 the present small one-story frame building (fifteen and a-half feet square) was erected expressly for the library. The first catalogue was printed in 1836, and contains forty pages. In 1850 it contained two thousand five hundred and fifteen volumes, divided into four folios, thirty quartos, eight hundred and seventy-two octavos, and one thousand six hundred and nine duodecimos; besides pamphlets. At that time, R. Adamson was the librarian; his successor, now, is Chas. H. Greger. It contains, at present, about two thousand and eight hundred volumes.

About the year 1830 a Cabinet of Natural Science was started, chiefly through the exertions of Peter A. Browne, Esq., of Philadelphia. It continued to flourish for several years, and quite an extensive collection of objects in natural history was obtained, especially in the geological and mineralogical departments. In the course of time it went down and its collections became dispersed, but we are pleased to say it is about coming to life again, we hope with renewed vigor after so long a rest. In September last, the first meeting for its re-organization was held, when a committee was appointed "to collect such of the property of the Cabinet as they may be able to find." Alan W. Corson was elected President, and Samuel Tyson Secretary. If specimens of each of the various kinds of stones and minerals to be found in Montgomery were collected, they would form a highly interesting collection for study, independent of the other departments of natural history.

Four weekly newspapers are at this time published in the borough. First in the order of time is the "*Norristown Herald and Free Press,*" which is published by Robert Iredell. This paper was the first printed in the place, and was commenced by David Sower, June 14th, 1799, under the title of "*Norristown Gazette,*" at one dollar per annum. In size it would now be considered a newspaper in miniature, the sheet being twelve by twenty inches, with three columns to a page. The "*Norristown Register,*" now published by Dr. E. L. Acker, was the second, and begun its career in 1801, and was at that time the same in size as Sower's paper. The "*Norristown Republican,*" now published by Moses Auge, has gone by this title since the beginning of 1857, but was started, we believe, about fourteen years ago. The "*National Defender,*" now published by Edwin Schall, was commenced in August, 1856. The aforesaid papers are now published at two dollars per annum, and are all issued on Tuesday, except the *Republican*, which appears on Saturday. We have spoken of David Sower, the first printer in the place; a further account may be interesting. He was the son of Christopher Sower, was born in 1764, and was brought up to the printing business. We have said that he began his paper here in 1799. This was the first newspaper published in Montgomery county. In 1800 he changed the title of his paper to its present one of *Norristown Herald.* About 1809 the establishment passed into the hands of his eldest son, Charles, who continued the publication until 1812. In 1816 another son, David Sower, Jr., took charge of it and continued it till 1834. Mr. Sower died in this Borough, after a lingering illness, in October 1835, aged seventy-one years. David Sower, Jr., is still living in this place, where he established the first book store, now in the hands of his son, Franklin D. Sower. In 1832 five papers were published in the county, of which three were here. At present there are eight papers in the county. The "*Montgomery Watchman*" was commenced by D. Fry, in April, 1849, and was merged, last November, into the *Norristown Register.* Several works have been written by residents of this Borough. B. F. Hancock, Esq., is the author of "The Law, Without the Advice of an Attorney," published in 1831. Elijah W. Beans is the author of "A Manual for Practical Surveyors." E. F. Freedley is the author of the "Legal Adviser," "A Practical Treatise on Business," and a recent work on the "Manufactures of Philadelphia." L. E. Corson prepared a map of the Borough before its enlargement, which was published several years ago, and Thomas A. Hurley, in 1857, issued quite a large map, showing its late improvements.

Norristown, at the present time, contains thirteen churches, among which are several large and handsome edifices. The St. John's Episcopal church was the first erected in the place. It was commenced in 1813 and finished the following year. It is in the Gothic style of architecture and its dimensions are fifty by eighty feet. The Rev. Nathan Stem is the present pastor. The first Presbyterian church was built in 1819, under the charge of Rev. Joseph Barr, who was at the same time pastor of the Providence church. It stood till 1855, when it was torn down and the present splendid edifice was erected in its place. It is certainly the most costly church in the Borough, and, excepting the court house, has the highest steeple. It belongs to the Old School Presbyterians. Its present pastor is the Rev. J. F. Halsey. The Baptist church was built in 1833, and is a commodious building, on Swede street, and is in charge of Rev. R. Cheney. The first Methodist church was erected in 1834, and in the summer of 1857 the present large two story brick edifice was erected in its place. The Methodist church, in Oak street, was erected in 1854. St. Patrick's Catholic church was built in 1837, and is a three story stone edifice, near the river. Its pastor is the Rev. Jeremiah O'Donoghue. The German Reformed church of the Ascension was founded in 1847, and is in charge of the Rev. John S. Ermentrout. The Lutheran church was built in 1849, and the Rev. Charles H. Baer has recently become its pastor. The Central Presbyterian church, on Main street, is probably the largest in the place, and was built in 1856. It is in charge of the Rev. D. G. Mallory. The Old School Covenanters have a church at which the Rev. Joseph Nesbitt officiates. In addition to the above the Quakers have a meeting house, and the colored Methodists two houses of worship. In 1842 there was but five churches in the place and in 1849, eight.

The "Bank of Montgomery County," at Norristown, was chartered the 29th of August, 1815, with a capital of four hundred thousand dollars. Its officers are John Boyer, President, and William H. Slingluff, Cashier. The present banking house was erected in 1854. It is a two story brick building with a marble front. Its name for a long time was not misapplied, for it was the only bank in the county until 1857, when the bank of Pottstown was chartered. By the statement of this bank, in September last, it had discounted bills and notes to the value of over six hundred thousand dollars, and had notes in circulation to the amount of one hundred and fifty-eight thousand dollars. The post office was established at this place before 1799, and was probably the second in the county, one having been in Pottstown in 1794. John Davis was post master in 1799, which office is now held by H. G. Hart. The Odd Fellows' Hall is a large three story brick building, erected in 1850. An account of the Court House and Prison is given near the close of this article.

As both the township of Norriton and Norristown received their names from Isaac Norris, of Philadelphia, some account of him in this work may not be amiss, as little has been published concerning him. He was a native of England, where he was born about the year 1671. At what time he arrived in Pennsylvania we are unable to tell, but he early commenced his career in Philadelphia as a successful merchant. During his life he was a leading member of the society of Friends. With William Trent, in 1704, he purchased all of what is now called Norriton township, containing seven thousand four hundred and eighty-two acres. In 1712 he bought out Trent's right and thus became its sole owner. He was elected to the Assembly in 1713, and was continued in the same for eighteen years. He chiefly resided at Fair Hill, his country seat, which was in the present vicinity of Broad street, below Monument Cemetery. He was, for a number of years, a member of theG overnor's Council, and at the time of his death was Chief Justice of the province. He died suddenly in the beginning of June, 1735, of an apoplectic fit, while attending the Germantown meeting. At the time of his decease he was about sixty-four years of age. He made his will the 17th of January, 1731, and appointed Mary, his wife, and sons Isaac, Charles and Samuel, jointly his executors. His eldest son Isaac, one of the aforesaid executors, was also distinguished as a merchant, and for his services in public life. He was long an alderman of the city and for twenty years Speaker of the Assembly. He died July 13th, 1766, aged sixty-five years. The Pennsylvania Historical Society have, in their collection, a portrait of him. He is represented as rather full faced and of a stout and heavy appearance, and in a plain dress. The William Trent alluded to was also an early merchant of Philadelphia. He had also been a Speaker in the Assembly and was one of the Judges of the Supreme Court from 1705 to 1716. He shortly afterwards removed to where is now Trenton, New Jersey, and commenced the first settlement of the place by erecting severalmills in 1719. He died there the 29th of December, 1724, and at that time was Chief Justice of that province. Trenton was called in honor of him.

William Penn, the proprietary and governor

of Pennsylvania, by a patent dated the 2d of October, 1704, granted to his son, William Penn, Jr., a tract of land containing seven thousand four hundred and eighty-two acres, on the north side of the Schuylkill, which he called the "Manor of Williamstadt," but since known as Norriton township, and from which nearly the whole of the present Borough of Norristown has been taken. At this time William Penn, Jr., lived in this country and the allowance money he received through his father, from James Logan, not being sufficient to defray the expenses of his youthful follies and extravagances, he sold this manor, after holding it but a few days, to Isaac Norris and William Trent, the 7th of October, of the same year, for eight hundred and fifty pounds. The 11th of January, 1712, Isaac Norris became the sole proprietor of this tract, by purchasing William Trent's right to the same, for five hundred pounds. In the year 1730 the Court of Quarter Sessions for the county of Philadelphia, granted a petition for erecting the manor of Norriton into a separate township, which rights its citizens continued to hold uninterrupted till the formation of this Borough, in 1812. It appears that Isaac Norris must have sold off portions of this tract some time before his death, for in 1734 there resided in this township twenty land holders and tenants, whose names appear in the article on Norriton. Isaac Norris died in 1735, and his family retained the property for some time after, though occasionally selling portions of it. However, the greater part of the land on which the borough now stands came in possession of Charles Norris, son of the aforesaid, who erected a mill by the side of the Schuylkill, a few yards above the present dam, and made other valuable improvements. After his death, Mary, his wife, sold, on the 17th of September, 1771, the mill and five hundred and forty-three acres, situated on the east side of the river, to John Bull, of Limerick township, for the sum of four thousand six hundred pounds, which, in our present currency, would be twelve thousand two hundred and sixty-five dollars. In addition to the aforesaid, and included in the purchase, was Barbadoes Island, which is stated to contain eighty-eight acres. Mr. Bull continued to reside here till the spring of 1777, having sold it the 2d of November previous, to the Rev. Dr. William Smith, of Philadelphia, for six thousand pounds. On Scull's map of 1770, an inn, called the "Norrington House," is marked as being situated on the south-east side of where the Ridge road crosses Stony creek. This, it is supposed, was the first house in Norristown. As John Bull was a native of this county and an early resident here, as well as a conspicuous character in the Revolution, a biographical sketch of him is given in the appendix.

But two days after the defeat of Washington, at Brandywine, he despatched General Armstrong, with a portion of militia, along the Schuylkill, to throw up redoubts at the different fords which were to be occasionally occupied, that in case the British should attempt to cross they might be opposed. At this time the principal crossing place was at Swedes' Ford, and on this account it was expected that they might cross here, and for this reason, under the direction of Chevelier Du Portail, an engineer, formerly in the French army, Armstrong's men threw up entrenchments and breastworks opposite that place, and now in the Borough, and it is said that they were scarcely completed before the British made their appearance on the other side, but in consequence changed their line of march towards Valley Forge. Remains of these works were still visible a few years ago. While Washington was near Pottsgrove the enemy crossed the Schuylkill at Fatland ford, five and a-half miles above Norristown, on the night of September the 22d, and proceeded leisurely on their march to the city. On the 23d a portion of their army was over night in or near the present borough, on which occasion they burned the barn of Mr. Smith, erroneously published as having, at the time, belonged to Mr. Bull, this latter gentleman having parted with all his property here the previous fall. While in this neighborhood, we learn from the Rev. H. M. Muhlenberg's Journal, the American light cavalry captured five English soldiers, who, at the time, we presume, were out marauding, and brought them through the Trappe, on their way to the American army.

When Washington broke up his camp at Whitemarsh and proceeded with the army to Valley Forge, for winter quarters, it was in this borough where, on the 11th of December, they crossed the river by making a bridge of their wagons by backing them together. Major Mathias Holstein, who witnessed the proceeding, relates that a number of trees then grew upon the banks. While the British had possession of the city it is said they offered a reward of one thousand pounds for the head of Colonel Andrew Knox, and another officer of the army who lived in the vicinity, and who had, as ardent patriots, incurred their displeasure. Prompted chiefly by this offer, seven tories undertook the office of assassins. They arrived about midnight and called him up, telling him the enemy were upon him. He replied that they must be the enemy, when one of the number fired at him through the window, but fortunately missed his aim. He then seized a heavy broad sword and came down stairs and met them at the door. They fired through the door and broke the lock, by which they were enabled partly to force open the door. Col. Knox now attacked them as they advanced and wounded two of them so severely that they were caught the next day and executed at the present village of Centre Square. Washington and Franklin, shortly after this occurrence, visited him at his house and complimented him for his bravery, and was presented with their arms, which they had left behind to facilitate their escape. The Colonel, in this attack, received a musket ball through his thigh, and some fifteen slight bayonet wounds, from all of which he soon after recovered. This house is still standing, in Whitpain township, nearly three miles north of the borough, where the bullet holes, seven in number, are shown in the door. His grandson, Colonel Thomas P. Knox, late Senator from the county, resides within the present limits of Norristown. From the "Pennsylvania Packet" of October 27th, 1778, we extract the following, from an advertisement, which is not without interest in the history of this place, and which bears Dr. Smith's name: "To be let for a term of years, that valuable plantation at Norriton, on Schuylkill, lately occupied by Colonel Bull. Such persons as desire to lease the same are requested to make their propositions to the subscriber, at the college, as soon as possible, as the farm and meadows now suffer for the want of a tenant."

After an arduous struggle the Revolution at length passed away and the country achieved its independence, and on the 3d of September, 1783, a definitive treaty was signed with Great Britain. Peace, happy peace, now reigned within our borders, and industry soon brought returning prosperity to the long-neglected fields and workshops. Above all, confidence was now restored, and the laborer was secure in his reward. Up to this period all the territory at present in the county was comprised in that of Philadelphia, which, from the distance that many had to go to attend to county affairs, caused a great inconvenience. Petitions were accordingly got up and numerously signed by the people, praying for the erection of a new county. The petitions were heard and graciously acted upon by the Legislature, and an act was accordingly passed the 10th of September, 1784, "for erecting part of the county of Philadelphia into a separate county." Thus did the present county of Montgomery, rich and populous as it now is, spring into origin. In the said act constituting it a separate county, is found the following extract: "At the time appointed by law the freemen of the county of Montgomery shall meet at the house of Hannah Thompson, inn-keeper, in the township of Norriton, and there elect four Representatives, one fit person for Sheriff, one fit person for Coroner, and three Commissioners, and one member of the Supreme Executive Council. That it shall be lawful for Henry Pawling, Jr., Jonathan Roberts, George Smith, Robert Shannon and Henry Cunnard, all of the aforesaid county, yeoman, or any three of them, to purchase and take assurance to them, in the name of the commonwealth, of a piece of land, situated in some convenient place in the neighborhood of Stony run, contiguous to the river Schuylkill, in Norriton township, in trust and for the use of the inhabitants of the said county, and thereon to erect and build a Court House and Prison, sufficient to accommodate the public service of said county."

At that time, where is now the large and populous Borough of Norristown, the land chiefly belonged to the Trustees of the University of Pennsylvania, to whom it had been transferred by the Rev. Dr. Smith, who had been the provost of the same. His son, William Moore Smith, however, became the final owner, under certain reservations to the trustees of that Institution, and got it laid out as the town of "Norris" into streets and lots. The lots were each divided into the width of fifty feet front, but of different depths. Those most advantageously situated brought as high as four dollars per foot, while others less desirable were sold as low as one dollar and forty cents. There were in all at this time (1785,) sixty-four town lots, bounded on the north by Airy street, east by Green alley, south by Lafayette street and west by Cherry street. This may be considered the original size of the town. As it was of course now satisfactorily ascertained that it had become the county seat, and that the county buildings would soon be erected, the lots were soon all sold and a number of buildings commenced, though, as will be seen, its growth at first was very slow.

A further account of Wm. Moore Smith may not wholly be without interest. His father was considered one of the most accomplished scholars of Philadelphia, and it was through his exertions that the University owes its origin and of which he was elected its first provost. He was early admitted to the ministry of the Episcopal church in Philadelphia, and of which he was a pastor for many years. Wm. Moore was his eldest son and was born in the city, June 1st, 1759. It appears as if he had inherited a taste for letters, for he was early distinguished for the extent and variety of his acquirements. In his general character he was a gentleman of the old school, of highly polished education and manners, and, in his day, a poet of considerable reputation. He lived in Norristown for some time, and we know as late as 1789, if not later. He afterwards moved near Philadelphia, where he died the 12th of March, 1821. His remains were interred by the side of his father, in Laurel Hill cemetery. The late Richard Penn Smith was his son.

As the court house and jail were not built for several years after the erection of the county, the courts had to be held wherever they could get the most proper accommodations. The first court was held at the public house of John Shannon, the 28th of December, 1784. Frederick A. Muhlenberg, James Morris, Henry Scheetz and William Bean, Esquires, Justices, presided—the former being president. To show the spirit of the times, we learn from the records of the court, that one person, for committing two larcenies, was sentenced on the 28th of September, 1785, to receive on his bare back fifteen lashes, well laid on, and on the following 8th of October, the same number, to be repeated for the second offence. "Negro William" was sentenced, at the same time, to receive nineteen lashes.

The court house and jail were both commenced in 1787, and were built of stone. The dimensions of the former were seventy by forty feet, two stories high, and surmounted with a cupola and bell. The stairs were placed on the outside to reach the second story, similar to those of the court house in Philadelphia, and which was common in those days, even with churches and private houses, when two stories high. The cost to the county, for erecting these buildings, was £4,774 11*s.* 9*d.* Of this amount, £1828 19*s.* were received from Philadelphia county, as the share coming to Montgomery from the proceeds of the sale of the old prison there, according to the act of Assembly in establishing the county. The building containing the county offices was not erected till 1791. Several years after, it was enlarged to fifty by thirty-six feet. It is said that Colonel Thomas Craig, who had been an officer in the Revolution, in 1784, and for several years afterwards held at one time the offices of prothonotary and clerk of the several courts.

An act was passed June 14th, 1777, that the elections of Norriton, Providence, as well as several of the adjoining townships, be held at the house of Jacob Wentz, in Worcester township. Previously, the elections of the whole county were held at the inn opposite the State House, in Philadelphia. By the act of 13th of September, 1785, Montgomery county was divided into three election districts. The first comprised the townships of Norriton, Plymouth, Whitpain, Upper Merion, New Providence, Worcester, Skippack and Perkiomen, and were to hold their elections at the court house. They were held there for all these townships till 1797, when the county was divided into five districts, of which Norriton, Providence, Worcester, Plymouth, Whitpain, Upper Merion and Lower Merion continued for some time after to hold their elections at the same place.

Francis Swaine, a resident of the Trappe, while sheriff of the county, on the 12th of April, 1788, executed John Brown, who had been sentenced to death for burglary, and who it appears was an old offender. He was executed in the rear of the jail, on Airy street. This affair, for some time after, was the occasion of considerable controversy, if not excitement, between the sheriff and several citizens of the town. It originated chiefly through the execution having been performed on the highway and in the most public manner. The sheriff, on the other hand, defended himself on the ground that he could not get the permission of any holders of lands in or near the place to permit him, as an officer, to fulfil the due performance of that which was required of him by law. This, it is believed, was the last, if not the first, execution in the present county.

It is time, at this period, that we should have something more to say about the improvements and progress of the town in its early career. In 1790, it contained the court house, jail, four or five inns, eight dwelling houses, mill, school house and a barn—in all, but eighteen buildings. An intelligent lady of near eighty, who was raised in the place and still lives in its vicinity, gave us the following reminiscences: that the town in 1793 contained four taverns —one was the General Washington, then kept by Alexander More, and is the same house now occupied by David Heebner; one was the Rising Sun, kept by Jesse Roberts; and one, the Eagle, kept by a person of the name of Rudolph. There were, at this time, two stores, one of which was kept by John Young. There was not a house then within the present borough below the Montgomery House. She well remembers when shad, herring and rock fish were caught here in abundance, and remembers canoes and flats, on the river, but she has no recollection of batteaux. On one occasion she went with her father to Philadelphia in a canoe, and was considerably frightened in going through the falls this side of Manayunk. In returning with the canoe, at the most difficult places, it had to be poled to stem the current.

On Reading Howell's map of Pennsylvania, published in 1792, this place is marked as "Norristown." Scott, in his U. S. Gazetteer of 1795, speaks of it as then containing about twenty houses, besides the county buildings. An aged gentleman gives us his recollections of the place in 1803. He says it then contained about fifty houses, and that most of them were but one story high, and built of frame or logs. Besides these, were the court house, jail, three taverns, one store and a small school house, two or three lawyers and one doctor. He also informs us that back of Airy street, in the vicinity of the present prison, was the old jail lane, with a stake and rail fence on each side, which was a favorite place for horse-racing and playing bullets; that in the spring and fall, when the condition of the roads became almost impassable, the people hauled tan from the old tan-yard and made walks of it before their doors. Swede street, at this time, was the only road that extended to the river; and that there was a splendid walk along the banks of the river, from the mouth of Stony Creek to Swedes' Ford, which was beautifully shaded with a number of buttonwood and beach trees.

After the county had been formed and the town laid out twenty-seven years, application was made by a number of its citizens to have it incorporated with the rights and privileges of a borough. The act was accordingly passed the 31st of March, 1812, and among its provisions were that the burgess, town council and high constable should be elected annually. The borough, as laid out at this time, was wholly taken from Norriton township, to which it had previously belonged, and contained an area of five hundred and twenty acres, being nearly a mile square. It extended on the river from the mouth of Stony Creek to the Plymouth line, somewhat over a mile. The population of the town, at this time, was probably five hundred, and we know, by the census of 1820, that it then contained but eight hundred and twenty-seven inhabitants, showing a slow growth after being laid out as a town and county-seat thirty-six years. Saw Mill Run, which rises in Whitpain township and is about four miles in length, at this time divided the borough into nearly two equal parts.

The island in the Schuylkill, at this borough, is called Barbadoes, and, though not named, is given with tolerable correctness on Holmes' map of original surveys, made between the years 1682 and 1695. It belonged, from the earliest period, to the manor of Norriton, and, from the records we know that it bore its present name in 1771. It is very probable that this name was given it by Isaac Norris, who, as a merchant, carried on an extensive trade with Barbadoes, one of the British West India Islands, which had been first settled by the English in 1605. In the purchase of the island here, by Colonel Bull, in 1771, mention is made that it was then four hundred perches in length, and at the broadest part sixty perches, and that it contained eighty-eight acres. In the beginning of this century there was a race-course on this island, which was kept up for this purpose many years, and is still in the recollection of some of our oldest citizens. In consequence of the Navigation Company building a dam across the river, below the island, it was the means of considerably reducing its area; and to avoid the expense of litigation, the company purchased it and by whom it is still owned. This island is under cultivation, and contains farm buildings. Immediately below it there was a smaller island, which, by the erection of the dam, has disappeared.

Norristown did not become a manufacturing place till after the completion of the Schuylkill Navigation, when the dam erected here gave an impetus to the business. In 1832 the following manufacturing establishments were here: B. McCredy's cotton mill, of stone, five stories high, containing seven thousand spindles; Mr. Freedley's cotton mill, with nine hundred spindles; and Mr. Jamison's weaving factory, with one hundred and forty-three looms. According to the census of 1840, the business had considerably increased, the three factories having nineteen thousand one hundred and sixty-four spindles, and a dye and print establishment, which, together, manufactured products to the value of $454,958 and employed five hundred hands. Of course, since that time, the business has been considerably extended, and probably at this time they give employment to three times that number.

In consequence of the rapid increase of population, it became necessary to divide the borough into two wards, which was done by an act of Assembly, passed the 8th of February, 1847. The upper ward, in 1849, contained 579 taxables and the lower ward 410, making 989 taxables. Through an additional increase an act was passed in 1852, dividing the borough into three wards, which remain to the present time. In 1858, the upper ward contained 957 taxables; the middle ward, 393; and the lower ward, 604—making a total of 1954 taxables in the borough at that time. On petition of a number of its inhabitants, an act was passed the 26th of March, 1853, to enlarge the area of the borough, which was accordingly done, to its present size. By its extended limits, it is fully one and three-fourths of a mile square, and has an area of about two thousand acres, which was all taken from Norriton township, excepting a small, narrow strip from Plymouth, probably containing one hundred and fifty-eight acres.

The county buildings in this borough are the court house and prison. The old court house and prison, mentioned as having been built here in 1787, were torn down in 1855. The present fine buildings were erected in 1853-6. The court house is one of the finest buildings of the kind in the State, and is built of white marble, procured in the county. It contains the various county offices, and was erected at a cost of $150,000. The prison is situated on Airy street, and is very substantially built, two stories high, and the cells arranged for solitary confinement. Its cost was about $86,000. The Montgomery Cemetery, beyond Stony creek, on the west side of Main street, is a neat affair. Here the dead repose amidst shady lawns, shrubbery and flowers. Another, called the Norris Cemetery, has been recently erected on Swede street, just beyond the borough limits. The lot of ground on which the old court house and public offices stood has, within the last two years, been beautifully laid out in walks, planted with trees and ornamented with a fountain. The streets of Norristown are regularly laid out and generally cross at right angles. Main or Egypt street, beyond Stony Creek, contains a number of handsome residences, and is neatly planted with trees. Swede street, north of the court house, is another pleasant, shady street. Not many towns of equal size excel this in the number of its splendid three and four story private residences. The frequent use of white marble, of late years, as a material for building purposes, has given a neatness to the appearance of the houses and streets that is not generally found elsewhere.

XV.

NORRITON.

The township of Norriton is bounded north by Worcester, north-east by Whitpain, south-east by Plymouth, south by Norristown and the Schuylkill, and west by Lower Providence. Its greatest length is nearly six miles and width three and three-fourths, with a front on the Schuylkill of about two and a-half miles. Its original area was seven thousand four hundred and eighty-two acres, but by the erection of Norristown into a borough, in 1812, five hundred and twenty acres were taken off, which by the act of 1853 was increased to about two thousand acres, thus leaving its present area five thousand five hundred acres.

The surface of Norriton is slightly rolling and the soil is a clay and red shale, which makes its present appearance in this township as we proceed up the Schuylkill. Naturally the soil is much inferior to that of Plymouth, Whitemarsh and Springfield. Now, no more, for future descriptions in this work, need be mentioned the rich lime stone bottoms—the never-failing, copious, chrystal springs—the noble chestnut timber and the vigorous under-brush in woods and thickets, for these will be missed. The best and most fertile lands will be found along the river. The principal streams are Stony creek, Indian creek, Five Mile run and Saw Mill run. They all furnish water power to grist mills, saw mills and clover mills.

Norriton, in 1734, contained twenty land-holders and tenants; in 1741, twenty-five tax-ables; in 1828, two hundred and forty-five; in 1849, three hundred and eighty, and in 1858, three hundred and forty. According to the census of 1810, it contained one thousand three hundred and thirty-six inhabitants; in 1820, one thousand and ninety-eight; in 1830, one thousand one hundred and thirty-nine; in 1840, one thousand four hundred and eleven; and in 1850, one thousand five hundred and ninety-four. The population was somewhat decreased by the erection of Norristown, in 1812, and its enlargement, in 1853. By the triennial assessment of 1858, the real estate was valued at $359,105, and the horses and neat cattle, $18,215. The census of 1850 gave the township two hundred and eighty-six houses and one hundred and forty-eight farms. In May, 1858, it contained four inns, four stores, six grist mills, two saw mills, two clover mills and one plaster mill. Two turnpike roads pass through Norriton. The German-town and Perkiomen, but better known as the Reading pike, has a course of four miles, being the entire width of the township. The Ridge pike traverses it about two miles. Since the borough extension, there are no manufactories, excepting those mentioned. There are some well improved and cultivated farms in Norriton. Its villages are Jeffersonville, Norritonville, Penn Square, Port Indian and Springtown. At the first three named places are post-offices. The public schools are five in number, and for the school year ending with June 1st, 1857, were eight months open and attended by two hundred and seventy-seven scholars. The sum of $1,411 was levied to defray the expenses of the same.

Jeffersonville is the largest village in the township and is situated on the Ridge turn-pike, two miles above Norristown and eighteen and a-half from Philadelphia. It contains an inn, store, a two story stone school-house and a blacksmith and wheelwright shop, and thir-teen houses. The elections of the township are held here and at Penn Square, alternately. The post-office was established in January, 1829. In 1832 it contained a tavern, store and six or eight dwellings. A quarter of a mile below this village on the pike by the toll-gate are eight houses. About half a mile above Jeffersonville the Presbyterians have a two story stone church, erected about twelve years ago.

Norritonville is situated on the Germantown and Perkiomen turnpike, eighteen miles from Philadelphia. It contains a church, school house, post office, blacksmith and wheelwright shop, and twelve houses. The church here is under the charge of trustees and is free to all denominations, several of whom hold worship in it alternately.

The village of Penn Square is situated at the intersection of the State road, leading from Doylestown to Norristown, and the German-town and Perkiomen turnpike. It is two miles northeast of Norristown and sixteen and a-half from Philadelphia. It contains an inn, store, post-office, school house and a blacksmith and wheelwright shop, and eleven houses. The school-house is a two story stone building, erected in 1847, the upper story of which is used for public meetings, lectures and debates. This village has considerably improved within the last twelve years.

Springtown is situated on the Germantown and Perkiomen turnpike, about half a mile be-low Penn Square, and contains an inn and seven houses. Here are the exhibition grounds of the Montgomery County Agricultural Society, in the centre of which is a handsome large two story frame building, for the display of vegeta-bles and manufactures. There are also on the grounds extensive sheds for horses and cattle. This society was started in 1847, but did not exhibit here, we believe, till several years afterwards. It is said that it originated with six farmers, who met in a small room in this township, and of whom three are still living. Their object was, by this means, to further ad-vance the agricultural interests of the county. Little did they then think that from that germ should spring such a noble and expanded institution, whose grounds and buildings would cover twelve acres, and be witnessed with gratifying interest annually by thousands of persons. The present officers are William B. Roberts, president, and George F. Roberts, secretary.

Port Indian is situated on the Schuylkill, at the mouth of Indian creek. It contains a grist mill, two lumber yards and six houses. In this vicinity are several fertile and well-improved farms. Indian creek has its source in Lower Providence township, is about two miles in length, and propels, in Norriton, two grist mills and a saw mill.

The oldest house of worship now standing in the county—if we except the Lower Merion meeting-house—is undoubtedly the Presbyterian church on the Germantown and Perkiomen turnpike, about three miles northeast of Norristown. We judge, both from the style and architecture of this building, that it must have been erected previous to 1740, which is the year of the earliest date found on the tombstones. This church is a small one-story stone building, and from its appearance has undergone no material alteration since its erection. The grave-yard comprises about a quarter of an acre of ground and contains a number of handsome tombstones. The most common names found on the stones are Armstrong, Hoowen, Smith, McCrea, Bryant, White, Christey, Hanna, Freeman, Porter, Trump, Thompson, Zeigler, Stuwart, Darrah, Burns, Richards, Curry, Patterson, Dunn, Stroud, McGlathery and Fitzwater. The oldest stone informs us of the death of Joseph Armstong, who died April 29th, 1740, aged four years. Among the patriots of the Revolution, reposing here, may be mentioned Col. Archibald Thompson, who died on November 1st, 1779, aged thirty-nine years, and Col. Christopher Stuart, who died May 27th, 1799, aged fifty-one. In the Revolution, it is said, this church was considerably injured, by the soldiers using it as quarters. There is a tradition in the neighborhood that a man at that time was killed in it, and that his blood stains may be still seen on the floor. There was formerly a superstitious belief that the shutters of a certain window could not be kept shut and a certain pane of glass stay whole. In consequence of the damages this church suffered through the war, the Assembly passed an act the 17th of September, 1785, permitting money to be raised by means of a lottery for repairing the same. Between the years 1781 and 1810, the time of his decease, the Rev. William M. Tennent, of Abington, occasionally preached here, at stated times. Both the church and grave-yard are now considerably dilapidated and need repair; and neither, we believe, has been used by the congregation for a long time. There is here a cross-roads, three houses and a blacksmith and wheelwright shop. A short distance east of this church lived for many years the celebrated philosopher, David Rittenhouse, of whom a biographical sketch is given in the appendix.

As the early history of both Norristown and Norriton are so much identified till their separation, in 1812, is our apology for omitting here a number of particulars which may be found under the former head. The "Mannor of Williamstadt" is marked on Thomas Holmes' map of original surveys, with the same extent as the present township before 1812. William Penn, the proprietary and governor of Pennsylvania, by a patent dated October 2d, 1704, granted to his son, William Penn, Jr., a tract of land on the Schuylkill, containing seven thousand four hundred and eighty-two acres, called in said patent the manor of Williamstadt. This spendthrift son, but five days afterwards, sold the same to Isaac Norris and William Trent, both distinguished merchants of Philadelphia, for the sum of £850, or of our present currency, $2,266 61. On the 11th of January, 1712, Isaac Norris purchased all William Trent's right to the same for the sum of £500.

The bounds of the manor, in this latter conveyance, are thus set forth: "Beginning at a hickory by the said Skoolkill, being the corner of Plymouth township, thence northeast by the same township nine hundred and fifty perches to another hickory, thence northwest in the line of a tract of land called Whitpain's township, eleven hundred and sixty-nine perches, to a corner oak in the line of the said Proprietary's Manor of Gilberts, thence southwest along the said Manor line eighteen hundred and forty-eight perches to a dog tree by the said river Skoolkill, thence down the same river on the several courses thereof to the place of beginning."

By the year 1730, it appears, the population had sufficiently increased within the manor for them to apply to the Court of Quarter Sessions of Philadelphia county to erect Norriton into a township, which was granted, with the same extent and boundaries already given. The landholders that resided here in 1734 were Aaron Roberts, Job Pugh, Jesse Pugh, Ellis Roberts, John Hatfield, Bartle Bartlestol, Thomas Warner, Joseph Armstrong, William Hays, Nicholas Robinson, John Eastburn, John Coulston, Samuel Evans, Henry Johnson and Evan Hughs. Francis Meheny, Robert Roger, Robert Shannon, Charles Morris and William Robinson, tenants—making in all, at this time, twenty landholders and tenants in the township. Isaac Norris died near Philadelphia, in the beginning of June, 1735, and it appears made his will the 17th of January, 1731, by which he appointed his wife, Mary, and sons, Isaac, Charles and Samuel, executors. Isaac Norris, previous to his death, sold off several small portions to most of the aforesaid settlers, amounting to about seventeen hundred and twenty acres. Though afterwards the family retained possession of the estate, they still occasionally kept selling off tract after tract, as the township increased in population. On the 16th of November, 1738, they sold one hundred acres to Cadwallader Evans, who, in 1748, sold the same to Dennes Conrod.

XVI.

LOWER PROVIDENCE.

The township of Lower Providence is bounded northeast by Perkiomen and Worcester, southeast by Norriton, south by the river Schuylkill, and west by the Perkiomen creek, which separates it from Upper Providence. Its greatest length is five and a-half miles, and greatest width five, with an area of nine thousand one hundred and forty-three acres. The surface of the country is gently undulating, and the land slopes quite gradually from the Schuylkill and Perkiomen, with no elevations along those streams worthy of notice. Methacton hill commences near the east corner of this township and extends into Worcester, nearly to the Wissahickon creek. It is about six miles long and runs in a northeasterly direction. It is of considerable elevation and is mostly under cultivation—the greater portion of the timber having been cut off. The soil on it is not naturally fertile, being a light-colored clay. On Scull's map of 1770 it is called Matateken, and in a dispatch of 1777, Metuchen. It is sometimes called Methatchen, and is an Indian name. The soil of this township is generally a red shale, and along the Schuylkill and Perkiomen is very productive.

Besides the Perkiomen, which forms the western boundary of the township, it is watered by the Skippack creek and Mine run, both branches of the former stream. The Skippack has its source in Franconia township, a few yards from the Bucks county line. Its principal branches are Little Branch, Towamencin and Zachariah creeks. It is about seventeen miles in length, and is remarkable for flowing in a straight southwest course nearly its whole distance. It is a very sluggish-looking stream, of very little current, and appears almost to be a succession of pools, yet at times is subject to high freshets. The water is never clear, but turbid, and is tinged with a yellowish red color. According to Heckewelder, Skippack is an Indian name, signifying a stagnant stream or pool of water. The earliest mention we have found of this stream is in 1734. It is also called by this name on Lewis Evan's map of 1749, and on Scull's of 1770. The Perkiomen, in this township, propels four grist mills, and the Skippack, two. Mine run rises near Methacton hill and is over three miles in length, but furnishes no water power, and empties into the Perkiomen below Shannonville.

Lower Providence is rich in mineralogical specimens. The greater portion of the township is occupied by the red shales and sandstones of the middle secondary formation, among which are found a variety of minerals. Not far from the mouth of the Perkiomen lead mines have been wrought, at times, for many years, but never, we believe, with much profit. Scott, in his Geography, speaks of this lead mine having been discovered in the year 1800, and we know it was worked by Mr. Wetherill before 1818. It appears that through working the lead mines copper was first discovered. In January, 1848, several gentlemen associated together as the "Perkiomen Mining Association," and purchased a considerable tract of land, lying between the Perkiomen and Shannonville, for $10,000, with the intention of working for copper. By the close of 1849, they had a twenty-five horse power engine in operation for pumping out water and for raising, washing and breaking the ore. At this time, also, they had sent one thousand four hundred tons of copper to market, and in procuring it had sunk a perpendicular shaft five hundred and eighty-five feet deep, with side-drifts of one thousand four hundred and one feet, making the whole length of work in the mine one thousand nine hundred and eighty-six feet, or over the third of a mile. The 20th of August, 1858, we paid a brief visit to this mine. We were told that but five hands were then working it, and that they were under the charge of a Mr. Wheatley, of New York. These copper works are about a quarter of a mile northwest of Shannonville; and four steam engines have been erected in as many large buildings for the purposes of pumping out water from the shafts and raising and washing the ore. A considerable amount of money must have been expended here, especially in machinery, which has been built on a large scale. Both the works and machinery show that they have not been used evidently for some time, and we have not a doubt that more money has been sunk by the operation than the value of the copper raised. Several shafts have been worked to the depth of four or five hundred feet. Close to these works a small stream flows by and empties into the Perkiomen, and is, in consequence, called Mine run. The lead mine, we have been informed, has not been worked for over thirty years past. The copper obtained here, it is said, yielded, on an average, twenty-two per cent. of pure metal. In and around these mines have been procured the following interesting mineralogical specimens: carbonate of copper, in minute chrystals and in very small quantities, of a beautiful dark blue color; also, green carbonate of copper, red oxide of copper, copper pyrites, sulphate of iron, scaly red oxide of iron or red iron froth, arsenical pyrites of iron, galena or sulphuret of lead, carbonate of lead, sulphate of lead, molydate or yellow lead, phosphate of lead, brown and green lead, blende or sulphuret of zinc and sulphate of barytes—certainly a goodly variety of specimens, some of which were exceedingly beautiful and several rare.

As Lower Providence was separated from Upper Providence in 1805, and having previously been one township, called Providence, it will therefore be impossible for us to give to each, before that time, the number of early landholders, tenants and taxables, as heretofore. The two present townships in 1734 had 74 landholders and tenants, and in 1741, 146 taxables—showing a considerable population for that early period. According to the census of 1810, Lower Providence contained 904 inhabitants; in 1820, 1146; in 1830, 1193; in 1840, 1413; and in 1850, 1961. It contained, in 1828, 237 taxables; in 1849, 434; and in 1858, 401. By the triennial assessment of 1858, the real estate of this township was valued at $411,560, and the horses and cattle, $22,982. The census of 1850 gives three hundred and thirteen houses and one hundred and sixty-four farms. In May, 1858, it contained three inns, six stores and six grist mills. The Germantown and Perkiomen turnpike traverses the township a distance of two miles. The Ridge pike crosses its whole width of about five miles. Both these roads connect at the Perkiomen bridge. Within the limits of Lower Providence, two bridges cross the Perkiomen, and one the Schuylkill. The public schools are seven in number, and for the school year ending with June 1st, 1857, were open seven months and were attended by three hundred and ninety-three scholars. The sum of $1,779 was levied to defray the expenses of the same. The villages of Lower Providence are Shannonville, Eagleville, Evansburg and Providence Square. At the first two places are post-offices.

Evansburg is the largest village in the township and is situated on the Germantown and Perkiomen turnpike, one mile from the Perkiomen bridge, seven from Norristown, and twenty-three from Philadelphia. It contains two churches, a two story stone school house, grist mill, store, blacksmith and wheelwright shop, and thirty-two houses. At the lower end of the place the pike crosses the Skippack creek by a substantial stone bridge, built by the county in 1792. The Methodist church is a one story stone building, erected in 1841. Of the Episcopal church an account will be given hereafter. This village is a very old place, having been settled at a very early period by Welsh Episcopalians, among whom can be mentioned the Beans, Evans, Shannons, Lanes, Pawlings and others. In 1832 it contained nineteen dwellings, and since has considerably improved. Sherman Day, who was here in 1841 gives, in his "Collections," the following account of one of its residents.

"Jesse Beans, Esq., who is still living in the village, about eighty years of age, was a boy at the time of the Germantown battle. He well remembers the dismay that prevailed the night after the battle, when the fugitives were quartered in every house. The old gentleman is one of the most active men in the place, and in 1841 was performing the arduous duty of a superintendent of the turnpike." There is a fertile and well cultivated country in this vicinity. At its lower end, on the west side of the pike, near Skippack creek, stood, for a long time, what was called Funk's Menonist meeting house, which was a small one story stone church, and was torn down several years ago. The grave yard, which is quite small, still remains, and is enclosed by a stone wall. The most common names on the tombstones are Funk, Gotwals, Detweiler, Croll and Keiter. The earliest date found on a stone is that of 1815.

Shannonville is five miles distant from Norristown, and contains an inn, two stores, a post-office, church, school-house, two smith shops and twenty-four houses. The Union church, as it is generally called, is a one story stone building with a steeple. It is now only used as a house of worship by the Episcopalians, under the charge of the Rev. G. Mintzer, of Evansburg. Robert Shannon, of Norriton township, is the only person of the name in our list of 1734. He was a native of Wales, where he was born in 1667, and came early with his family to this country, where he settled. He died July 15th, 1747, in his eightieth year, and was buried at St. James' church, at Evansburg. There was a John Shannon, who died in 1771, aged fifty-eight years, and is buried at the same place. This village received its name from the descendants of this family. About three-fourths of a mile from this place is the lower bridge over the Perkiomen. It is of frame, covered, resting on one stone pier, and is over two hundred feet in length, between the abutments, and twenty-two feet wide. It was built by the county and is one and a-half miles from the mouth of the stream.

Eagleville is situated on the Ridge turnpike, four and a-half miles from Norristown and twenty-one from Philadelphia. It contains one hotel, which is a large and well-kept house, a store, post-office, smith shop and ten houses. The elections of the township are held here.

Providence Square is on the Germantown and Perkiomen turnpike, nearly a mile below Evansburg, and on the line of Worcester township. It contains a store, school-house, blacksmith and wheelwright shop, and five houses. At the south end of the Perkiomen bridge is a store, tin-ware factory and four houses. Here the Germantown and Perkiomen and Ridge turnpikes meet.

Pawling's bridge, over the Schuylkill, is situated a mile above Valley Forge, and a road leads direct to it from Shannonville, from whence it is two and a-half miles, and which passes through the centre of the Wetherill manor. The company that erected this bridge was incorporated April 3d, 1809. The bridge was destroyed by ice in a high freshet, in 1820, and was shortly afterwards rebuilt. Near this bridge was Pawling's ford, well known in colonial days.

The Saint James Episcopal church, at Evansburg, was the first house of worship erected in Lower Providence. It is a large one story stone edifice, with a tower at the west end, which is without a spire. The church yard comprises over an acre of ground, on which are preserved a number of ancient oaks of the forest. Opposite is the old grave-yard, which contains about the fourth of an acre, enclosed by a wall, and nicely laid with sod and planted with shrubbery and trees—the whole bearing evidence of taste and management. There are some elegant tombstones here. The most common family names on them are Clay, Tyson, Casselberry, Evans, Christman, Burr, Shupe, Hallman, Rhoades, Saylor, Munshower, Fry, Force, Deeds, Dill, Boyce, Nungesser, Coffey, Fronefield, Reed, Dewees, Custer, Pugh, Hobson, Bringhurst, Skeen, High, Assheton, Gray, Coates, Davis, Markley, Lane, Gouldy, Bean, Keel, Jacobs, Morton, Church, Shannon, Pawling, Lewis, Vanderslice, Rambo, Prizer, Harwood, Wilson, Jones, St. Clair, Wolmer, Fox, Moore, Newberry, Prevost, Bate, Yorke and Robeson. The oldest stone containing an inscription is that of a person who died November 24th, 1723, aged forty-six years. It is extremely difficult to decipher and appears to be a mixture of English and German. The next is "In Memory of Humphrey Bate, who departed this life September 3d, 1727," aged nearly sixty years. There is on a stone the following brief announcement of an officer of the Revolution: "In Memory of Capt. Vachel

D. Howard, of Maryland Light Dragoons, who departed this life March 15th, 1778, aged 30 years, in defence of American Liberty." The Rev. Slater Clay, who died in 1821, and was for nearly thirty-five years the pastor of this church, is buried here. The Rev. Evan Evans, a native of Wales and a missionary of the Church of England, came to Pennsylvania about the year 1699 to visit the Episcopal congregations—especially those of his countrymen, and to establish churches among them. It appears that Mr. Evans met with tolerable success, and, with others, succeeded in collecting a congregation for worship, between the years 1708 and 1714, of which he says that many persons "became attached to the Episcopal Church, were baptized and committed to her Communion." About the year 1715 he went to England, but returned in 1716 and took charge of Christ church, Philadelphia, till the close of 1717, when he went to Maryland. In 1721 the congregation had sufficiently increased here that a church was built, of which James Shannon and Isaac Pawling were appointed church-wardens. The church was incorporated under an act of October 3d, 1788. In 1843 the old church was torn down to make room for the present commodious edifice, more suitable to the wants of an increasing congregation. The Rev. G. Mintzer is its present pastor.

The Providence Presbyterian church is situated on the Ridge turnpike, four miles above Norristown, and on the southwest end of Methacton hill. It is a large one story stone building. From the church yard a fine view is obtained in a southwest direction. The Rev. Henry S. Rodenbaugh is its present pastor and has a large congregation. The grave-yard covers an acre of ground and contains a number of handsome tombstones. The most common names here are Bowyer, Todd, Hamill, Knox, Hallowell, Crawford, Morgan, Major, Batt, Francis, Hamilton, Logan, Lyons, Sloat, Mongo, Adams, Chesnut, Cambell, Chain, Vanfossen, Kirkpatrick, Burnside, Vanderslice, Armstrong, Brown, Baker, Roberts, Umstead, Horning, Curry, Barnett, Porter, Bodley, Morris, Teany, Highly, Shambaugh, Cowden, Wilson, Zeiber, Barton, Getty, Shepherd, Detweiler, Foust, Wills, Henry, McEwen, Dehaven, Carson, Beck and Shearer. This church was founded in 1730 and rebuilt in 1844. It appears that the Rev. William M. Tennent, of Abington, preached here and at Norriton at stated times, between the year 1781 and 1810. The earliest tombstone containing a date is that of 1750. In the lower end of the yard is a tomb of white marble on which is an inscription to the "Memory of Mrs. Elizabeth Porter, widow of the late General Andrew Porter, who died May 18th, 1821, aged 69 years and 9 months." This lady was the mother of two Governors and a President Judge.

The Baptists have a meeting-house on the Ridge turnpike, about half a mile above Eagleville. It is a one story stone building, erected in 1836, and the Rev. David Jeffrey is its present pastor. It has a high situation and a splendid view is obtained from the church-yard, particularly in an east and southeast direction, among which can be seen the Oley hills, in Berks county. It is surrounded by a number of shade trees, which, we regret to say, are often found wanting at such places. The grave-yard comprises nearly an acre of ground and is enclosed by a newly erected stone wall. The family names on the tombstones are Sisler, Morgan, Baker, Fimple, Trites, Rees, Strawbridge, Brumback, Miller, Grigg, Kurtz, Johnson, Munshower, Casselberry, Funk, Zimmerman, Custer, Reiner, Norris, Umstead, Dau, Roberts, Philips, Davis, Jones, Pennepacker, Hughs and Allen. As some of these stones date back to 1816, it appears as if the grave-yard had been here some time before the erection of the present building.

How the name of Providence became applied originally to the two townships is not easily ascertained. We know they were so called as early as 1734. Perhaps it was derived from Roger Williams' settlement, in Rhode Island, which he had so called in 1636. From Holmes' map of original surveys and early records we learn that these two townships, before 1712, were called the "Proprietary's Manor of Gilberts." Penn very probably gave this name of Gilberts in honor of his mother's family, who were of this name.

Providence was settled at an early period, for in 1734 it contained seventy-four land owners and tenants, whose names were as follows:—Caspar Stull, John Bideler, Derick Rumsawer, Aubery Richardson, Edward Richardson, James Hamer, Conrad Rupel, Thomas Wyatt, Thomas Valuntine, Samuel Lane, John Jacobs, Adam Hammer, Arnold Francis, Thomas Morgan, Morris Lewis, Henry Pawling, Philip Fasset, Robert Dunn, Woodrick Myor, Conrad

Knoos, Conrad Steine, Catharine Castleberry, Derick Castleberry, Daniel Rees, Edward Roberts, Arnold Hancock, Lewis Morgan, Thomas David, John Deemer, Stephen Bowyer, Paul Castleberry, John Morris, John Bull, George Phillips, John Lewis, Wm. Lane, Richard Adams, Isaac Adams, Philip Cheadle, Peter Rambo, Abraham Adams, John Pierce, David Phillips, John Wyatt, Mathias Coplin, Wm. Adams, Jacob Shrack, Harman Indehaven, Jacob Miller, Jacob Pobulus, Richard Jones, Hanical Crisman, John Hanpull, Anthony Vandersluice, John Hendrick, Henry Hooven, Francis Plum, Bastian Miller, Thomas Howe, Daniel Longacre, Lewis David, John George Wagemill, Roger North, Daniel Dismond, Henry Jones, Joseph Wills, George Burston, Thomas Roseter, Henry Holstein, John Edwards, Thomas James, Evan Pugh, Benj. Walkins, and John Colling. The seven last were tenants.

The Pawling family of this township, and after whom Pawling's ford was called, appears from an early time to have been conspicuous in the history of the county. Isaac Pawling was one of the wardens in 1721 of St. James' Church, at Evansburg. Henry Pawling, sr., in 1734, owned 500 acres of land opposite Valley Forge, in the present Wetherill manor, where he resided. His son Henry owned at the same time 1200 acres in Perkiomen township. In February, 1747, he was elected a captain of a company of Associaters, and in October, 1751, a member of Assembly from Philadelphia county. In 1761 he was appointed one of the commissioners for improving the navigation of the Schuylkill. Henry Pawling, jr., was appointed by the act of Sept. 10th, 1784, a commissioner for laying out the present county, and locating the county seat and buildings. Nathan Pawling was sheriff of the county in 1795. Henry Pawling, Esq., lived on his estate during the revolution, and which we believe the family retained down to the beginning of the present century.

Fatland ford is in this township, a short distance below Valley Forge, on the present property of Dr. Wm. Wetherill, It was here, on the night of September, 22d, 1777, where the British army crossed the Schuylkill on their march to Philadelphia, which they entered on the 26th. Washington at this time was near Pottsgrove, thirty-six miles from the city. In their passage here they drove a scouting party of the American light infantry for some distance, but who the following night encamped at the Trappe.

By a petition of the citizens of Providence to the Court of Quarter Sessions of Montgomery county, leave was granted in November, 1805, to have the same divided into two separate townships, making the Perkiomen creek the division line. This was accordingly done, and to which Upper and Lower Providence owe their origin.

Wm. Bakewell, a wealthy English gentleman, purchased in the beginning of this century the large farm that had formerly been in possession of the Pawling family at Fatland ford. He was a man of extensive scientific acquirements, and was a brother of the celebrated sheep raiser of the same name. He made on his farm valuable improvements, and had among the rest a valuable library and philosophical apparatus. He was an intimate acquaintance of the distinguished Joseph Priestley, and through him no doubt became interested in philosophic investigations. Mr. Bakewell died here in 1822. The family consisted of his wife Rebecca, and children Wm. Gifford, Thomas Woodhouse, Lucy, Eliza, Sarah and Ann. John J. Audubon, the celebrated ornithologist, resided for a number of years on the adjacent farm belonging to his father, and through this circumstance became acquainted with Mr. Bakewell and. his family, and was married about 1806 to Lucy, his eldest daughter. In 1810 Mr. Audubon removed to Louisville, Kentucky, where he engaged in mercantile pursuits, and the Bakewell family subsequently followed him in 1823. A biographical sketch of Mr. Audubon is given in the appendix. Both Mr. Bakewell's and Audubon's properties are now comprised in the extensive estates, belonging to Dr. Wm. Wetherill and his brother, the late John Price Wetherill, containing together nearly nine hundred acres.

XVII.

UPPER PROVIDENCE.

The township of Upper Providence is bounded on the northeast by Perkiomen, east by Lower Providence, from which it is separated by the Perkiomen creek, southwest by the Schuylkill, and northwest by Limerick. Its greatest length is nearly six miles, and breadth five, with an area of twelve thousand and ninety-five acres. The surface of the township is rolling and the soil red shale. The most productive land is in the vicinity of the Perkiomen and Schuylkill below Black Rock. Above the latter place to the Limerick line the country may be regarded as hilly, the greatest elevation being the Black Rock Hill, situated on the Schuylkill, about half a mile above Quincyville, which attains a height of about one hundred feet perpendicular. With this exception the land rises gradually from the river. This hill has given a name to the dam near by, which was erected by the Navigation company for the purpose of feeding the canal.

The Perkiomen creek is the largest stream in Montgomery county, and rises by two branches in Lower Milford township, Lehigh county. Following its meanderings is nearly thirty miles in length, and with its tributaries waters half the area of the county. Its general course is south and receives the following streams :—West Branch, Macoby, Deep, Swamp, North East Branch, Great Swamp and Skippack creeks. Where it empties into the Schuylkill the country is rather level and is subject to great freshets. Perkiomen is an Indian name, and, according to Zeisberger, signified, in their language, "where the cranberries grow." The earliest mention of this stream is in Penn's deed of purchase in 1684, where it is called "Pahkehoma;" on Holmes' map of original surveys "Perquamink," and on Lewis Evans' map of 1749, "Perkiomy." By the latter name it is still called by the German inhabitants of the county. Mingo creek rises in Limerick township and after a course of about six miles empties into the Schuylkill. Its stream is weak, but subject to considerable freshets, and at its mouth the Reading railroad crosses on a stone bridge of two arches fifteen feet high. A few yards above the road crosses it also by a two-arched stone bridge, built by the county in 1847. Here is a large grist and saw-mill, and Wissimer's ford near by across the Schuylkill. This creek propels two grist-mills and one saw-mill, all in this township. A small stream rises near the Trappe and empties into the Perkiomen, which propels a grist and saw-mill.

As previous to the year 1805 this township was connected with Lower Providence, we must refer the reader to that head for any information we may have been enabled to procure relative to statistics. According to the census of 1810, Upper Providence contained 1395 inhabitants; in 1820, 1670; in 1830, 1682; in 1840, 2244; and in 1850, 2457. In 1828 it contained 326 taxables; in 1849, 567; and in 1858, 591. By the triennial assessment of 1858 the real estate was valued at $462,230, and the horses and neat cattle, $36,455. The census of 1850 gave four hundred and twenty-four houses and one hundred and ninety-six farms in the township. In May, 1858, it contained eight inns, eight stores, four grist-mills, three saw-mills and two coal yards. For the school year ending with June 1st, 1858, it contained eleven schools, open six months, and attended by seven hundred and ten scholars. The sum of $2,865 was levied to defray the expenses of the same. There are, besides, three large private schools, which will be described hereafter. The villages are the Trappe, Port Providence, Perkiomen Bridge or Freeland and Quincyville. The first three contain post offices. The Reading turnpike passes through Upper Providence a distance of three and a-half miles. Within its limits are two bridges over the Schuylkill and the same number over the Perkiomen.

The largest as well as the most ancient village of Upper Providence township is the Trappe; and, as it is a place rich in historical associations, we have concluded to defer a further account till the next article. The second in size is Port Providence, situated on the east side of the Schuylkill, a mile below the borough of Phœnixville. It contains one hotel, store, school-house, post-office, a hall, in which the Methodists hold worship, and thirty-four houses. Hammond's axe factory is an extensive building between the canal and river, and was propelled by steam, but has not been in operation for nearly two years. Samuel L. Hall has a boat-yard, established in 1855, for repairing canal boats. For this purpose he has a dry dock adjoining the canal. There are in this village several fine brick houses. Between this place and the lower bridge on the Perkiomen are some very fine farms with good buildings, among which we observed barns containing two threshing floors.

Freeland or Perkiomen Bridge is situated on the Reading turnpike, seven miles from Norristown. It contains two hotels, a store, post-office, church, Pennsylvania Female College, Freeland Seminary, public school house, grist mill, carriage manufactory, blacksmith shop, and twenty-six houses. The Pennsylvania Female College was established in 1851 and incorporated by an act of Assembly in 1853, of which J. W. Sunderland, L. L., D., is president. It is a large four story building, and a large number of young ladies have been educated here. Near by is the Freeland Seminary for young men and boys, of which Henry A. Hunsicker is principal. The Christian or Menonite church was built in 1854, and is a handsome one story building. There are several fine three story dwellings in this village, and the country in the vicinity is rolling, fertile and well cultivated. On Scull's map of Pennsylvania, published in 1770, there are two inns marked at this place—one at the present bridge called "Lanes," and farther up the road to Reading, the "Duke of Cumberland." The bridge over the Perkiomen, at this place, is a noble structure for its day, and was built by the county at an expense of $60,000. It is made entirely of stone and has six arches, and was begun in 1798 and finished the following year. The county commissioners at this time were Frederick Conrad, Samuel Mauldsby, Conrad Boyer, James Bean and Henry Sheetz. It is about five miles from the mouth of the creek, which is here one hundred feet in width. By an act of February 21st, 1797, the sum of $20,000 was permitted to be raised by lottery towards beginning this enterprise. Another act, of March 28th, 1799, allowed the commissioners to raise sufficient money by toll for its completion. From the Journal of the Rev. H. M. Muhlenberg we learn that during the Revolution there was no bridge here nor over the Skippack creek on the Reading road. Four turnpike roads at present meet at this bridge, the first of which was commenced in 1801.

Quincyville is situated on the Schuylkill, opposite Phœnixville. It contains an inn, store, steam saw mill, lumber yard, and seventeen houses. There was formerly an iron foundry and machine shop here, which has been converted into a paper-mill, and is now carried on by Joseph Jordine. There was also a post office here, which was discontinued in the spring of 1858. The bridge across the Schuylkill was incorporated in 1844. The school house is situated half a mile east of the village.

A mile from the mouth of the Perkiomen and half a mile from the Schuylkill is a small village, which, in consequence of a large pine tree (over six feet in circumference) standing at the corner of the meeting house, has received the name of the Green Tree. It contains six houses, a school-house, smith-shop, and, till recently, a tannery. The Dunkard meeting house, here, was erected about ten years ago, and is a large one story stone building. The presiding elder of it is John H. Omstead, and it numbers about two hundred communicants. In the summer of 1858 the grave-yard was enlarged. The most common names on the tombstones are Bean, Umstead, Gotwals, Keyser, Shunk, Oberholzer, Davis, Dettra, Schrauger, Rodda, Miller, Walt and Schrack. Half a mile from this place and about a mile below Port Providence is a large island in the Schuylkill, which is cultivated and belongs to Mr. Omstead.

About one and a-half miles northeast of Port Providence is the Friends' meeting house—a small one story stone building, with a graveyard, both considerably dilapidated. It is shaded by several fine and venerable buttonwood trees. We know, by Scull's map of 1770, that there was a meeting house here before that time: the present one was erected in 1828. We were informed of the following names of families belonging to this meeting: Ambler, Tyson, Hopkins, Rogers, Taylor and Barnet. The land between this meeting-house and Quincyville appears to be of inferior quality, the soil being a light-colored clay, and the stone approaching a dark-colored slate.

Near the banks of the Perkiomen and about two miles south of the Trappe, at the intersection of two roads, is the Menonist meeting-house, a small one story stone building, with a school-house attached. Henry Johnson, we believe, is the principal preacher of the congregation. The most common names on the tombstones are Kolb, Johnson, Ashenfelter, Kindy, Kepner, Reiner, Landis, Wair, Horning, Shoalter, Rittenhouse, Bean, Alderfer, Rosenberger, Hallman, Wismer, Tyson, Buckwalter, Hunsicker, Godshall, Bechtel, Detweiler and Kratz. From the Journal of the Rev. H. M. Muhlenberg we learn that when he first came to the Trappe, in 1742, there were but two houses of worship in Providence—one was the Episcopal church, at Evansburg, and the other at this place. There is an old grave-yard in this township, near the Schuylkill and Limerick line, which contains a number of tombstones, on which are the names of Rambo, Dismant, Tyson, Stahl, and others. It is generally called Dismant's grave yard.

The Poor House of Montgomery county is situated on the east bank of the Schuylkill, in this township, and is ten miles above Norristown and three southwest of the Trappe. There are three commodious buildings: one is used by the steward and male paupers, one by the females and children, and one is a hospital for the sick and insane. In January, 1832, it contained one hundred and ten paupers; in January, 1849, one hundred and ninety-eight; and in January, 1858, two hundred and thirty-three. The farm comprises two hundred and sixty-five acres of ground, of which thirty are wood sufficient to furnish the place with fuel and fencing. For the year 1857 the produce sold from the place amounted to $1059 78, and the expenses, $13,290 33. The land of the farm is quite rolling, and appears to be under better cultivation than some of the adjoining farms. This institution was established according to an act of Assembly passed the 10th March, 1806, and subsequent acts of January 26th, 1807, and December 22d, 1810. The government of the entire place is under the complete control of three directors, one of whom is elected every year. They appoint all officers of the institution, viz: stewards, matrons, clerks, physicians, &c., &c. They are required by law to meet at least every month at the place and to see to the proper regulations of the same. On the first Monday of January, of every year, the directors, county auditors and treasurer, meet here to adjust and make out the accounts of the previous year. The expenses of this place are met by funds raised by tax levied by the county commissioners on requisition of the directors and disbursed by the county treasurer by their order.

A short distance above the Poor House, the Reading railroad crosses to this side of Schuylkill by a splendid stone bridge of four arches, each of seventy-two feet span, and, with the ice-breakers, cost $47,000. Opposite this bridge the railroad passes through a tunnel of solid rock one thousand nine hundred and thirty-four feet in length, or over one-third of a mile.

This township, with Lower Providence, was originally called the "Manor of Gilberts," in which Thomas Penn, in 1738, owned three thousand two hundred acres, valued at £2,240, or, of our present currency, $5,972. The aforesaid was the son of William Penn, and after his father's death was the chief proprietary of Pennsylvania. By order of the Court of Quarter Sessions, in November, 1805, Upper and Lower Providence were erected into separate townships. Before this time, it was known as Providence township, for the settlers of which, for the year 1734, see Lower Providence. Together, in 1741, they contained one hundred and forty-six taxables.

XVIII.

THE TRAPPE.

The ancient village of the Trappe, so rich in historical associations and the birth place of several distinguished men, is situated in Upper Providence township on the Reading turnpike, eight miles from Norristown, twenty-five from Philadelphia, and twenty-six from Reading. Its situation is high and healthy and the land descends gradually in every direction. The houses are chiefly confined to a single street on the pike, and the village is said to extend to the toll-gate, which is regarded as its southern limits; from thence to the Perkiomen bridge, being included in the village of Freeland. The Trappe contains two inns, three stores, three churches, the Washington Hall Seminary, a post-office, library, school-house, Odd Fellows' hall, tannery, brickyard, cabinet, wheelright and blacksmith shops, and about forty houses. Washington Hall is situated in the centre of the village, and is a seminary for the education of young men and ladies. It was established in 1830, and Abel Rambo, A. M., is its present principal. The library is kept in this building, and contains over four hundred volumes. The German Methodists have a one story brick church, erected in 1851, and stands a short distance back from the old Trappe church. The Odd Fellows' Hall is a large two story stone building erected in 1849. A handsome omnibus runs daily on the pike, from this village to Norristown, where a connection is made with the railroad. The Hon. Jacob Fry, late member of Congress, and at present Auditor General of Pennsylvania, is a resident of the place.

One of the first settlers of this place was Jacob Shrack, who arrived from Germany in

1717, accompanied by his wife Eva Rosina and four children. He purchased in the present village two hundred and fifty acres of land, at which time there was but comparatively few inhabitants in the vicinity. It appears he took a considerable interest in getting a church erected in the place, and for this purpose at different times wrote letters to London and Halle for help and Lutheran preachers. He died February 22d, 1742, at the age of 63 years. He is buried in the Lutheran church-yard, and the oldest stone there containing an inscription was erected to his memory. His widow lived till 1756. His son, Christian Shrack, resided here till his death in November, 1780.

There has been much speculation concerning the origin of the name of Trappe. It is undoubtedly original and of local origin. Of all the various theories on this subject, the most feasible to us appears to be that given by the Rev. Henry M. Muhlenberg, the founder of the church. The following extract on this subject is taken from his journal, in which after speaking of Jacob Schrack and his family, he says: "they built a cabin and dug a cave in which they cooked. They kept a shop in a small way, and a tavern with beer and such things. As once an English inhabitant who had been drinking in the cave fell asleep and came home late and was in consequence scolded by his wife, he excused himself by saying he had been at the *Trapp*. From that time this neighborhood was called the Trappe and known as such in all America." This tavern must have been in the family as late as the year 1770, for Scull, on his map, has it marked as "Shrock." In the order of time Mr. Muhlenberg's statement is the first on this subject, and is sustained by other authorities. On Reading Howell's map of Pennsylvania, published in 1792, and in Scott's U. S. Gazetteer of 1795, it is called "Trap;" thus proving that this name did not originate from the German name of *Treppe* for steps, but from the English word *Trap*, signifying a snare, or rather a *pit-fall*.

Mr. Muhlenberg first came here in November, 1742, when he found a congregation of fifty members, who worshipped in a barn. Chiefly through his efforts the church was commenced in the spring of 1743, and was not finished till the fall of 1745, when he made his residence in the place. He was absent from 1761 till 1776, when he returned and spent the remainder of his days here. From his journal we have been enabled to procure some information respecting the revolution in this vicinity, from which it appears the inhabitants suffered severely. On the morning of September 11th, 1777, the cannonading at Brandywine, thirty miles off, was distinctly heard. On the afternoon of the 19th the British camp was seen with a telescope on the opposite banks of the Schuylkill, below Valley Forge. The American army, with Washington in person, the same day crossed to this side at Parker's Ford, five and a-half miles distant, and marched through the village to the Perkiomen. The procession lasted the whole night, and he says he had numerous visits from officers, wet breast high, from wading through the river, who had actually marched in that condition the whole night, cold and damp as it was, besides suffering from hunger and thirst. On the 23d a portion of the army encamped in the vicinity, and besides breaking down the fences and making fires of the rails, several houses were entered and the trunks and chests forced open. On the 27th he found that a regiment of Pennsylvania militia had taken possession of the church and schoolhouse, and that they were filled with officers, men and arms, and the floors covered with straw and dirt. The same day the schoolmaster complained with tears that they had destroyed his buckwheat in the field, and plundered and trodden down his garden vegetables. Mr. Muhlenberg had three acres in with buckwheat, which was then in blossom, in which he found twenty head of horses and oxen grazing. He says, when complaint was made about it by those sustaining damage, they were called tories, and their houses and stables threatened with fire. Major Gen. Armstrong, with about twenty-five hundred militia, continued in the vicinity till the 2d of October, when he joined the main division of the army near Skippack. He says the country in the neighborhood of the village looked as if it had been ravaged by an army of locusts, and that they had cut down and consumed for him near the church ten acres of woodland. The foregoing is an illustration of the evils attending a war and which will be occasioned more or less by any army, let it be friend or foe.

This village, according to Scott's Gazetteer, in 1795 contained about twelve houses. Gordon, in his Gazetteer of 1832, mentions it as then having two taverns, two stores and fifteen houses. By the foregoing it will be observed that the place has been steadily increasing to the present time. According to an act of Assembly, passed January 19th, 1802, the elections for the townships of Providence, Limerick and Perkiomen, being the 7th district, were ordered to be held here at the public house then kept by David Dewees.

On the Reading pike, about a quarter of a mile below the old church, is a large substantial two story stone house, now owned by the Hunsberger family which is not without interest. After the return of the Rev. H. M. Muhlenberg to the Trappe, in 1776, he made it his residence. He continued to live here till his death, which occurred the 7th of October, 1787. Some time afterwards it became the residence of the Rev. Henry Geisenhainer, who also breathed his last within its time-honored walls. Not long since it was owned by Dr. Philip Wack, and for awhile was the residence of Mathias Haldeman,Esq. General Peter Muhlenberg, Hon. Fred. Augustus Muhlenberg,Rev. Henry Ernest Muhlenberg and Gov. Francis R. Shunk were residents of the Trappe, the last four being natives of the place. Biographical sketches of these individuals appear in the appendix.

The present new Lutheran church, built in 1853, will rank nearly with the finest houses of worship in the county. It is situated in the northern part of the village and about one hundred feet northwest of the old church. It is built of brick, two stories high, and its dimensions are eighty-five by fifty-five feet. The steeple is one hundred and ten feet high, and from its elevated situation is a conspicuous object for many miles around. The congregation possesses also a school-house, with a dwelling for the sexton or teacher, and a parsonage, erected in 1836, and five acres of land, together with a field to contain carriages, &c., during worship. The present pastor of the church is the Rev. Adam S. Link.

Adjoining the church is the grave-yard, which comprises about an acre and a-half of ground, and from its elevated situation affords a fine prospect of the surrounding country. It contains a great many tombstones, among which are several of interest. It is to be regretted that this yard is so deficient in shade. Trees should have been planted here long ago, which would not only have improved its appearance, but as a place of resort would have made it more attractive. The most common family names on the tomb-stones are Zoller, Emrich, Heiser, Wald, Rawn, Fry, Heebner, Hallman, Wack, Spare, Royer, Garber, Fritz, Goodwin, Prizer, Rambo, Miller, Culp, Horning, Morgan, Allabaugh, Gross, Gristock, Shupe, Lonacre, Rittenhouse, Roudenbush, Essick, Prutzman, Weidner, Hildebeidle, Neiman, High, Harpel, Young, Yerger, Sailor, Berk, Dehaven, Stetler, Schrack, Pennepacker, Fuchs, Custer, Graff, Trumbauer, Boyer, Bean, Ritter, Croll, Kleine, Casselberry, Walter, Beck, Shontz, Cressman, Buckwalter, Hatfield, Welcher, Johnson, Fox, Pawling, Reiff, Marsteller, Hollebush, Moyer, Derricks and Kugler. The oldest stone, containing an inscription, bears the date of 1742, and the next of 1755. Amongst the distinguished dead reposing here can be mentioned the Rev. Henry Melchior Muhlenberg, General Peter Muhlenberg and Governor Francis R. Shunk, of whom a further account will be given hereafter. Jacob Custer, who was treasurer of the church from 1830 to 1857, kept a record of all those buried here within that time. The number was six hundred and ninety-two, of which the two oldest were females, aged respectively upwards of ninety-nine and one hundred and four years.

The old Trappe church is still standing, though upwards of one hundred and fifteen years have passed away since its erection. It was used by the congregation as a house of worship until the close of October, 1853, when the new church was completed. Since that time it is only used by the Sunday school attached to the church, which was established in 1836, and numbers upwards of one hundred and twenty scholars, with a library of five hundred volumes. In its architectural style it is certainly unique, and in its day is said to have been considered a great affair. It is built of stone, two stories high, fifty-four feet in length and thirty-nine wide. At the ends of the roof are two iron vanes, each bearing the date of 1743. Its interior is well calculated to give one an idea of a building in the olden times. From the floor to the ceiling of the roof is about thirty feet. The original pulpit is still here with its sounding board, all of black walnut. The four pillars, as well as the joists that support the galleries, are of hewn oak, twelve by fifteen inches in thickness. The pews have never been painted—in fact, all the wood work of the church is done in a very rude rough manner, denoting simplicity, solidity and strength. With a little repair it may be preserved for a long time. Near its entrance stands a pump in which has lately been placed a large wooden handle, copied after its original.

In the month of November, 1742, the Rev. Henry Melchior Muhlenberg arrived in this country from the kingdom of Hanover, where he had been pastor of a congregation in the village of Great Hennersdorf. In September, of the previous year, he had accepted a call of the congregations in Philadelphia, Providence and New Hanover. When he first came here, he found the country very fertile, but almost unimproved; a few houses scattered miles apart, along roads leading principally through forests yet unreclaimed. In Providence, by which we mean the Trappe, he found about fifty heads of families, with whom he held worship in a barn. Chiefly through his exertions it was determined to build a church and school-house. The latter was built of logs and finished before the former was commenced. On the 2d day of May, 1743, the corner-stone was laid by Mr. Muhlenberg, on which occasion he preached in English and German. On the following 12th September the church was roofed, when he preached in it for the first time. He resided in the village from 1745 until the 18th of October, 1760, when he preached his farewell sermon, and moved with his family to the city of Philadelphia. On the 17th of June, 1750, a general Synodical meeting was held here, which was attended by sixty-nine clerical and lay delegates. Another similar meeting was held here the 18th of October, 1760. To the time of Mr. Muhlenberg's return, in 1776, the congregation was attended by the Rev. Messrs. Hartwig, Van Buskirk and Voigt. During the Revolution the church was repeatedly used by the American soldiers in wet and cold weather as quarters.

After the death of Mr. Muhlenberg, in 1787, the entire charge devolved upon the Rev. Mr. Weinland, who continued until his death in 1808. It was during his ministry that the church was incorporated by an act of Assembly passed March 20th, 1805. It is stated to be a remarkable fact that the congregation worshipped in this church without any fire during the winter seasons for a period of sixty years, or from the time it was first built to about the year 1803, and that even then its introduction was strongly opposed by several of its members as an impious innovation. From the death of Mr. Muhlenberg to the year 1823, when the Rev. Frederick Wm. Gaisenhainer received the charge, the preaching was wholly confined to the German language, but from that time the English has been gradually getting the ascendency. One of the most important events in the history of the church was the centennial anniversary held in commemoration of its foundation, May 2d, 1843. On this occasion the sermon was preached by the Rev. J. W. Richards, of Germantown, a grandson of Mr. Muhlenberg, the founder. The following grandchildren were also present: the Hon. Henry A. Muhlenberg, Hon. M. S. Richards, Mrs. Charlotte F. Oakeley and Mrs. Hetty Heister. As has been stated the last worship held in this venerable building was in the latter part of October, 1853, when the present church was completed. To a stranger this church is an interesting object of visit, particularly its interior, and is well calculated to carry the mind back to the early history of the country. It is sincerely hoped that the old building may be preserved not only as an object of antiquarian interest, but as a place for the instruction of the rising generation in the moral duties of life.

Near the lower end of the village on the east side of the pike, is St. Luke's church, belonging to the German Reformed congregation. The present building was erected in 1835, and is of stone, two stories high, and forty by fifty feet in dimensions. Its pastor is the Rev. A. B. Shingle. The churchyard comprises upwards of an acre of ground, and a few of the ancient forest trees stand near the entrance. The earliest tombstone here with an inscription announces the death of "Lodwick Eualt, who departed this life, March 16th, 1760, aged 69 years." The following are the most common names on the stones: Paul, Reed, Shenkle, Netz, Buckwalter, Hillborn, Casey, Ricknor, Daringer, Smith, Dull, Francis, Wiland, Schneider, Eselin, Spare, Stauffer, Tyson, Thomas, Spear, Everhart, Garber, Eisenberg, Longabough, Koons, Espenship, Wanner, Hanger, Shade and Beidler. From Wm. Scull's map of Pennsylvania, published in 1770, we learn that a church then stood here and which is marked as the "Dutch Meeting." We were informed that the old church was built of logs, and was left standing till the erection of the present commodious edifice.

XIX.

LIMERICK.

The township of Limerick is bounded northeast by Frederick, southeast by Perkiomen and Upper Providence, southwest by the river Schuylkill, west by Pottsgrove and northwest by New Hanover. Its greatest length is nearly five miles and its breadth four and a half, with an area of fourteen thousand one hundred and fifty-one acres, and, excepting Lower Merion, is the largest township in the county. The surface of the country is rolling, and in its northern part is hilly, where the highest elevation is called Stone Hill. For about the distance of a mile and a-half along the Schuylkill, between Limerick station and Royersfordville, there are pretty steep hills, rising immediately from the water's edge to a height of from sixty to a hundred feet, which are covered principally with small pines and bushes. Between these places are extensive quarries of hard red sandstone, which can be taken out in huge square blocks. From Limerick station up the river for more than a mile, the land recedes quite gradually. The soil along the Schuylkill is fertile and productive, but the remainder is generally a stiff clay. Although the second in extent, it does not contain a stream that furnishes water power. Mingo creek has its source near Limerick Square, and, after a course of four miles, turns into Upper Providence. Lodle and Mine creeks have also their sources in this township. Swamp creek, for a short distance, passes through the north corner. There are several other small streams, but in consequence of being easily affected by drought are not of much account.

Limerick, in 1741, contained 58 taxables; in 1828, 315; in 1849, 461; and in 1858, 536. According to the census of 1810, it contained 1282 inhabitants; in 1820, 1577; in 1830, 1748; in 1840, 1786; and in 1850, 2165. By the triennial assessment of 1858, the real estate was valued at $372,969, and the horses and neat cattle, $30,791. In May, 1858, the township contained six inns, seven stores, two lumber yards, two coal yards and one steam grist and saw mill. In 1850 it contained three hundred and seventy-three houses and two hundred and forty-three farms. The Reading railroad traverses the township its entire length on the Schuylkill a distance of about five and a-half miles and has two stations, one at Royer's Ford, and the other at Limerickville. The Reading turnpike crosses for five miles through its centre, and the Limerick and Colebrookdale pike for about three miles. Limerick has eleven schools, and for the year ending with June 1st, 1857, were open only four months, and attended by six hundred and seventy-five scholars. The sum of $1,440 was levied to defray the expenses of the same.

The villages of this township are all small, but within the last fifteen years have considerably improved. The largest is called Limerick Square, and is situated on the Reading pike, twenty-eight miles from Philadelphia. It contains a store, brick yard, two smithships and sixteen houses. George Gilbert has also here a large steam grist mill, saw mill and machine shop. This place has chiefly grown up within the last twelve years and contains several fine three story brick houses. At the lower end of the village the German Methodists have a small one story brick church, built in 1851, and a school-house near by. At the upper end of the place the Limerick and Colebrookdale turnpike strikes the Reading road, and is above nine miles in this county, and was finished in 1855. This turnpike is located on the Swamp road, which is marked on Scull's map of 1770. At its confluence with the Reading road, as we learn from the same, was "Widow Lloyd's inn."

Limerickville is a station on the Reading railroad and is situated on the Schuylkill, thirty-four miles from Philadelphia. It contains an inn, store, post-office, an extensive lumber yard, coal yard and twelve houses. Samuel Kulp has also an extensive steam planing mill and sash and door factory. The post-office here is called Limerick Bridge. A short distance above this village is what is generally called Lawrenceville bridge, which was built in 1849. The name is applied from Lawrenceville, on the opposite side of the river, in Chester county. In the vicinity of Limerickville are several fertile farms which produce good crops.

Royersfordville is also a station on the Reading railroad, and is situated on the river thirty-two miles from the city. It contains two inns, a store, post-office and nine houses. There are several handsome dwellings here built within the past few years. The bridge over the Schuylkill here was built in 1840, and was washed away September 2d, 1850, and rebuilt the following year. Opposite, in Chester county, is Springville, a place of about fifty houses. Half a mile above the village is the Aramingo Telegraph office, belonging to the railroad company. Limerick Church is a small village on the Reading turnpike, twenty-nine miles from Philadelphia. It contains two inns, a church, school-house, carriage factory, wheelwright and blacksmith shop and eight houses.

The present Limerick church was built in 1817 and is a two story stone building held by the German Reformed and Lutherans in common. The German Reformed pastor is the Rev. N. C. Strassberger, and the Lutheran, Rev. George F. Miller. This church is situated on elevated ground and affords from the churchyard a fine view of the surrounding country. We regret to say that we were not enabled to ascertain when it was first erected, but no doubt considerably over a century ago. The grave and church-yard contain about two acres of ground and should be planted with trees. A great many have been buried here, particularly of the name of Evans. The oldest stone bears the date of 1754 and several of 1787. The most common names on the tombstones are Evans, Shaner, Brooke, Kraus, Smith, Snell, Messimer, Nettles, Kohl, Groff, Klein, Miller, Wagner, Christman, Schaffer, Barlow, Hallman, Beyer, Boyer, Fox, Geiger, Royer, Walt, Mench, Brant. Hunsberger, Grubb, Linderman, Johnson, Schwenck, Kendall, Warley and Stetler.

Limerick no doubt derived its name from a city and county of this name in Ireland. It was erected into a township at an early period. The following is a list of residents and landowners in 1734: Edward Nichols, John Davy, Enoch Davis, John Kendall, Owen Evans, Wm. Evans, Joseph Barlow, Peter Umstead, Cliff Pennypacker, Henry Reynor, Wm. Woodly, Jonathan Woodly, Wm. Maulsby, Henry Peterson, Peter Peterson, Nicholas Custard, Hironius Haas, Lawrence Rinker, Stephen Miller, Barnaby Coulson and Martin Calf.

Owen Evans was an early settler in this township, where he took up four hundred acres of land. He was appointed a justice of the peace in 1732, and continued to hold the office till his death. He appears to have been a conspicuous man in the neighborhood, and died in 1754, aged 55 years. Peter Umstead first settled in or near Germantown some time previous to the year 1700, and afterwards removed to Limerick where he had purchased two hundred and fifty acres. From our list of 1734 we learn that at that time there resided in the present county two of the name of Pennapacker. Henry purchased one hundred and fifty acres in Perkiomen township and Cliff two hundred and fifty acres in Limerick. The origin of the name is singular. It appears the father of the aforesaid, whose name was Beerman, came from Holland and settled at quite an early period at Skippack, where he carried on tile-making. In the Dutch language *pauny* is the name of tile, which, added to *backer*, the German for baker, gives the clue to the origin, namelyPaunybacker, which, literally translated into English, is *tilebaker*. In consequence of his business this name was bestowed on him by his German neighbors, and which he and his family finally adopted as their surname. The Pennypackers can therefore say, what very few in this country can, that their name is of American origin. The Evans, the Umsteads and the Pennypackers at this time are very numerous along the valley of the Schuylkill.

Parker's Ford on the Schuylkill, is a quarter of a mile above the village of Limerickville and five miles below the borough of Pottstown. The road from the ford to the Trappe was laid out at an early period, and is about five miles and a-half in length. The land rises gradually from the river, but on the Chester county side is more elevated. It was at this place on the 19th day of September, 1777, were the following incident occurred, which we extract from the journal of the Rev. H. M. Muhlenberg. "In the afternoon we had news that the British troops on the other side of the Schuylkill had marched down towards Providence, and with a telescope we could see their camp. In consequence of this the American army, four miles from us, forded the Schuylkill breast high, and came upon the Philadelphia road at Augustus church. His excellency General Washington was with the troops in person, who marched past here to the Perkiomen. The procession lasted the whole night, and we had numerous visits from officers, wet breast high, who had to march in this condition during the whole night, cold and damp as it was, and to bear hunger and thirst at the same time." For the first time on the 19th of August we stood at this place and as we gazed on the river mused on this occurrence, and after surveying the surrounding scenery, we were struck with the idea what a glorious subject it would be for a painting. The crossing of the American army, breast deep, over the Schuylkill! May some artist take the hint.

XX.

POTTSGROVE.

The township of Pottsgrove is bounded northeast by Douglas and New Hanover, southeast by Limerick, south by the Schuylkill, southwest by Pottstown, and west and northwest by Berks county. Its length is five miles, and average breadth three and a-half, with an area of eleven thousand, six hundred acres. The entire southern part of the township, especially that portion which lies between the Reading turnpike and the river, is fertile and well cultivated. The eastern part is more rolling, and towards the Douglas, New Hanover and Limerick line is quite hilly. Some of the eminences are of tolerable elevation, among the most prominent of which can be named Ringing hill, Stone hill, Prospect hill and the Fox hills. The soil on these elevations is generally thin and very stony.

Pottsgrove is pretty well watered by the Manatawny and Sprogels creeks, Saratoga and Goose runs and their various branches, the largest of which is the Manatawny, which rises in Rockland township, Berks county, and after a general southeast course of about eighteen miles, empties into the Schuylkill at the borough of Pottstown. Of its length two miles are in this township, in which distance it propels three gristmills, the remainder being in Berks. The earliest mention we have found of this stream, is from a visit of Governor Gordon in its vicinity in 1728. He calls it the "Mahanatawny." It is an Indian name, and Heckewelder says in their language it signified "where we drank." Sprogels run is wholly in this township and rises in the Fox hills, and after a southeast course of four miles empties into the Schuylkill. It propels only a clover and chopping mill. It is called by this name on Scull's map of 1770. Formerly on its banks near the centre of the township a copper-mine was worked. Saratoga run, though only about three and a-half miles in length, furnishes valuable water-power. It rises by two branches in New Hanover township, with a general southwest course, and propels in Pottsgrove four grist and three saw mills. This stream has an Indian name, and we find it variously spelled. On Scull's map of 1770, Senitoga, on Howell's map of 1792, Saraloga, and on the county maps of 1849 and 1857, Saratoga.

Among the natural curiosities of Montgomery county, may be mentioned the Ringing Rocks, as they are called on Stone hill, which are situated about three miles northeast of Pottstown. After enjoying the hospitalities of Isaac F. Yost, Esq., late county commissioner, who resides near by, he accompanied us to this noted place on the morning of the 21st of August, and pointed out the most interesting objects for inspection. To him of course we are much indebted for some valuable information. The Ringing Rocks consist of a bed of trap rocks, exceedingly hard and compact, and which on being struck with a hammer ring like iron. They cover about one and a-half acres of ground, and consist of a number of rocks piled on one another, within which space no trees or bushes are found growing. They are entirely surrounded by woods and are on the property of Abraham Mench. The largest rocks we suppose would weigh from five to twenty-five tons each, and some of the apertures are visible to the depth of twenty-five feet. A great many names have been pricked or scratched on these rocks by visitors, some not without considerable labor. A number of impressions on them were shown us, among which were three closely resembling the human foot, from three to six inches in depth, and also a number resembling the tracks of horses, elephants, and cannon balls of from six to twelve inches in diameter. The sounds emitted by these rocks are various, depending on their size and shape; for some, when struck, resemble the ringing of anvils, others of church bells with all the intermediate tones. In fact there is not a note in music that has not here a corresponding key. As Aristotle has stated that in every block of marble there is a statue, but it took a sculptor to find it, so it might be said of those rocks, in every one there is some note in music, but it would still require the aid of a musician to verify it. In consequence, it has been proposed to hold a concert here, under the direction of some experienced master, on some Fourth of July, for the purpose of playing our national airs by the music of these rocks alone. By the impressions and hardness of them we are led to infer that they were originally soft, but by being subjected to an intense heat deep in the earth, have, by a violent eruption, been upheaved to the surface and then cooled off. Geologists thus account for the formation of trappean matter and which we are led to believe is the cause of their shape, hardness, color and position, in small surfaces of great depth. The German inhabitants of the neighborhood from an early period have given this hill the name of Klingleberg, signifying Ringing hill. Of late years these rocks have become quite a harbor for foxes, who commit considerable depredations on the poultry of the neighborhood. On the west end of Stone hill, about two miles from Pottstown, a fine view is obtained of the surrounding country. The hills of the Schuylkill can be traced in Chester and Berks counties for thirty or forty miles.

Pottsgrove, according to the census of 1810, contained 1571 inhabitants; in 1820, 1882; in 1830, 1302; in 1840, 1361, and in 1850, 1689. In 1828 it contained 252 taxables; in 1849, 351, and in 1858, 406. By the triennial assessment of 1858, the real estate was valued at $348,511, and the horses and neat cattle at $15,136. In May, 1858, it contained three inns and three stores. Pottsgrove contains eleven schools, and for the school year ending with June 1st, 1857, were open only four months, and attended by four hundred and eighty-five scholars. The sum of $1,450 was levied to defray the expenses of the same. The Reading railroad passes nearly through the whole length of the township, a distance of five miles, but has no station. The Reading turnpike passes through it nearly six miles. The only villages are Glasgow and Crooked Hill. At the latter place there is a post-office. In 1850 Pottsgrove contained three hundred and eight houses and one hundred and sixty-eight farms. We are satisfied from the number of houses erected in this township within the last six years that the population must have considerably increased. Three copper mines were formerl[illegible]ed between the borough of Pottstown and Ringing hill, among which the most noted was Blaine's copper mine on Sprogel's run. However, they have all for some time been discontinued, and we believe have never proved profitable.

Glasgow is the largest village in the township, and is situated on the Manatawny creek, about a mile north of Pottstown. It contains about twenty houses and a large merchant, grist and sawmill, belonging to Gen. James Rittenhouse, who also owns the old forge and furnace. It is said, in consequence of the decline in the iron business, the village is not as prosperous as formerly. Iron works are mentioned as having been established on the Manatawny as early as 1728; but we are unable to say whether at this place. From Scull's map we know that "McCall's Forge" was here before 1770.

Crooked Hill is the name of a village on the Reading turnpike, three miles below Pottstown and thirty-two from Philadelphia. It contains an inn, post office, two blacksmith shops, a large grist mill, propelled by the Saratoga run, and thirteen houses. The land in the vicinity is quite rolling and well cultivated.

Near the mouth of Saratoga run is Rees' grist mill and two houses. The Reading railroad crosses the stream here by a handsome stone bridge of two arches, twenty-eight feet above the water. Near by is Heister's ford, over the Schuylkill, which is considerably traveled by wagons to and from Chester county. The country in this vicinity is extremely rugged and hilly. Just below the borough of Pottstown, near the Reading railroad, is a very ancient grave-yard, where are buried members of the families of Sprogel, Grob, Bechtel and Rhoades. Some of the stones were deciphered with difficulty. The most ancient announces a death in 1716.

Pottsgrove was erected into a township in 1807, and its territory was taken from the townships of Douglas and New Hanover. The upper half of its area was originally comprised in Douglas and the remainder in New Hanover. William Penn, the 25th of October, 1701, conveyed to his son, John Penn, a tract of twelve thousand acres of land, which the latter, the 20th of June, 1735, sold to George McCall, a merchant of Philadelphia, for the sum of 2,000 guineas, or, in our present currency, $9,333. On a re-survey it was found to contain fourteen thousand and sixty acres. This purchase comprised all of the present township of Douglas and the upper half of Pottsgrove and the whole of Pottstown to the Schuylkill. We know from the records that down to 1753 it was commonly called "McCall's Manor." John Potts, in 1753, lived in Pottsgrove, now called Pottstown, after whom both the borough and this township have been called. The elections of Pottsgrove in 1807 were ordered to be held at Pottstown.

Among the first settlers of the township was John Henry Sprogel, who, with his brother, Lodwick Christian Sprogel, by invitation of William Penn, came to this country from Holland. In the beginning of 1705 we know they were both naturalized. John Henry purchased here about six hundred acres, on which he settled with his family. The present Sprogel's run was called after him and flows through this tract. From a stone in the ancient grave-yard, east of the borough line, we learn that his wife, Dorothea, died the 7th of August, 1718, aged forty years. From another stone we learn a son, Frederick, died in 1716, aged one year. By these dates we infer that he must have been nearly the first that resided in the vicinity of the present borough. Lodwick Christian Sprogel, we believe, resided in Philadelphia and was a man of education. In December, 1728, he presented a donation of books to the library of Christ church, chiefly large folios, bound in parchment. The same year the congregation of the church purchased the organ from him for £200, which was used till 1763, when a larger one was substituted. These are all the facts we are at present enabled to give of this family.

XXII.

POTTSTOWN.

The borough of Pottstown is situated on the north side of the Schuylkill river, at the mouth of Manatawny creek, twenty miles from Norristown and thirty-seven from Philadelphia. It contains an area of two hundred and sixty-eight acres, which was wholly taken from Pottsgrove township, on its erection into a borough in 1815. It is bounded on the northeast and west by Pottsgrove, northwest by the Manatawny creek, and south and southwest by the Schuylkill river, on which it has a front of three fourths of a mile, and extends back from the same about half a mile. Few towns have a handsomer location; the land lies high and gently rolling, with plenty of room for its future growth. In its vicinity is a fertile country on which are a number of fine farms which have been much improved within the last ten years.

The streets of the town are laid out very regular and wide, and cross each other at right angles. Beginning at the river and running parallel with it, are the following streets: Water, Laurel, Cherry, South, Queen, High, King, Chesnut, Walnut and Beech. At right angles with these, and beginning at the Manatawny creek, are York, Hanover, Penn, Charlotte, Evans, Franklin, Washington and Warren. The Reading railroad is located on Queen street and the Reading pike on High street. The bridge over the Schuylkill is at the extremity of Hanover street. Besides the aforesaid, there are several smaller streets, as Apple and Hubley.

The borough of late years has rapidly increased in population. According to the census of 1830 it contained six hundred and seventy-six inhabitants; in 1840, seven hundred and twenty-one, and in 1850, sixteen hundred and sixty-four. In 1828 it contained one hundred and forty-one taxables; in 1849, three hundred and eighty-eight, and in 1858, five hundred and nine. From the census of 1850 we learn that it then contained three hundred and twenty-eight houses and three farms. By the triennial assessment of 1858, the real estate was valued at $346,675, and the horses and cattle at $4367. At the present time it contains thirty-seven stores, as follows: six merchandise, five boot and shoe, five confectionery, four clothing, two stove, two hardware, two grocery, two jewelry, two drug, one trimmings, one hat, one dry goods, one leather, one book and stationery, one tobacco and one provision store, besides one lumber and six coal yards. It also contains seven churches, eight public and two private schools, five hotels, two rolling mills, two fire engines, a bank, library, tannery, gasworks and the extensive machine shops of the Reading railroad.

The first house of worship built in Pottstown was the Quaker meeting house which was erected some time previous to 1795. The present meeting house is a small one story brick building. The Lutherans and German Reformed hold worship in the Union church, which is a large two story brick edifice with a cupola. The Lutheran clergyman is the Rev. George F. Miller, and the German Reformed the Rev. N. C. Strassburger. Attached to this church is a fine graveyard containing about two acres. The Episcopal church is built of stone, in the Gothic style, with a high spire. Its pastor is the Rev. Aaron Christman. The present church was erected in 1847, when the previous one, which had been built in 1833, was torn down. The Presbyterian church is a large and handsome structure with the highest spire in the town. Its present pastor is the Rev. Robert Cruikshanks. The Methodist church is a one story building erected in 1838. The Catholic church at present is under the charge of the Rev. Mr. Davis. The Baptist church was built in the summer of 1858, and is a large and handsome two story building. The town contained one house of worship in 1795; two in 1832, and four in 1842. The Rev. Edmund Leaf, who is a native of this place, informed us that not thirty years ago all the preaching, (excepting by the Quakers,) was done in the German language. At the northeast end of the town is a cemetery which is laid out with walks and planted with shrubbery and trees. It contains a number of handsome monuments.

The borough contains eight public schools, which, for the school year, ending with June 1st, 1857, were open six months and attended by three hundred and ninety-two scholars. The sum of $1,400 was levied to defray the expenses of the same. The public school-house is a large two story brick building, erected in 1854. The academy, which was built in 1834, is a remarkably quaint looking edifice of stone, one story high. Pottstown contains several excellent schools. The Cottage Female Seminary is a fine large three story building, of which the Rev. Robert Cruikshanks is principal. Mr. M. Meigs has a fine building, on an elevation near the Female seminary, for boys. These institutions are both situated near the Reading pike at the east end of the town.

The Bank of Pottstown was incorporated in 1857, and went into operation in October of the same year. Henry Potts is President and Wm. Mintzer cashier. The library was founded about 1845, and contains at present one thousand and fifty volumes. D. H. Keim is librarian. There was a previous library here which was commenced before 1831, but several years afterwards went down. The gas-works went into operation in 1856. To this time the place possesses no waterworks. In 1828 S. Royer published here two weekly newspapers, the "*Montgomery Republican*" and "*Der Advocat*," in German. In 1832 "*The American Star*" was published here, which, not long after, gave way to the "*Pottstown Journal*." The only paper now published here is the "*Montgomery Ledger*," by Davis and Williamson, which commenced its career in 1844.

The Perkiomen and Reading turnpike road was made under the acts of March 20th, 1810, and February 13th, 1810, and passes through Pottstown. It was commenced in 1811 and finished in 1815, and extends from Reading to the Perkiomen Bridge, a distance of twenty-nine miles. It cost $7000 per mile, the State subscribing $53,000. The canal of the Schuylkill navigation company is on the opposite side of the river. The bridge over the Manatawny creek is built of stone and was completed in 1805. The county commissioners, by an act of March 25th, 1803, were empowered to collect toll on this bridge which was to go towards defraying its expenses while building. The bridge over the Schuylkill at this place was incorporated by an act of March 5th, 1819. It was commenced in 1820, and was made passable in 1821. It measures between the abutments three hundred and forty feet, is twenty-eight feet wide and eighteen feet above the water. Its total cost was nearly $14,000, of which sum the State subscribed $3,000. The Reading railroad crosses the Manatawny a short distance below the turnpike by a substantial stone bridge of five arches and one thousand and seventy-one feet in length.

Of the various improvements passing through the place none singly have contributed so much to the prosperity of the town as the Reading railroad. The company by whom this grand work was constructed was chartered the 4th of April, 1833. Surveys were shortly after made and before the lapse of another year it was placed under contract as far as this borough. On the 9th of December, 1839, the road was opened from the city to Reading, a distance of fifty-nine miles. It was not completed to Pottsville till the beginning of 1842, when it was opened with considerable display. The total length of the road is ninety-eight miles, and cost $19-262,720. For the year ending with January 1st, 1859, nearly one million, seven hundred thousand tons of coal were sent over this line, being three hundred thousand tons more than had passed within the same time over the Schuylkill navigation. The railroad company have erected several extensive machine shops in Pottstown, chiefly for repairs of tracks, bridges, cars and locomotives. The dimensions of the largest shop is one hundred and fifty-one by eighty-one, the second one hundred and eighty-one by forty-one, and the next in size is eighty-one by forty-four feet. The passenger depot is a handsome two story stone building with a cupola. At the east end of the town the company have an establishment by steam for preparing sills. It is said if all the locomotives and passenger and freight cars belonging to the company were placed together on a single track, they would extend in length a distance of over fifteen miles. The author has counted ninety-five cars loaded with coal on this road drawn by a single locomotive, and was told of the number being as high as one hundred and fifty-five.

The town received its name from John Potts, an enterprising miller, who, in 1752, resided here, and was then known as Pottsgrove. Not long previous he had lived on his extensive plantation and mills in Colebrookdale, in Berks county. It is said that he erected the first mill on the Manatawny creek, near the present borough, and that he built the large two story stone house, on the north side of the creek, now owned by Mr. Davis. Its dimensions are about forty-six by twenty-eight feet, and the stones have been nicely dressed into squares. It is said when this house was built, on account of its size, it was regarded with wonder by the people of this section of the country. There is a tradition that Washington in the Revolution, while in this vicinity, made it his head-quarters. Mr. Potts was the father of Isaac Potts, who erected the first forge at Valley Forge. Mr. Davis also owns the large three story flour mill near his residence. It was here where John Potts had his mill. The present building was erected in 1814.

Washington, with his army, crossed the Schuylkill at Parker's Ford, five miles below this place, September 19th, 1777, and proceeded to this vicinity, where the army remained while the British marched to Philadelphia. How long the army continued in this neighborhood is not exactly known, but probably not much over a week, for we know that on the 28th they were encamped at Skippack. In a letter from this place, dated September 23d, Washington says that more than one thousand of his men were barefooted, and that, owing to the want of shoes, he was unable to make forced marches.

From Scott's Gazetteer we learn that in 1795 there was a post-office here, which at that time was the only one in the county. By an act of Assembly, passed April 8th, 1802, the elections of Limerick and parts of Douglas and New Hanover were ordered to be held at the house of George Pfleiger, of this town. After the erection of the borough the town was laid out and surveyed by Thomas Baird, in September, 1828. In January, 1829, the name of the post-office was changed to its present one of Pottstown. In 1832 the place contained nearly one hundred dwellings, a mill, four stores, four taverns and two churches. In consequence of the increase of population, the borough, by an act of Assemby, passed March 16th, 1842, was divided into two wards, which continue to the present time, one being called the East and the other the West ward.

Benjamin B. Yost, formerly Register of the county, and now aged seventy-two years, informed us that he well remembers when they caught shad and herring in the river here in abundance. Hon. Jacob S. Yost, formerly member of Congress, but at present United States Marshal for the Eastern District of Pennsylvania, is a resident of this borough. The population of Pottstown, at this time, is probably two thousand eight hundred.

APPENDIX.

BIOGRAPHICAL SKETCHES.

John Roberts.

Among the first that came from Wales and settled in Lower Merion, was the Roberts family. They belonged to the Society of Friends and were distinguished for their industry, enterprise and respectability. The subject of this notice, we may say, was born to wealth, and from his position in society exerted more or less influence with those he came in contact. We may call him, by his business, a farmer; but he was generally known as John Roberts, the Miller, to distinguish him from others bearing the name in that vicinity. Our information respecting his early life is scant, indeed, but we shall cheerfully give such as we have been enabled to secure while prosecuting researches on other matters.

In 1773, with several others, he was appointed by the Assembly one of the commissioners to improve the navigation of the Schuylkill. A convention for the province of Pennsylvania was held at Philadelphia from the 23d to the 28th of January, 1775, of which he was one of the twelve delegates from Philadelphia county. The object of this convention was to endeavor to get the Assembly to pass a law to prohibit the future importation of slaves. The Revolution next followed, and as the contest waxed warmer and warmer, the people accordingly espoused the cause of one or the other of the parties. Mr. Roberts at first remained neutral, and it is said was not at least an active participant till after the banishment of several influential Friends by the Americans from Philadelphia under a guard to Reading, and from thence to Virginia. While the British were on their march with a powerful army to Philadelphia, in the fall of 1777, Mr. Roberts joined them and gave information how they might capture his friends, who were then on their way to exile.

After the British had taken possession of the city, Joseph Galloway was appointed superintendent general of the police, and Mr. Roberts acted as spy and agent for him, giving him information of the residence and whereabouts of the most prominent whigs who lived in the vicinity of the city. In June, 1778, the British evacuated Philadelphia and this placed Mr. Roberts in an unfortunate position, especially as the owner of valuable real estate. No doubt, if it would not have been for this, he would have followed their departure. The Americans arrested him, and after a long trial and close examination he was found guilty as a traitor to his country. Powerful efforts were now made by his friends, as well as a number of ardent whigs, to save him—but in vain. He was publicly executed in the city, with Abraham Carlisle, in November of the same year. His remains were interred by the side of his ancestors in the grave-yard of the ancient Lower Merion meeting house. His real estate was confiscated and ordered to be sold at the court house, in Philadelphia, the 21st of June, 1780. His homestead contained three hundred acres, with a good mansion house, two grist mills, a saw mill, paper mill and several tenant houses. Adjoining this was a farm of seventy-eight acres, and on the Schuylkill another property of three hundred acres, with three dwelling houses, a saw mill, powder mill and oil mill. The proceeds of these sales were ordered to be applied to the use of the University of Pennsylvania. All the aforesaid property was in Lower Merion, and a part of the homestead is now owned by Samuel Robeson.

CHARLES THOMSON

Was a native of Ireland, where he was born in 1730. He came to America in 1741, in company with his three elder brothers, and landed at New Castle, Delaware. They were all poor and entirely dependent on their own exertions for a livelihood. Charles received the greater part of his education from Dr. Allison, and afterwards became a teacher in an academy at New Castle. In the course of a few years he removed to Philadelphia and formed an intimate acquaintance with Dr. Franklin. The troubles of the Revolution were now approaching, and at the first meeting of the Continental Congress in the city, in 1774, he was called to the responsible duty of keeping the minutes of their proceedings. He continued to hold the office of secretary till after the close of the war, in 1789, when he resigned. He was married to Hannah Harrison, and settled on her extensive estate called Harriton, in Lower Merion, where he continued to reside for the remainder of his days. The Abbe Robin, who was attached to Rochambeau's staff, gives the following description of Mr. Thomson in the Revolution: "His meagre figure, furrowed countenance, his hollow sparkling eyes, his white, straight hair, that did not hang quite so low as his ears, fixed our thorough attention, and filled us with surprise and admiration." Mr. Thomson, from his position, had an excellent opportunity to judge not only the characters of all the members of Congress, but the contrast existing between the respective sessions, in virtue and ability in conducting the war. He often expressed himself unfavorably of the Congress of 1777–8, as not being near so zealous, patriotic and able a body as previously. It was in this Congress that a certain few wished to supplant Washington for Gates, and it was chiefly owing to their tardiness that the army at Whitemarsh and Valley Forge suffered so much from the want of proper clothing and other necessaries. Mr. Thomson terminated his long career the 16th of August, 1824, at the advanced age of ninety-four years. He was buried in a Presbyterian grave yard, near the Baptist meeting house, on the Gulf road, where several years afterwards his remains were removed to Laurel Hill cemetery, where they now repose. His mansion house is still standing near the present Green Tree tavern on the Gulf road, and is now owned by Levi Morris.

EDWARD FARMER.

The subject of this sketch arrived, with his father, Jasper Farmer, at Philadelphia, the 10th of ninth month, 1685, in the ship Bristol Merchant, commanded by John Stephens. Edward settled on a large tract of land near the present village of Whitemarsh, which had been purchased by his father. At an early period he here built a grist mill on the Wissahickon creek, which in its day was widely known. From the Colonial Records we know that this mill was erected some time previous to 1722, and stood on the same spot where is now Samuel Comly's merchant mill. From his remote situation in the woods, he early acquired a knowledge of the Indian language, and on several occasions acted as interpreter for the government. With John Sotcher, in May, 1701, he was sent as an agent to the Lehigh river, to ascertain the intentions of the Indians of that vicinity. In 1710 the St. Thomas' Episcopal church was built on a lot of ground which he presented for the purpose. An Indian council was held at his house the 19th of May, 1712, at which was present the Governor, Charles Gooken, and several of his friends, besides a number of Indians. The most prominent chiefs at this meeting were Sasunan, Ealochelan and Scolitchy, the latter being the principal speaker. Mr. Farmer was commissioned one of the justices of the courts of Philadelphia county, in September, 1704, and continued to hold the same for a period of nearly forty years. In 1716 he was elected one of the members of Assembly from Philadelphia county. He died the 3d of November, 1745, aged seventy-three years, and was buried in the grave-yard attached to St. Thomas' church, where a stone is erected to his memory. We believe there are none of the name of Farmer now living in Whitemarsh.

Nicholas Scull.

We are inclined to believe that he was the son of Nicholas Scull who arrived at Philadelphia, with Jasper Farmer, in 1685, and afterwards settled in Whitemarsh, where we know the subject of this article resided for some time. Mr. Scull, as a land surveyor, had few equals, and for a knowledge of the Indian language no superior. From what information we have been enabled to procure respecting him, we are led to believe he must have received a better education than was generally given at this early period of our colonial history. In 1722 he made the survey of the road leading from where is now the Willow Grove to Governor Keith's residence, in Horsham, and from this latter place another road on the county line to the York road. He was sent with his brother, John Scull, as interpreter, by Governor Gordon, in May, 1728, to hold a council with the Indians at Conestoga. The same year, in consequence of a disturbance between several Indians and whites, residing in the vicinity of New Hanover township, in this county, he was sent with presents to pacify the former, in which object he was completely successful. He was sent on a similar errand to Shamokin, in 1729. Mr. Scull, we know, in 1781 resided in Philadelphia, and for several years afterwards. Governor Thomas, in May, 1740, sent him to the Minesinks to settle a difficulty that had arisen between a white man of the name of Henry Webb and an Indian, by which the former was wounded. In October, 1744, he was commissioned sheriff of Philadelphia county, which office he held for several years. The Indians from Shamokin having visited Governor Thomas, in Philadelphia, in July, 1745, he was again solicited to serve as interpreter. Through ill health, William Parsons resigned the office of surveyor general of Pennsylvania, and in June, 1748, Mr. Scull was appointed in his place, and which he continued to hold to the close of his life—a period of thirteen years. Abigail, his wife, died in 1753, in her sixty-fifth year, and was buried in the family burying-ground, on Camp Hill, near the line of Whitemarsh and Upper Dublin townships. He published a map from his own surveys, in Philadelphia, in 1759, of the improved parts of Pennsylvania and Maryland. Mr. Scull died at an advanced age, in 1761, when John Lukens, of Horsham, was appointed his successor. His daughter, Mary Scull, was married to William Biddle, whose son, Edward Biddle, was an officer in the Revolution, a member of Assembly, a speaker of the House, and a member of Congress. William Scull, who published a large map of Pennsylvania, in 1770, was also a grandson. Mr. Lukens appointed him deputy surveyor-general. Afterwards he served in the geographical department, under Mr. Erskine, from 1778 to 1780.

Jacob Ritter.

His parents were Jacob and Elizabeth Ritter, who came from Germany, and when they had arrived in America bound themselves as servants to pay for their passage. His father served three, and his mother four years When their servitude was over, they married and settled in Springfield township, Bucks county, where Jacob was born in 1757. The Revolution breaking out he joined as a soldier, and at the battle of Brandywine was taken a prisoner by some Hessians and confined, with nine hundred others, in the prison at Philadelphia. Through the influence of his cousin and Joseph Galloway, the superintendent of police, he was discharged from confinement. In the spring of 1778 he married Dorothy Smith and moved to the city. After a residence there of several years he lost his wife, when, in the spring of 1794, he moved with his children to Springfield. In 1802 he married Ann Williams, of Buckingham. Having sold his farm in Richland and purchased one in Plymouth township, he moved on it in 1812 and continued to reside there for the remainder of his life. He was a minister among Friends for fifty years, and of Plymouth meeting nearly twenty-nine. He died the 15th of December, 1841, aged eighty-five years, and his remains were interred in Friends' burial ground at Plymouth. Though he never received more than an ordinary education, he wrote a journal and memoir of his life, which was published in 1844, with a preface, additions and notes, by Joseph Foulke, of Gwynedd. It is a small duodecimo of one hundred and eleven pages, from which we have chiefly prepared this sketch.

Andrew Porter.

Robert Porter was a native of Ireland and emigrated in early life to this country, and settled in Worcester township, in this county, where his son, Andrew Porter, was born September 24th, 1743. His father furnished him with a good education, and in the spring of 1767 he removed to Philadelphia and took charge of an English and mathematical school, until the spring of 1776. On the 19th of June, he was commissioned by Congress a captain of marines, and ordered on board the frigate Effingham. He afterwards left the navy and joined the army as a captain and served with great gallantry at Trenton, Princeton and Brandywine. At Valley Forge he was a major of a regiment of artillery, and during the war was in considerable service. With David Rittenhouse, in the spring of 1785, he was appointed a commissioner on the part of Pennsylvania to ascertain the boundary between this State and Virginia. In the spring of 1787, with Andrew Ellicott, he commenced the survey of the northern boundary of the State, which was completed by the middle of the following November. While engaged on this work, he says:—"The Indians appear friendly and have expressed no dissatisfaction to our running the line." For his services Governor Snyder, the 4th of April, 1809, appointed him surveyor general of Pennsylvania, which office he held till his death, which occurred November 16th, 1813, at the age of seventy years. He died at Harrisburg, where he was buried with military honors in the Presbyterian burying-ground, and a neat white marble monument designates the spot. At the close of the Revolution Mr. Porter was colonel of the Fourth Pennsylvania regiment of artillery and subsequently brigadier and major general of the second division of the militia. It is said that President Madison offered him the commission of brigadier general in the American army, and also the office of secretary of war, both of which he declined. Mr. Porter resided in the upper part of the borough of Norristown, near the Ridge turnpike, in the mansion now occupied by Col. Thomas P. Knox. Robert Porter, the general's father, died in 1770, at the age of seventy-two years, and is buried in the Norriton Presbyterian grave-yard, where a large stone is erected to his memory. The sons of Andrew Porter have been quite distinguished. Gen. David R. Porter was governor of Pennsylvania from 1838 to 1844. Gen. James M. Porter has been a member of Assembly, president judge of the twenty-second judicial district, and secretary of war under President Tyler. George B. Porter was judge, United States Marshal of the Eastern District of Pennsylvania, and subsequently governor of Michigan, in which office he died in 1834, in his forty-fourth year. All these sons are natives of this county, and the two former are still living.

David Rittenhouse.

As numerous biographical sketches of this distinguished philosopher have at different times appeared, an extended notice is therefore deemed unnecessary. He was the eldest son of Mathias Rittenhouse, and was born the 8th of April, 1732, at his father's place on the Wissahickon creek, near Germantown. While David was an infant his father, with his family, removed to a farm he had purchased in Norriton township, this county, a short distance east of the ancient Presbyterian church, on the Reading road. He was principally induced to settle here through his brother Henry who had preceded him several years and who had taken up his abode in Worcester township in the immediate vicinity. It was the design of his father that David should be a farmer, and from his earliest years we find him engaged in assisting in the laborious duties of the farm. It is said that in his fourteenth year, he was actually engaged in ploughing the fields, He exhibited his mechanical genius quite early, for when barely eight years of age he made a complete water-mill in miniature. His younger brother used to say, that while he was employed in the fields, he repeatedly observed the fences, and even the plough with which he had been working, marked over with mathematical figures. The construction of a wooden clock in his seventeenth year caused some astonishment, as it was known that he had not previously received instruction either in mathematics or mechanics. Owing to the delicacy of his constitution and the irresistible bent of his talents, with the consent of his parents, he gave up farming, and in his eighteenth year built himself a small but commodious workshop on his father's farm by the side of a public road, and having obtained the necessary tools, set up the business of a clock and mathematical instrument maker. Besides devoting himself to these labors, in his leisure he closely applied himself to the study of mathematics and astronomy. So industrious was he, and with but the aid of three or four books, before his twenty-fifth year he was enabled to read the Principia of Newton in Latin. It is even asserted that he discovered the method of Fluxions, and was not aware of it till several years afterwards that Newton and Leibnitz had contended for the honor of the discovery of which he had deemed himself the author. In 1764 Mathias Rittenhouse moved to his farm, which lay nearly adjoining in Worcester township, and gave the one he had previously resided on, of one hundred and fifty acres, to David, who, the 20th of February, 1766, married Elianor Colston, daughter of Bernard Colston, a respectable farmer in the neighborhood. After this event he continued to reside here for a period of about four years. In 1768 he made his first planetarium for the Princeton college, which is regarded as a wonderful piece of scientific mechanism, and which may still be seen there, and for which he received three hundred pounds, Pennsylvania currency. Dr. Gordon, writing in 1790, says of this work:—"There is not the like in Europe. An elegant and neatly ornamented frame rises perpendicular near upon eight feet, in the front of which you are presented, in three several apartments, with a view of the celestial system, the motions of the planets around the sun, and the satallites about the planets. The wheels, &c., that produce the movement are behind the wooden perpendicular frame in which the orrery is fixed. By suitable contrivances you in a short time tell the eclipses of the sun and moon for ages past and ages to come; the like in other cases of astronomy." He afterwards constructed another planetarium for the University of Pennsylvania. In 1769 Mr. Rittenhouse was named one of the committee appointed by the American Philosophical Society, to observe the transit of Venus over the sun's disk, which happened the third of June of that year. His assistants were the Rev. Dr. Wm. Smith, the provost of the University, John Lukens, Surveyor-General of Pennsylvania, and John Tellor, a member of Assembly from Chester county. Their observations on this occasion were made at his temporary observatory on his farm. It is said when he observed the contact of that planet with the sun at the moment predicted, his excitement became so great that he fainted. The same year he was employed in settling the boundaries between New York and New Jersey, afterwards between Pennsylvania and Virginia, Pennsylvania and New York, and the latter State and Massachusetts. In the autumn of 1770 he removed with his family to Philadelphia, where he continued to carry on his self-acquired occupation of a clock and mathematical instrument maker. While the British forces under Sir William Howe held possession of the city, Mr. Rittenhouse chiefly resided at Lancaster, while his family remained with his wife's relatives in Norriton and Worcester townships.

He held the office of treasurer of Pennsylvania from 1777 to 1789. He was elected a member of the American academy of arts and sciences, at Boston, in 1782, and of the Royal society of London in 1795. In 1791 he was chosen the successor of Dr. Franklin, as president of the American philosophical society, which office he held till his death. He was, also, in 1792, appointed director of the United States mint, and continued in the office till 1795, when ill health induced him to resign. His constitution was naturally feeble and his last illness was short and painful, but his patience and benevolence did not forsake him. He died in the city the 26th of June, 1796, aged sixty-four years. His remains were interred in the cemetery adjoining the Presbyterian church, in Pine street, where a plain marble slab indicates the spot. By order of the Philosophical Society, Dr. Rush delivered, in his ablest manner, a handsome eulogium on his life and virtues, which was afterwards published. Although Mr. Rittenhouse, in his youth, had enjoyed only the advantages of a very limited education, yet, in after life, by his industry, energy and application, became an accomplished scholar. He communicated several valuable papers on his favorite studies, which were published in the three first volumes of the Philosophical Transactions. He understood the German and Low Dutch languages well, and translated several articles from their most celebrated writers. The life of David Rittenhouse is an instance of what can be successfully accomplished by assiduity when almost unaided and under the most adverse circumstances.

JOHN BULL

Was a native of Providence township, in this county, where the family had resided for several generations. In the beginning of 1771 he lived in Limerick where he resided till he purchased the mill and plantation of Charles Norris the following 17th of September, where is now the present borough of Norristown. He was at this time a justice of the county court, which office he held for several years. In January, 1775, he was one of the twelve members of Philadelphia county that met in a provincial convention, whose object was to get the Assembly to pass a law to prohibit the future importation of slaves into the colony. This same year, in consequence of the revolutionary troubles, the Assembly authorized the enlistment of a battalion of eight companies for the continental service, to be under the command of Col. Bull, until January, 1778. With three others he represented Philadelphia county in the convention that framed the constitution of the State, and which was adopted the 28th of September, 1776. In November of this year he disposed of all his property in Norriton township to Dr. Wm. Smith of Philadelphia, for the sum of £6000. He was confirmed a justice of the courts by the Assembly, August 31st, 1778. Not long after this date he moved to Berkeley county, Virginia, where he erected a mill on the Opeckon creek. He was still living there in 1795, which is the last we know of him. Benjamin Rittenhouse, a brother of the celebrated philosopher, and who was commissioned by Governor Mifflin in 1791, as one of the associate judges of the Court of Common Pleas of this county, was married to a daughter of General Bull. Wm. Bull, who was probably a brother, resided in Norriton township in 1770, where he had purchased a farm of Henry Conard.

HENRY MELCHIOR MUHLENBERG.

The Rev. H. M. Muhlenberg, the founder of the distinguished family of this name, was born in Eimbeck, in the kingdom of Hanover, the 6th of September, 1711. His father died while he was quite young, and at an early period had to rely on his own exertions as a teacher for support. On the 19th of March, 1735, he entered the University of Gottingen, where he made rapid progress in his studies. In 1737 he was received in the Theological Seminary, where, after graduating, he entered the University of Halle for the purpose of fitting himself more perfectly for the ministry. About 1740, the early Lutheran settlers of Pennsylvania having become tired of those who officiated among them as clergymen, and whom they denounced as impostors, wrote to the professors of the University of Halle for a regularly ordained and commissioned pastor to take charge of their feeble flocks. For this purpose Mr. Muhlenberg was selected, and accordingly in the spring of 1742 he left Halle for London. He then embarked in a vessel, and after a perilous voyage, landed the 22d of September at Charlestown, South Carolina, from whence he journeyed to Philadelphia, where he arrived the 25th of November. On the 28th he preached his first sermon at the Swamp, in New Hanover township, this county. He found but three organized Lutheran congregations—one at Philadelphia, one at the Trappe, and one at New Hanover. The latter congregation had a log church and one hundred and twenty members. At the Trappe were about fifty members, who worshipped in a barn. Churches were soon built, and during his labors they prospered abundantly. His services were divided between the three congregations, and as may be supposed, were very arduous, requiring him to travel in his regular journeys many miles through the wilderness on horseback. In 1745 he received the assistance of several other brethren who arrived as pastors and teachers from Germany. The 30th of April of this year he married Anna Maria, daughter of Col. Conrad Weiser, the celebrated Indian interpreter, and immediately settled at the Trappe, where he continued to reside till October, 1761, when he moved to Philadelphia to take charge of the church there. In 1776 he returned again to the Trappe to take charge of its congregation, and where he continued now to reside for the remainder of his life. He died October 7th, 1787, aged 76 years. He was buried in the Trappe graveyard, where also repose the remains of several members of his family. The memory of his piety and usefulness will long be cherished by the numerous Lutheran churches which have since sprung from the three to which he ministered. Mr. Muhlenberg had seven children that reached maturity, three sons and four daughters. Peter was a Major General in the Revolutionary army; Frederick was a Speaker of Congress and Henry a distinguished botanist. Among the daughters, one was married to the Rev. John C. Shultz, and was the mother of Governor Shultz, and another was married to General Francis Swaine. Mr. Muhlenberg, we are aware, has been styled by several writers the father of the Lutheran church in America, and also the first regularly ordained minister sent here. This is an error which we will here take the liberty of contradicting. Long before he was born the Swedes had built Lutheran churches, and had regularly ordained ministers not only in Pennsylvania, but in several of the adjoining States, which churches exist to this day, though generally as respects worship we believe have before this become Episcopalian. Mr. Muhlenberg could speak Latin, German, Dutch and English well, besides having a knowledge of several other languages.

JOHN JAMES AUDUBON.

Had any person predicted, near the close of the last century, that a youth was then living in this country that almost unaided would in the course of time produce one of the most magnificent works on birds the world had ever seen, and that for only two hundred copies of which he should receive the enormous sum of $160,000, he would almost have been regarded as insane. Surely to have said this would, in the opinion of many, been looked upon as positive insanity, if not downright absurdity. But this is only one of the many instances that history can show where truth is stranger than fiction. Perhaps of all the many visionary schemes for literary success, none have been so extravagant as the above, which really came to pass. What we particularly admire in the genius of Mr. Audubon, is his remarkable perseverance and success in accomplishing one of the greatest literary undertakings, unaided by governmental appropriations, but relying solely on his own exertions. It has been too much the case, both before and since, in producing great scientific undertakings (and perhaps none of this magnitude) for governments to lavish great sums to assist their favorites in their particular avocations. It is especially when viewed in this respect, that we must award him a niche in the Temple of Fame, to which greater names in the world's estimation are not as deserving of being placed.

John James Audubon, the celebrated American ornithologist, was a son of John Audubon and Anne Moynette, his wife, both natives of the commune of Coucron, near the city of Nantes, in France. He had been an officer in the naval service of his country, but in consequence of Louisiana being then a French possession, he removed there, and settled on a plantation near New Orleans, where his son was born the 4th of May, 1780. Under the instruction of his father, who was a man of education, he was early taught a love of natural objects, to which he afterwards attributed his inclinations to those pursuits. While quite young he was sent to Paris to pursue his education. While there he attended the school of natural history and arts, and in drawing took lessons from the celebrated David. He returned in his eighteenth year, when his father resided in Philadelphia, and who had as early as March 28th, 1789, as we learn from the county records, purchased of Augustin Prevost, in Providence township, at the mouth of the Perkiomen creek, a tract of two hundred and eighty-five acres of land, with a grist and saw mill. Mr. Audubon, the younger, about the beginning of the present century, resided on this plantation, and in the charming preface to his "Birds of America," gives the following account of it: "In Pennsylvania, a beautiful State almost central on the line of our Atlantic shores, my father, in his desire of proving my friend through life, gave me what Americans call a beautiful 'plantation,' refreshed during the summer heats by the waters of the Schuylkill river and traversed by a creek named Perkioming. Its fine woodlands, its extensive fields, its hills crowned with evergreens, offered many subjects to agreeable studies, with as little concern about the future as if the world had been made for me. My rambles invariably commenced at break of day; and to return wet with dew and bearing a feathered prize, was, and ever will be, the highest enjoyment for which I have been fitted." It was here where he conceived the plan of his great work and in reality laid its first foundation; it was here too where he married his wife and his eldest son was born.

On an adjoining farm lived William Bakewell, an Englishman by birth, a gentleman of a highly refined mind and cultivated manners. He had a valuable library and an extensive philosophical apparatus. To his house, as may be well supposed from congeniality of taste and dispositions, Mr. Audubon was a frequent visitor, which resulted in an intimacy with Lucy, Mr. Bakewell's eldest daughter by a first wife, and which resulted in a marriage about 1806. Some time in the following year Mr. Audubon and Ferdinand Rozier entered into partnership as merchants, in Philadelphia, where he resided a portion of his time, till in the summer of 1809, when he and his partner removed to Louisville, Kentucky, to continue in the same business. He sold the farm given him by his father to Joseph Williams, in the spring of 1810. As a merchant he confesses that he was not successful and that his love for the fields, the flowers, the forests and their winged inhabitants unfitted him for trade. We find mention made of his visiting his father-in-law, in Lower Providence, in 1810 and 1812, in pursuit of rare and curious birds. Indeed, he several times mentions in his great work the discovery of new species of birds in this county, which had heretofore remained undescribed.

While at Louisville, in March, 1810, he was visited by the celebrated Alexander Wilson. He says he entered his counting-room and asked him to subscribe to his work on American Ornithology. By his own statement, Mr. Audubon appears to have received him rather coolly, perhaps, at that time, having formed the idea of becoming his rival. Shortly after this period of his life, Mr. Blake, in his Biographical Dictionary, thus speaks of Audubon: "His life was one of bold and fearless adventure, of romantic incident, and constantly varying fortune. Hardly a region in the United States was left unvisited by him, and the most inaccessible haunts of nature were disturbed by this adventurous and indefatigable ornithologist, to whom a new discovery or a fresh experience was only the incentive to greater ardor and further efforts in his favorite department of science." In April, 1824, he sought patronage in Philadelphia for the publication of his work, but he appears to have been unsuccessful, for he at least relinquished it. "America," he says, "being my country, and the principal pleasures of my life having been obtained there, I prepared to leave it with deep sorrow, after in vain trying to publish my illustrations in the United States. In Philadelphia, Wilson's principal engraver, amongst others, gave it as his opinion to my friends, that my drawings could not be engraved. In New York other difficulties presented themselves, which determined me to carry my collections to Europe."

In August of this year, while fifteen hundred miles from home, in Upper Canada, on one occasion he mentions that his money was stolen from him, when he took to painting portraits, by which he got plenty to carry him home. To meet with better encouragement he at last sailed for England, where he arrived in 1826. He commenced the publication of his work at Edinburgh, in 1827, but afterwards transferred it to London, where the first volume was completed in 1830, containing one hundred plates. William Swainson, Esq., in a review of this work, published in the Natural History Magazine, for May, 1828, says: "The size of the plates exceeds anything of the kind I have ever seen or heard of; they are no less than three feet three inches long by two feet two inches broad. On this vast surface every bird is represented in its full dimensions. Large as is the paper, it is sometimes (as in the male wild turkey) barely sufficient for the purpose. In other cases, it enables the painter to group his figures in the most beautiful and varied attitudes, on the trees and plants they frequent. Some are feeding, others darting, pursuing, or capturing their prey: all have life and animation. The plants, fruits and flowers which enrich the scene are alone still. These latter, from their critical accuracy, are as valuable to the botanist as the birds are to the ornithologist." The applause with which it was received was enthusiastic and universal. The Kings of England and France had placed their names at the head of his subscription list; he was made a Fellow of the Royal Societies of London and Edinburgh, and a member of the Natural History Society of Paris. With the first volume he obtained one hundred and eighty subscribers at eight hundred dollars each for the work, of which only six were in the United States. The second volume was finished in 1834. This edition contained in all about eight volumes, of which there is a copy in the library of the American Philosophical Society, in Philadelphia, which the writer has examined.

Mr. Audubon in 1839 returned to his native country and established himself with his family on the banks of the Hudson, near the city of New York. The following year he commenced the publication of his Birds of America, in seven imperial volumes, of which the last was issued in 1844. The plates in this edition, reduced from his larger illustrations, were engraved and colored in a most elegant manner by Mr. Bower, of Philadelphia, under the direction of the author. His labors as a naturalist did not cease here, for with the assistance of the Rev. John Bachman, he prepared for the press "The Quadrupeds of America," in three large octavo volumes, illustrated byfine colored drawings which, was published the year of his death by his son, V. G. Audubon. The last years of his life were spent on his country seat, in a quiet and retired manner, mixing little with the world at large. The celebrated naturalist Cuvior, in speaking of his great work, said it was "the most splendid monument which art has erected in honor of ornithology." His death took place the 27th of January, 1851, at the age of 71 years. It is a singular fact that Wilson and Audubon, the two greatest writers on American birds, both caught their first inspirations on the banks of the Schuylkill. On this stream, too, Dr. Godman, the zoologist, and Say, the entomologist, also pursued their favorite studies.

Peter Muhlenberg.

He was the eldest son of the Rev. H. M. Muhlenberg and was born at the Trappe, in this county, October 1st, 1746. When sixteen he was sent, with his two younger brothers, Frederick Augustus and Henry Ernest, to Halle, in Germany, to receive an education. While here he became restive from the restraints imposed on him and ran away and joined a German regiment, from which he was only extricated through the influence of an English officer, with whom he came to America. On his return home he completed his studies under the direction of his father who prepared him for the ministry of the Swedish Lutheran church. Episcopal ordination being necessary he went to England in 1772, with Bishop White, then also a candidate for holy orders, when both were ordained to the priesthood by the Bishops of London and Ely. On his return he took charge of several parishes near Woodstock, Dunmore county, Virginia. He was not long here before the difficulties between the mother country and the colonies were becoming wider and wider, with every prospect of war. From the beginning he was an ardent whig and was quite zealous in the cause of his country, and was sent by his republican friends a delegate to the House of Burgesses. A circumstance now transpired which showed that his martial spirit was too strong to be bound any longer to the pulpit. About the middle of January, 1776, he preached his farewell sermon to his congregation on "The duties men owe their country," and at the conclusion of the services he exclaimed that "there was a time for all things—a time to preach and a time to fight—and now was the time to fight." Suiting the action to the words, as he descended from the pulpit he deliberately took off his gown for the last time, which had thus far covered his martial figure, and stood, to the surprise of all, before them in full uniform, as a girded warrior. He then read his commission as colonel, and ordered the drummers to beat for recruits. The excitement that followed became intense, and three hundred men of the several frontier churches enlisted that day under his banner and thus, without difficulty and in a short time, had his regiment full. His first campaign was in Georgia and South Carolina, and he became quite popular with his soldiers, and from Washington he received flattering commendations. On the 21st of February, 1777, he was promoted to the rank of a brigadier general, and in the autumn of that year was an active participant in the battles of Brandywine and Germantown. With his brigade he spent the terrible winter at Valley Forge, and was engaged in the battle of Monmouth and the capture of Stony Point. He was present at the siege of Yorktown, which closed the struggle between the two countries, where he commanded the first brigade of light infantry. He continued in the army until it was disbanded, when, for his many services, he was promoted to the rank of major general. On the termination of the war he again made the Trappe his home for a brief time. He was immediately elected to the Supreme Executive Council of this State, and in 1785 was chosen its vice president. In 1789 he was elected to the first Congress of the United States, from this State, in which he served three terms. In February, 1801, he was elected a member of the United States Senate from Pennsylvania, but on the following 30th of June he resigned the office, and was appointed by Mr. Jefferson supervisor of the revenues for this State. In 1803 he was appointed collector of the port of Philadelphia, which situation he held to the time of his death, which occurred October 1st, 1807, at the age of sixty-one years. His remains repose in the Trappe grave yard, by the side of his parents and wife. The following extract from his tomb-stone sums up his character in a few words: "He was brave in the field, faithful in the cabinet, honorable in all his transactions, a sincere friend, and an honest man."

Frederick Augustus Muhlenberg.

He was the second son of the Rev. H. M. Muhlenberg and was born at the Trappe the 2d of June, 1750. He remained at the University of Halle several years after his brother, Peter, had left, and became an accomplished scholar. He also studied the theological course and was ordained there to the ministry. On his return to this country, he took charge of a country congregation, but not long after was called to a church in New York. The Revolution breaking out and the city coming in possession of the British, he retired to the Trappe, which he made his home for some time, while he had for several years in charge several congregations in this county. Like his brother, he was a firm and ardent patriot, and in 1779 he was elected to the Continental Congress, in which he served two terms. He was next sent three years to the Assembly. On the formation of this county, in 1784, he served for a short time as president of the courts. In 1787 he was elected a delegate to the State convention to ratify the constitution of the United States, and was chosen president of this body. He was elected to serve in the first Congress, in 1789, by the citizens of this county, and had the honor of being its first speaker. He remained in Congress until 1797, when shortly after he was appointed by Governor Mifflin register of the land office, which he held till his death. He died in 1802, aged fifty-two years.

Henry Earnest Muhlenberg

Was born at the Trappe, November 17th, 1753, and was the third son of the Rev. H. M. Muhlenberg. With his two elder brothers, he received his education at the University of Halle, in Germany. He returned in 1770, and several years afterwards was ordained an assistant pastor of the Lutheran church in Philadelphia. He remained in the city until the approach of the British in the fall of 1777, when, for his personal safety, he sought refuge in flight. Having been, like his brothers, an ardent patriot, the enemy several times endeavored to capture him, but without success. He now retired to the country, and being, for several years without a congregation, he devoted the greater portion of his leisure to scientific pursuits, particularly to botany and mineralogy. In 1780 he moved to Lancaster, where he took charge of the Lutheran church, in which he remained till his death, which occurred May 23d, 1815. He was distinguished for his talents, piety, usefulness and extensive scientific acquirements. Though he died young he was a member of several learned societies at home and abroad, and held correspondence with several of the most learned and scientific men of Europe. His chief works are *Catalogus Plantarum*, *Gramina Americæ Septentrionalis*, and *Flora Lancastriensis*. They are remarkable for their proficiency, and place him favorably amongst our early scientific writers. From the earliest period even to this day, the Muhlenberg family has been distinguished for its talents; it has mattered not whether as clergymen, statesmen, warriors, physicians, authors, naturalists or professors of colleges, for they have alike been celebrated in these various departments.

FRANCIS RAHN SHUNK.

Francis Shunk, the governor's grandfather, arrived from the Palatinate, in Germany, about the year 1715, and settled, not long after, in Providence township, in this county. His son, John Shunk, married Elizabeth Rahn, a woman of great excellence and talents, and who did much toward giving her son a careful instruction, which no doubt did much towards laying the foundation of his future fame. Francis was born, at the Trappe, in this county, August 7th, 1788. His parents being in humble circumstances, he was compelled, in his sixteenth year, for his support, to teach a small school, and subsequently the village school of his native place. When not thus occupied he spent his time in manual labor on a farm. General Andrew Porter, of this county, having been appointed surveyor general by Governor Snyder, in 1812, the former selected Francis R. Shunk his clerk. While thus employed he commenced and prosecuted the study of the law with Thomas Elder, Esq., of Harrisburg. In 1814 he performed the duty of a soldier in the defence of Baltimore. Not long after he was elected an assistant and then principal clerk of the House of Representatives of this State, in which capacity he served several years. In 1829 he was appointed clerk to the Board of Canal Commissioners. He was chosen by Governor Porter, in 1838, Secretary of State, and on retiring from that office he established himself in the practice of the law at Pittsburgh. In 1844 he became Governor of the State, and at the expiration of three years was re-elected to the same. He had not entered long on the duties of his second term, when, on account of ill-health, he was induced to resign. His disease terminated his career, July 20, 1848, at the age of sixty. According to his request, he was buried at the Trappe church-yard, and his funeral was attended by a large number of people. A handsome white marble monument, twenty-five feet high, was erected over his remains, July 4th, 1851, by the citizens of his native State, as a testimonial of their high regard for his public character, services and private worth. There are still living, in Upper Providence, several of the name and family.

WILLIAM POTTS DEWEES

Was a native of Pottstown, in this county, where he was born, May 5th, 1768. He was early left fatherless, with but little property; and he did not receive the advantages of a superior education, but by his industry he nevertheless improved himself by all the means at his command. While quite young he studied Latin and French, served awhile with an apothecary, attended medical lectures, and in 1789, without a diploma, commenced the practice of medicine, at twenty-one years of age. In 1793 he removed to Philadelphia, where, through his knowledge of obstetrics, he obtained a successful practice. To this branch of the profession, from his skill, he was induced especially to devote himself with a view of extending his knowledge. His reputation in this department spread throughout the community, and he very shortly commenced giving lectures to medical students. He was so successful in his labors that he was chosen one of the professors of the University of Pennsylvania, but from ill-health was compelled to resign in 1835. In 1823 he published a volume of Medical Essays; next followed his System of Midwifery; then, his Treatise on the Treatment of Children; then, a Treatise on the Diseases of Females; and, lastly, a Treatise on the Practice of Medicine. He died at Philadelphia, May 20th, 1841, aged seventy-three years. He was remarkable for his industry and attachment to his profession, which accounts for his proficiency and success.

INDEX.

ERRATA.

In the following list, p stands for page, c for column, and l for line.

4 p., 1 c., 2 l., insert a comma after "learning."
4 p., 1 c., 4 l., for "Douglasville," read Douglassville.
4 p., 1 c., 7 l., from bottom, for "Gazateer," read Gazetteer.
24 p., 1 c., last line, for "Andrew Boude," read Andrew Bonde.
25 p., 1 c., 36 l., omit the comma after "Mathias," and read Mathias Holstein.
25 p., 1 c., 4 l. from bottom, after "this" insert tract.
26 p., 1 c., 6 l., insert the word "one" after "some."
27 p., 2 c., 8 l., from the bottom, read the sentence to begin with "A."
28 p., 1 c., 9 l., from bottom, for "Gunna," read Gunner.
29 p., 2 c., 14 l. from bottom, after "of" insert the.
30 p., 2 c., 27 l., for "draper," read diaper.
31 p., 1 c., 6 l., omit "off."
31 p., 2 c., for "Charles Thompson," read Charles Thomson, and for "Harrington," read Harriton.
33 p., 2 c., 3 l., insert "a," before "cross-road."
34 p., 1., 7 l., for "Wm. Pennin," read Wm. Penn in," and omit the comma.
34 p., 2., 20 and 24 l. from bottom, let "1790" and "1797," read 1690 and 1697.
36 p., 2 c., 22 l. from bottom, for "exclusively" read extensively.
40 p., 1 c., 10 l. from bottom, insert "If," at the beginning of the sentence.
41 p., 2 c., for "Der Coudray," read Du Coudray.
44 p., 1 c., 22 l. from bottom, for "county." read country.
50 p., 2 c., 23 l. from bottom, for "day," read dry.
50 p., 2 c., 19 l. from bottom, omit the first "the."
54 p., 1 c., 10 l., omit "the."
54 p., 2 c., 19 l., for "save," read saving.
55 p., 2 c., 31 l., for "quarters," read quarter.
68 p., 1 c., 27 l., for "1760," read 1769.
74 p., 1 c., 20 l., for "measere," read measure.
75 p., 1 c., 29 l. insert "present," before "owner."
75 p., 2 c., 23 l., for "muskets," read musket.
77 p., 1 c., 14 l. from bottom, for "six," read sixty.
77 p., 2 c., 13 l. from bottom, omit "the."
78 p., 2 c., 11 l. from bottom, insert "laid," before "out."
86 p., 1 c., 13 l., omit "and."
99 p., 1 c., 19 l., for "Benjamin Walkins," read Benjamin Watkins.
99 p., 1 c., 17 l., for "Joseph Wills." read Joseph Wells.
108 p., 1 c., 5 l., for "mused," read musing.
111 p., 2 c., 13 l., for "1810," read 1811.
118 p., 1 c., 5 l., for "three first," read first three.
118 p., 1 c., 31 l., for "battallion," read battalion.
121 p., 1 c., 22 l. from bottom, for "Bower," read Bowen.
121 p., 1 c., 11 l. from bottom, for "Cuvior," read Cuvier.

CORRECTIONS.

Righter's Ferry, in Lower Merion, was not at Flat Rock, but nearly two miles below, nearly opposite the mouth of Wissahickon creek. Worship is still held at stated times in the Norriton Presbyterian Church.

www.ingramcontent.com/pod-product-compliance
Lightning Source LLC
LaVergne TN
LVHW021419110826
845150LV00007B/1992

* 9 7 8 1 4 2 5 5 0 8 8 3 8 *